HERBERT KNÖTEL's GERMAN ARMIES IN COLOR

Also in the Series

The Ackermann Military Prints

British Army Uniforms in Color

Queen Victoria's Army in Color

The Kaiser's Army in Color

In the Service of the Kaiser

Uniforms of Imperial & Soviet Russia in Color

HERBERT KNÖTEL's GERMAN ARMIES IN COLOR

AS ILLUSTRATED IN HIS WATERCOLORS & SKETCHES

Andrew Woelflein

Schiffer Military History
Atglen, PA

Acknowledgements

The author would like to acknowledge Anita Tauber, née Knötel, for providing her personal reflections as Herbert Knötel's only child. Mrs. Tauber's biographical essay offers unique insight into her father's life and work. The author also gratefully acknowledges the late Mr. Robert Kenny of the Anne S.K. Brown Collection. Bob wrote the first book on Knötel's Russian watercolors and started the groundwork on this book before sadly passing away. Alfred Umhey in Germany was another key resource who helped bring the book to life. Alfred helped identify troop units, pointed out interesting uniform features, expanded and edited the image captions, and graciously supplemented the watercolor work with Knötel sketches from his personal collection. Peter Harrington, Curator of the Anne S.K. Brown Military Collection, provided invaluable assistance in pulling together all of Knötel's German watercolor images. James VanHook, Phd. provided initial German translations.

Picture Credits

Anne S.K. Brown Military Collection at Brown University provided all of the watercolor images used in this book. Sammlung Alfred und Roland Umhey (Collection Alfred and Roland Umhey) in Germany provided all of the Hessian, Brunswick and World War II sketches.

Dedication

This book is dedicated to Andrew F. Anderson, a Brown University man who left us far too soon.
In Deo Speramus.

Book design by Robert Biondi.

Library of Congress Catalog Number: 2007925273.

Printed in China.
ISBN: 978-0-7643-2784-1

Published by Schiffer Publishing Ltd.
4880 Lower Valley Road
Atglen, PA 19310
Phone: (610) 593-1777
FAX: (610) 593-2002
E-mail: Info@schifferbooks.com.
Visit our web site at: www.schifferbooks.com
Please write for a free catalog.
This book may be purchased from the publisher.
Please include $3.95 postage.
Try your bookstore first.

In Europe, Schiffer books are distributed by:
Bushwood Books
6 Marksbury Ave.
Kew Gardens, Surrey TW9 4JF
England
Phone: 44 (0)20 8392-8585
FAX: 44 (0)20 8392-9876
E-mail: info@bushwoodbooks.co.uk
www.bushwoodbooks.co.uk
Free postage in the UK. Europe: air mail at cost.
Try your bookstore first.

HERBERT KNÖTEL's GERMAN ARMIES

This book follows Robert W. Kenny's 2001, *Uniforms of Imperial & Soviet Russia in Color as Illustrated by Herbert Knötel*. Anita Tauber, née Knötel, graciously provided the Anne S.K. Brown Military Collection at Brown University with the following personal and poignant biographical essay on her father's life. Mrs. Tauber's biographical essay provides a rare view into Knötel's personal life and some of the important events that influenced his art.

• • •

Anita Tauber's biographical commentary on her father, Herbert Knötel.

Herbert Knötel was a Berliner throughout his life. Born on April 6, 1893, in Berlin, my father stayed in this city all his life and felt like a real "Berliner". As the son of the painter and specialist in military items professor Richard Knötel, Herbert Knötel got interested in both painting and uniforms at an early age. He visited the *Prinz Heinrich Gymnasium* and was happy to leave it, as he hated some of the rather sadistic teachers. This is vividly illustrated by the fact that when he had bad dreams as a grown-up, it was the school that haunted him, not the events of war.

After having served in the Prussian army, he visited the Berlin Academy of Arts until the outbreak of World War I, when he was mobilized: he was wounded at one of the first great battles in Eastern Prussia, at Tannenberg in 1914. A bullet went right through his right shoulder, which meant that he had to train extremely hard in order to be able to paint again with his right hand. Through all his life this wound troubled him, whenever the weather changed.

After the war my father settled down in Berlin together with his mother – his father having died in 1914 and his brother having been killed in the war in 1916.

In April 1923 my father married my mother Svea, née Månsson, who was born in South Sweden as the only child of a farmer and horsebreeder. I was born in April 1924. Since neither my father nor my mother had any sisters or brothers and I was the only child, we were a very close little family, and I had the privilege of growing up surrounded by warmth and understanding.

During the inflation after World War I life was hard in Germany, and particularly difficult for an artist who had agreed upon a price for his work and then had to hurry to have it done and buy what was needed as soon as he had the "millions" in hand. In the 1920s my father made mostly illustrations and worked for the magazine *Kasket*. In 1930 we moved from the center of the city to a suburb, and the following years my father was quite busy working on cigarette albums for *Sturm* cigarettes, that meant small pictures attached to cigarette packages showing German uniforms. He was also called upon as a consultant in historical films. As a teenager I was once introduced to some of the actors, which was quite a sensation for me. But my father warned me not to become an actress! Well, I didn't.

My father's comprehensive knowledge within the field of uniforms and militaria as well as his kind and generous nature procured him many friends all over the world. He was an enthusiastic collector and was overjoyed whenever he found something new either in letters, books, articles or lectures. He was a very disciplined worker; always rose early and painted as long as the light would permit. Dark afternoons and evenings were reserved for his collection; cutting and pasting in his portfolios and for his vast correspondence.

I will always remember my father happy with his brushes, pens and colours. Luckily his work was his hobby. When I was a child we sometimes were on holidays in the mountains in Silesia, now Poland, where the Knötel family comes from. I still see us: my father and I singing while we wandered downhill, my mother and grandmother behind us. Music meant quite a lot to him, so at times in the late afternoon at home, he played the piano, while my mother and I listened. After dinner we usually played cards in those good old days without a television.

Regarding religion my father was a tolerant man. He was brought up as a Catholic, but only went to church for midnight mass at Christmas. He married my Lutheran mother in a Lutheran church in Sweden. Due to my German grandmother's insistency I was also brought up as a Catholic. However, during summer holidays in Sweden near the Baltic Sea, and often *in* it, I used to follow my Swedish grandmother to the services in the Lutheran church. Back in Berlin I confessed to a Catholic priest that I had attended Lutheran services, and he exclaimed: but that is not God's house – *kein Gotteshaus*. My father was furious when he heard that. "Here fights the one with the cross in hand against the one with the bible – although they both believe in the same God," he said.

Throughout the years the *Gesellschaft für Heereskunde* was an important meeting place for those interested in militaria. This society was founded among others by my grandfather Richard Knötel in 1898, and my father acted as its president for many years. Once a month Tuesday evening was reserved for this society. Besides the meetings there was an edited leaflet with articles and drawings.

One of the greatest tasks for my father, and a matter dear to him, was the publishing of a new edition of the *Handbuch der Uniformenkunde*, originally written by my grandfather and published in 1896, which my father revised and brought up to date in 1937.

The same year my father was called upon as *Kustos* i.e. scientific head at the *Zeughaus* (Army Museum) in Berlin. For the first time in his life he had a regular income as my grandmother happily remarked. Here he came to his proper place. The cooperation with both the director, Admiral Lorey, who became a real friend, and the staff was extremely good and resulted in fine exhibitions.

In late April 1945 my parents' flat was hit by Russian artillery, and they had to start life from scratch with two suitcases as their only belongings. When one of my father's friends supplied him with a child's water colour set he started to paint again, and the first result of his work were pictures of Russian soldiers in Berlin. He had to be careful, that means he observed them closely in order to remember all details of the uniforms until he got home to paint what he had seen.

The first customers to contact him after World War II were French officers, who traded paintings for cigarettes, which my mother immediately exchanged for food, food being being very scarce. Soon after, contacts with Americans were established, and their care parcels were extremely welcome. There was feast and happiness whenever a parcel from the U.S. arrived! Many contacts in foreign countries could be taken up again, and step by step my father started collecting militaria again.

My parents economic situation was secured when my father received his pension for the years as a civil servant in the *Zeughaus*. Eventually, they got a nice little flat and life became normal.

Even during the battle of Berlin and the hard times after the war, my father never lost his optimistic view. I had been recruited in January 1945 to become a military cartographer and was sent to a barracks in Altenburg/Thüringen, in central Germany, so I did not know what was going on at home. When the infrastructure was somewhat re-established in the autumn of 1945, I received quite a number of letters from my father, in which he described what had happened to them during and after the battle of Berlin. However, he never complained but ensured me that better times would be coming. And so they did!

My father died in November 1963. Both he and my mother are buried at Hörup in South Sweden near the city of Ystad. It is a family grave of my Swedish grandparents. Since a bridge has been built between Denmark and Sweden it is easy for me and my family to get there.

End Anita Tauber's biographical commentary.

• • •

Three prominent American friends of Herbert Knötel's were the late Anne S.K. Brown, founder of the extensive Anne S.K. Brown Military Collection at Brown University, the late Colonel Frederick P. Todd, former West Point Museum Curator and the late Colonel John R. Elting, renowned uniformologist and military historian. Mrs. Brown, Colonel Todd, and Colonel Elting all commissioned works by Knötel after World War II and were among those who sent the care parcels that Anita Tauber writes about so glowingly. The vast majority of the watercolors included in this book are from Colonel Todd's albums that Mrs. Brown acquired. She bought the Todd albums on the proviso that Colonel Todd could continue to add to his collection. When he passed away his widow forwarded the almost 700 albums to Mrs. Brown. Anita Tauber donated some of her father's watercolors several years ago to the Anne S.K. Brown Military Collection and a portion of those water colors also appear in this book along with Knötel work that Mrs. Brown and Colonel Elting commissioned directly from the artist.

The surreptious Russian military paintings that Anna Tauber refers to were in fact contracted for by the Military Intelligence Section, G-2, Berlin command in 1945 and were done by Herbert Knötel to help educate U.S. and Allied military personnel on the Soviet Army. The *Zeughaus*, where Knötel worked during World War II, was heavily damaged and restored in the 1950s. Today, it operates as the German Museum for History. The *Zeughaus* is described by the Berlin Tourism Board as, "one of the oldest and most important Baroque buildings in Berlin". In 2003, world renown architect I.M. Pei completed an impressive addition to the *Zeughaus*.

This volume contains watercolors depicting German units of the 18th through 20th century which are reproduced here for the first time. These German military units fought in campaigns from the American War of Independence to World War II. The infantry, cavalry and artillery are complimented by an array of musicians and other support personnel such as engineer and supply troops. The accompanying sketches, from Alfred Umhey's collection, provide unique insight into how Knötel initially approached his subject matter. The attention to detail in the drawings is impressive and clearly provided a solid base for the watercolors.

Knötel's work is so engaging because, whether mounted or on foot, his figures across the centuries have an ageless swagger. When

Herbert Knötel died in 1963 his two friends and world renown uniformologists, Col. John R. Elting and Col. Frederick P. Todd, wrote a summary of Knötel's life in the 1963 Winter issue of *The Military Collector and Historian* concluding that, "Soldiers of every nation, in every age, took shape under his fingers. These were not elegant fashion plates, drawn to merely illustrate some uniform regulation of years gone by. Instead, they were a soldier's soldier – infantrymen who knew the dragging weight of a pack and an empty belly; fussy, officious administrative personnel; cavalrymen and panzer troops with eyes alert for the first flicker of hostile movement; gay, gaudy, galloping aides-de-camp."

Herbert Knötel's watercolors are all signed, "Knötel d.J." meaning "Knötel the younger" to distinguish Herbert's work from his father Richard, best know for his *Grosse Uniformenkunde* which consisted of eighteen volumes with 1,060 full color plates. Charles Woolley, author of *The Kaiser's Army in Color* wrote, "*Grosse Uniformenkunde* remains the finest single source of uniformology today". In this book there is one pencil drawing by Richard Knötel of two late 17th century Saxons which illustrates his impressive artistic skill.

The Plates

The 137 watercolors and sketches in this book are presented in chronological order. The first image is of two late 17th century Saxons drawn by Herbert Knötel's father, Richard Knötel and a second Saxon of the Janissary Corp from 1730 by Herbert Knötel. There are seventeen Bavarian troops from the mid-18th century and one mid-18th century Prussian sketch followed by twenty-eight watercolors and sketches of Hessian troops that fought in the American War of Independence. Approximately 30,000 Germans fought for the British during the American War of Independence, including 20,000 Hessians and 6,000 troops from Brunswick. Exact figures are debateable but thousands of these German troops deserted and stayed in America after the war, primarily in Pennsylvania. There are twenty-five watercolors and sketches of Brunswick troops that also were deployed to North America during the American War of Independence. The Brunswick troops operated out of Canada.

The Napoleonic era watercolors are among the most spectacular in the book and comprise thirty-three images. Several of the German states are represented including Münster, Kingdom of Westphalia, Hanover, Prussia and Bavaria. The two dramatic battle scenes, Jena 1806 and Polotzk 1812, are extremely effective at evoking both the grandeur and horror of 19th century warfare. The Kingdom of Westphalia is particularly well represented here with twenty watercolors.

The sixteen images of the *Hermann Göring* division from World War II are easily discernible by the black armband worn on the right arm. The *Hermann Göring* division consisted of panzer, armored artillery and infantry battalions. The division saw action in Poland, Italy and Russia during the war. Of the 60,000 troops that served in the *Hermann Göring* division, only 15,000 survived the war. The division's casualty rate on the Eastern Front was 90%. The remaining fifteen images are of other German World War II military figures.

Sources

www.americanrevolution.org/hessindex.html

www.berlin-tourist-information.de/cgi-bin/sehenswertes.pl?id=13526&sprache=english

www.custermen.com/ItalyWW2/Luftwaffe.htm

Kenny, Robert W., *Uniforms of Imperial & Soviet Russia in Color as Illustrated by Herbert Knötel*, Atglen, Pennsylvania: Schiffer Publishing Ltd., 2001.

Lowell, Edward J., *The Hessians and the other German Auxiliaries of Great Britain in the Revolutionary War*, New York, New York: Harper and Brothers Publishers, 1884.

Seidel, Jochen. www.jochen-seidel.de/ab-troops.

Tauber, Anita, *Biographical Essay on Herbert Knötel*, Denmark, 2004.

Woolley, Charles, *The Kaiser's Army in Color*, Atglen, Pennsylvania: Schiffer Publishing Ltd., 2000.

THE PLATES

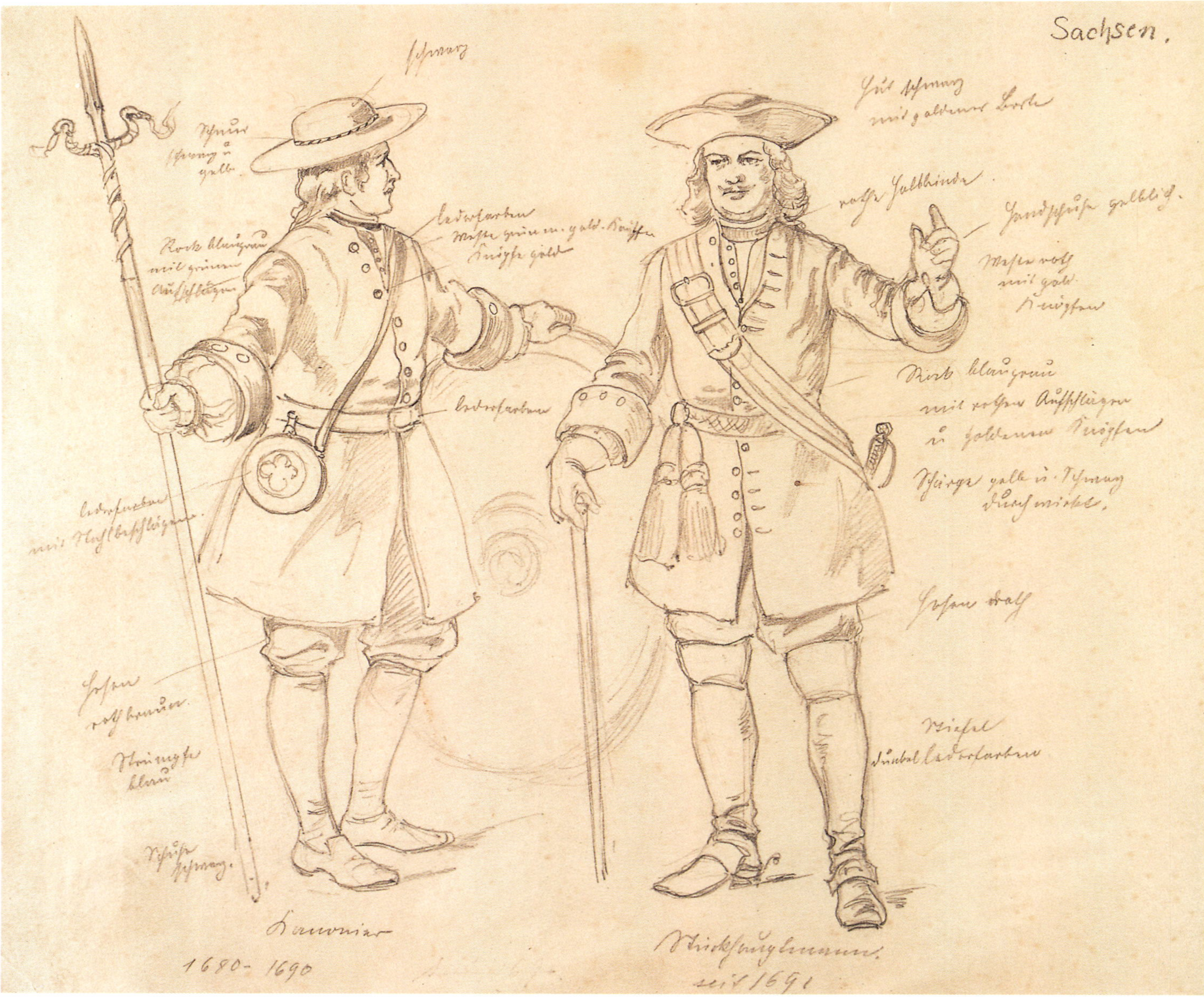

Two Saxons 1680-1690. Sketch by Herbert Knötel's father, Richard Knötel. Herbert Knötel clearly inherited his artistic genius from his father.

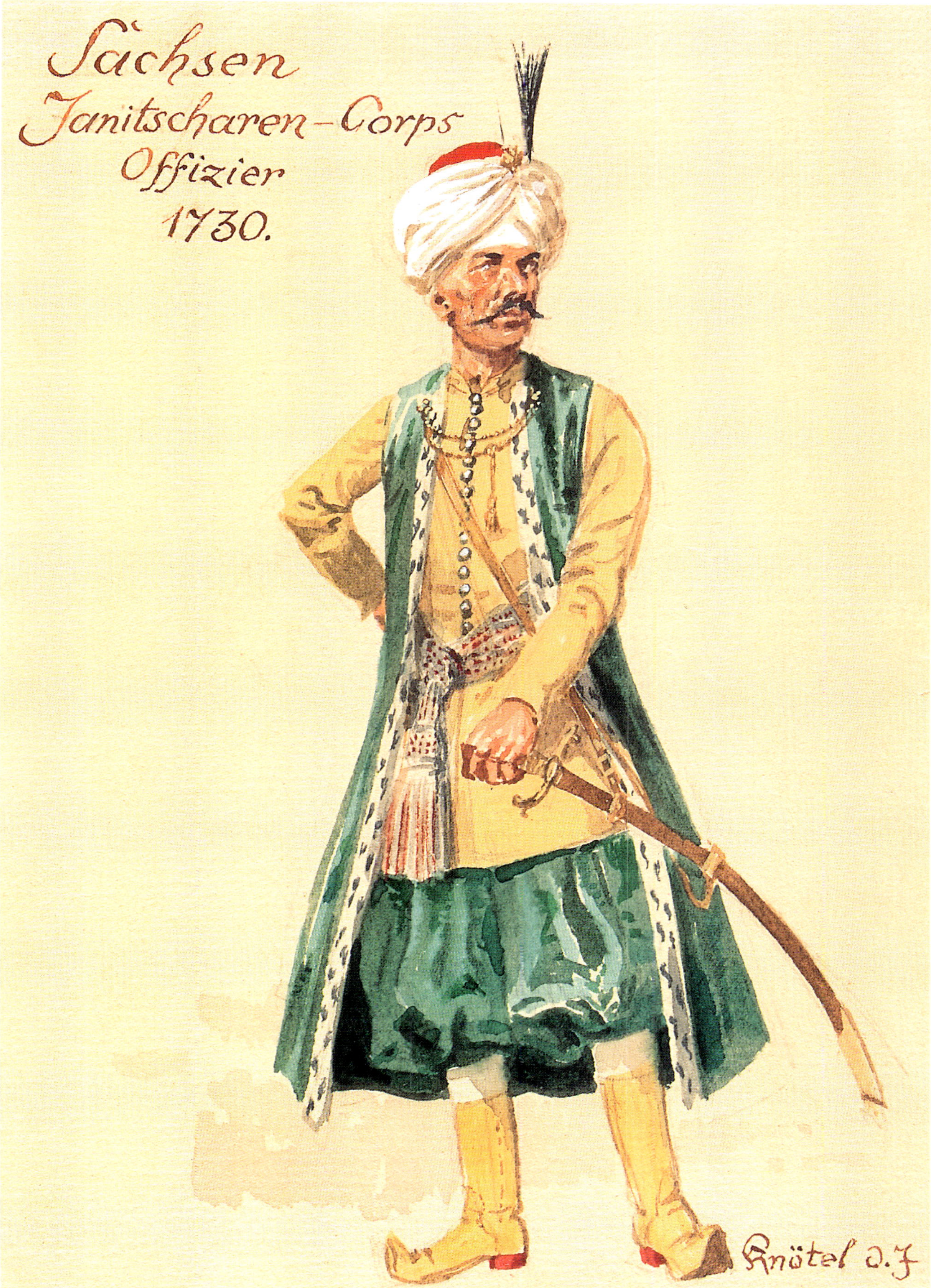

Officer, Janissary Corps, Saxony 1730. This was a unique court-unit, only for parade purposes, imitating the dress of the Turkish élite infantry.

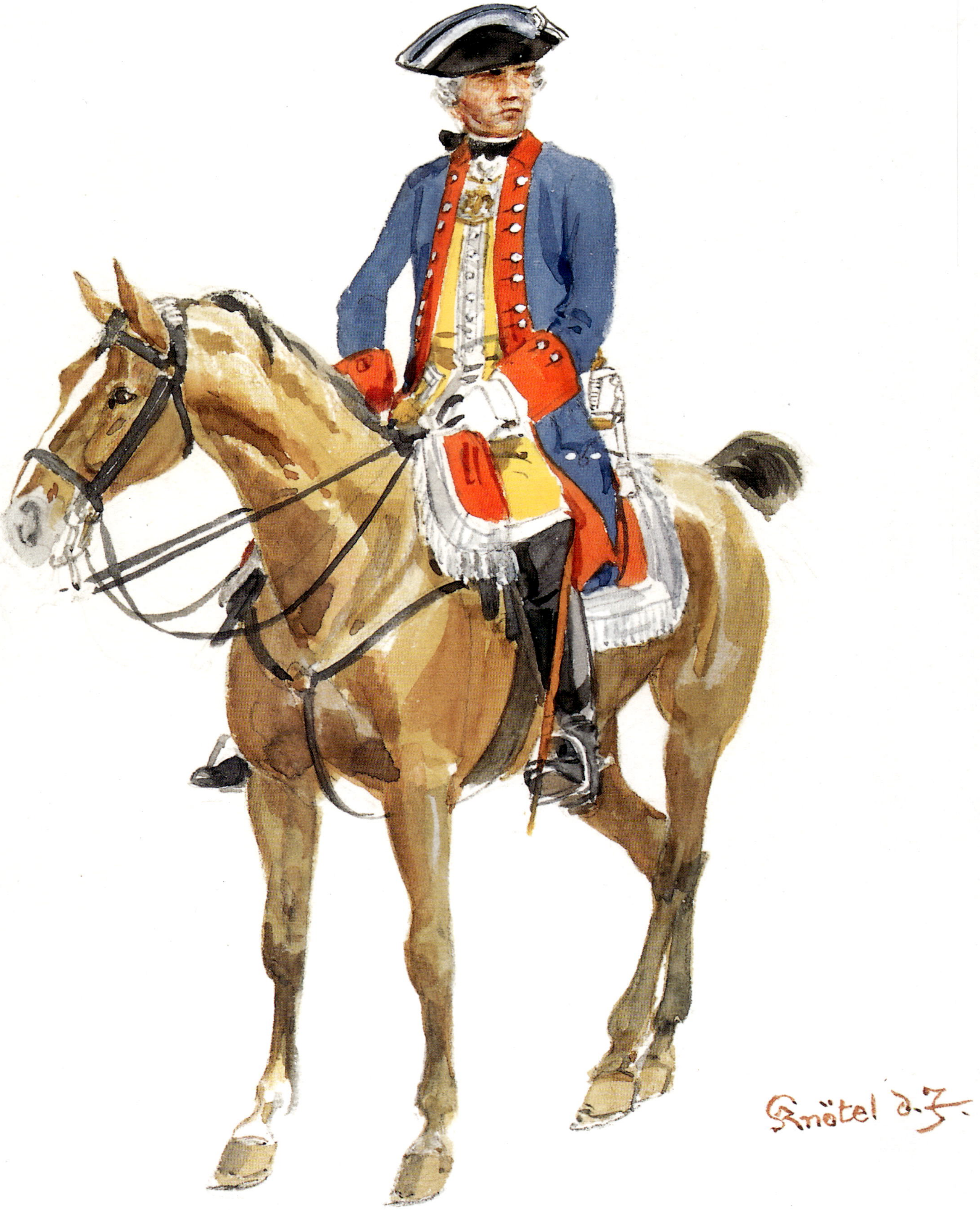

Staff Officer, Preising Infantry Regiment, Bavaria 1755.

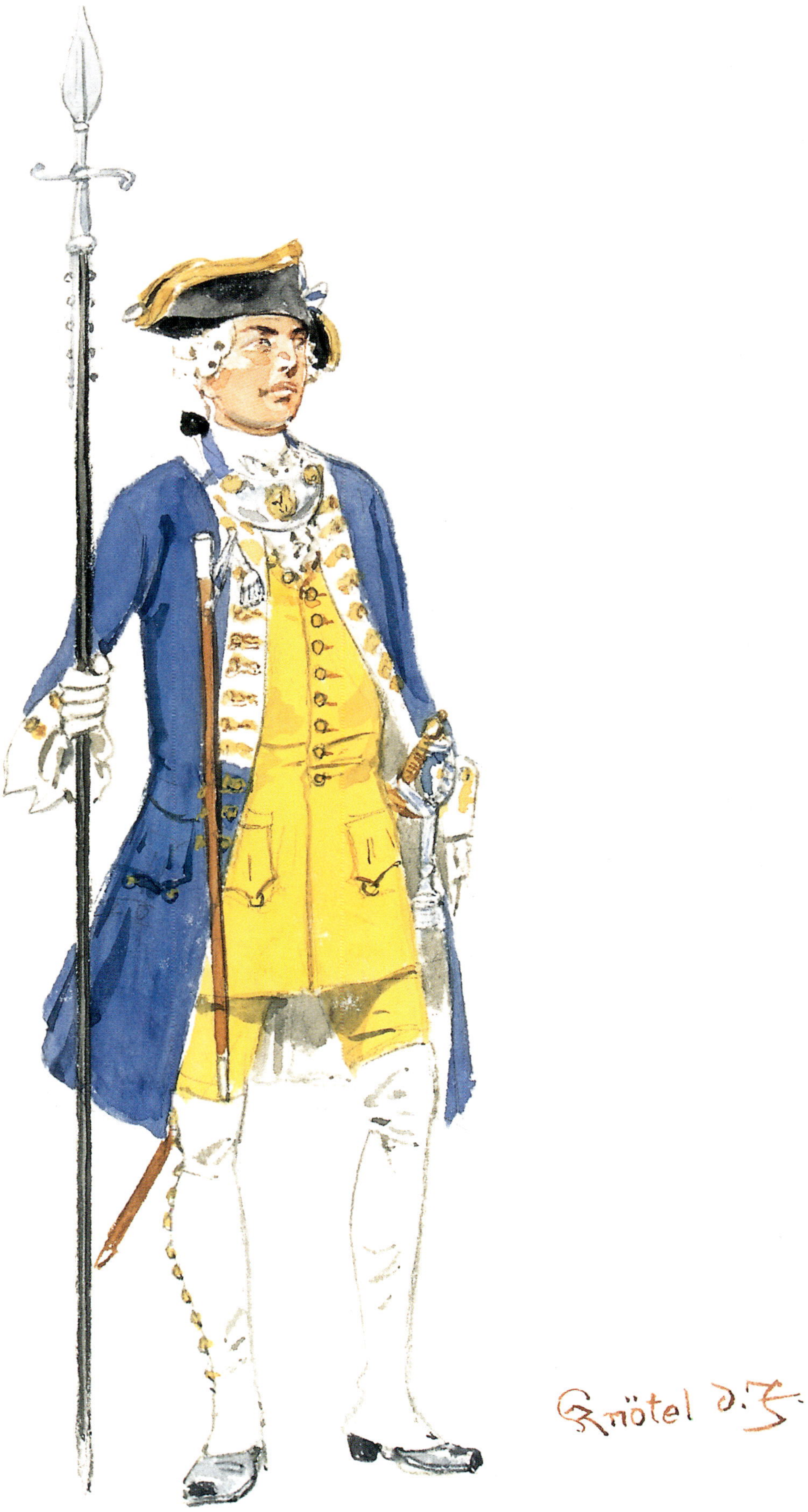

Officer, Prince Elector Infantry Regiment, Summer Uniform, Bavaria.

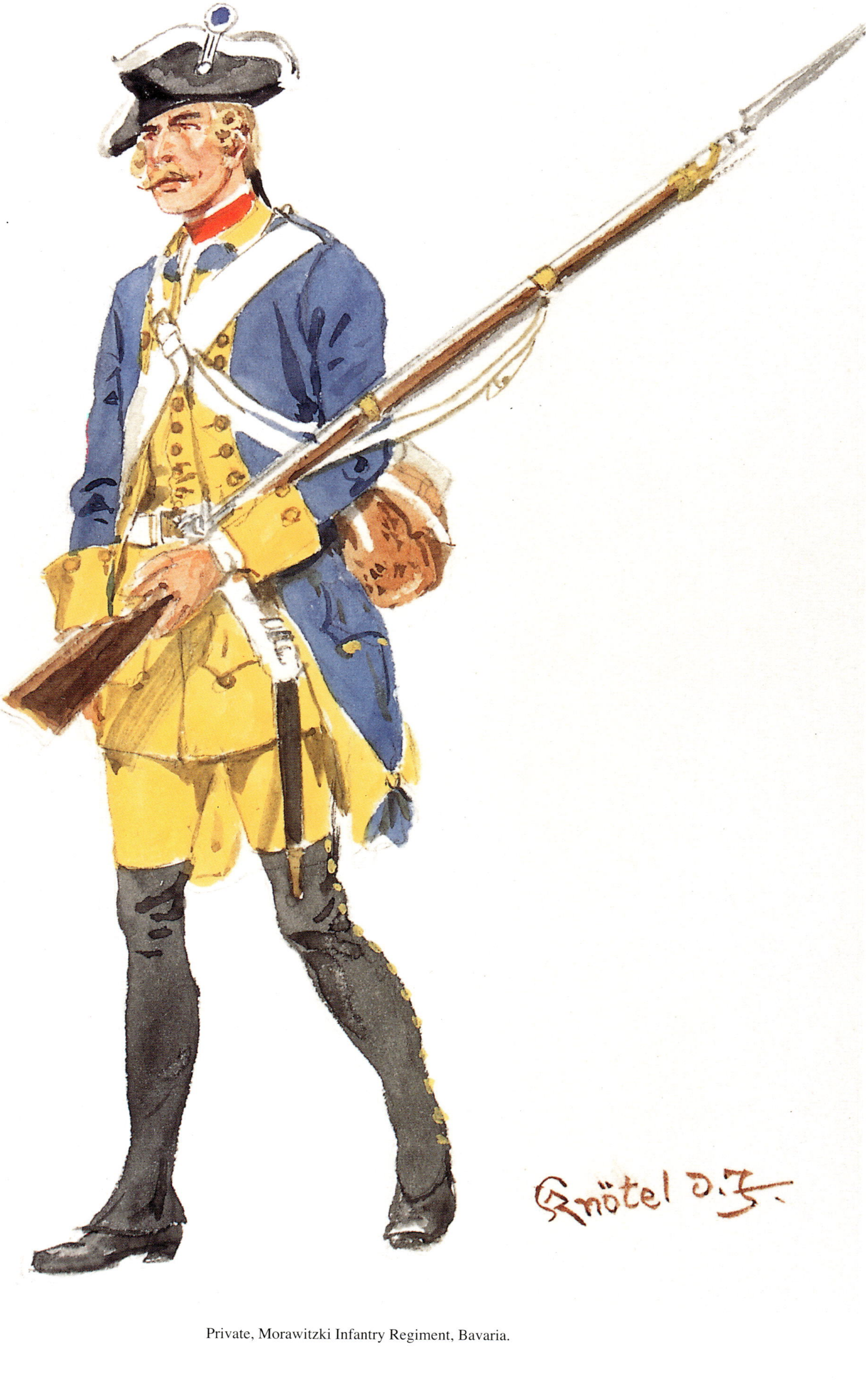

Private, Morawitzki Infantry Regiment, Bavaria.

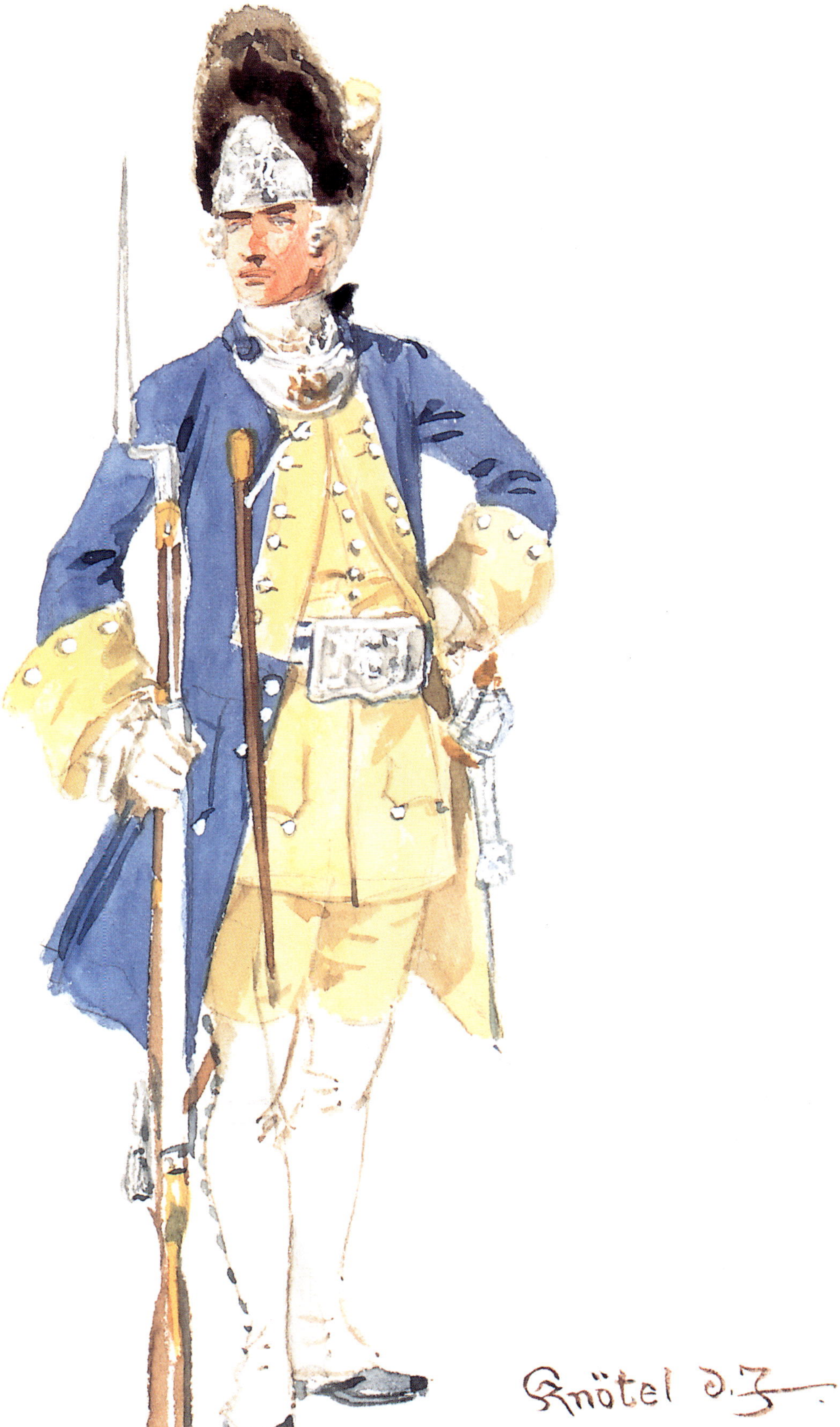

Grenadier Officer, Minucci Infantry Regiment, Bavaria 1755.

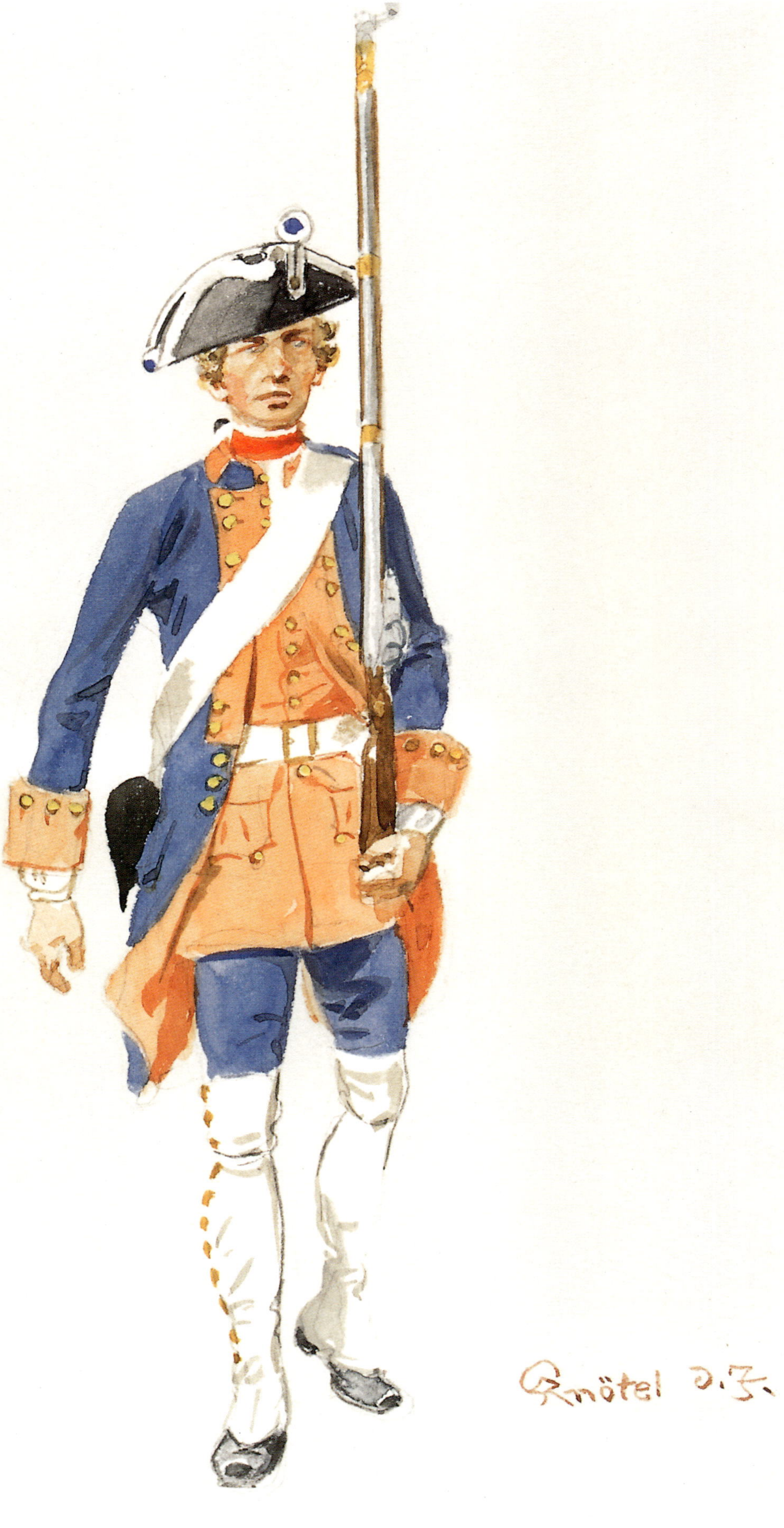

Private, Clemens Infantry Regiment, Bavaria 1755.

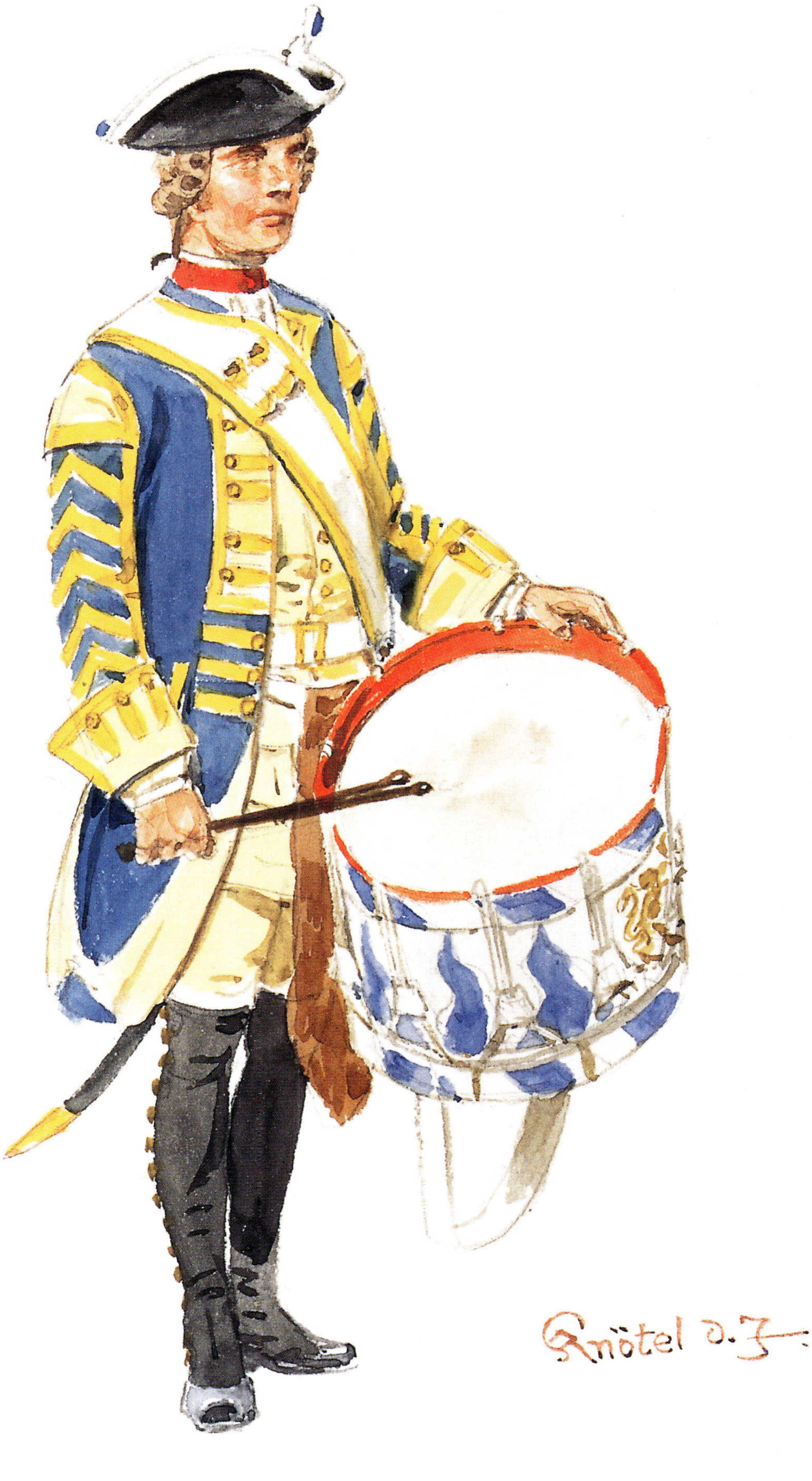

Drummer, Pechmann Infantry Regiment, Bavaria 1755.

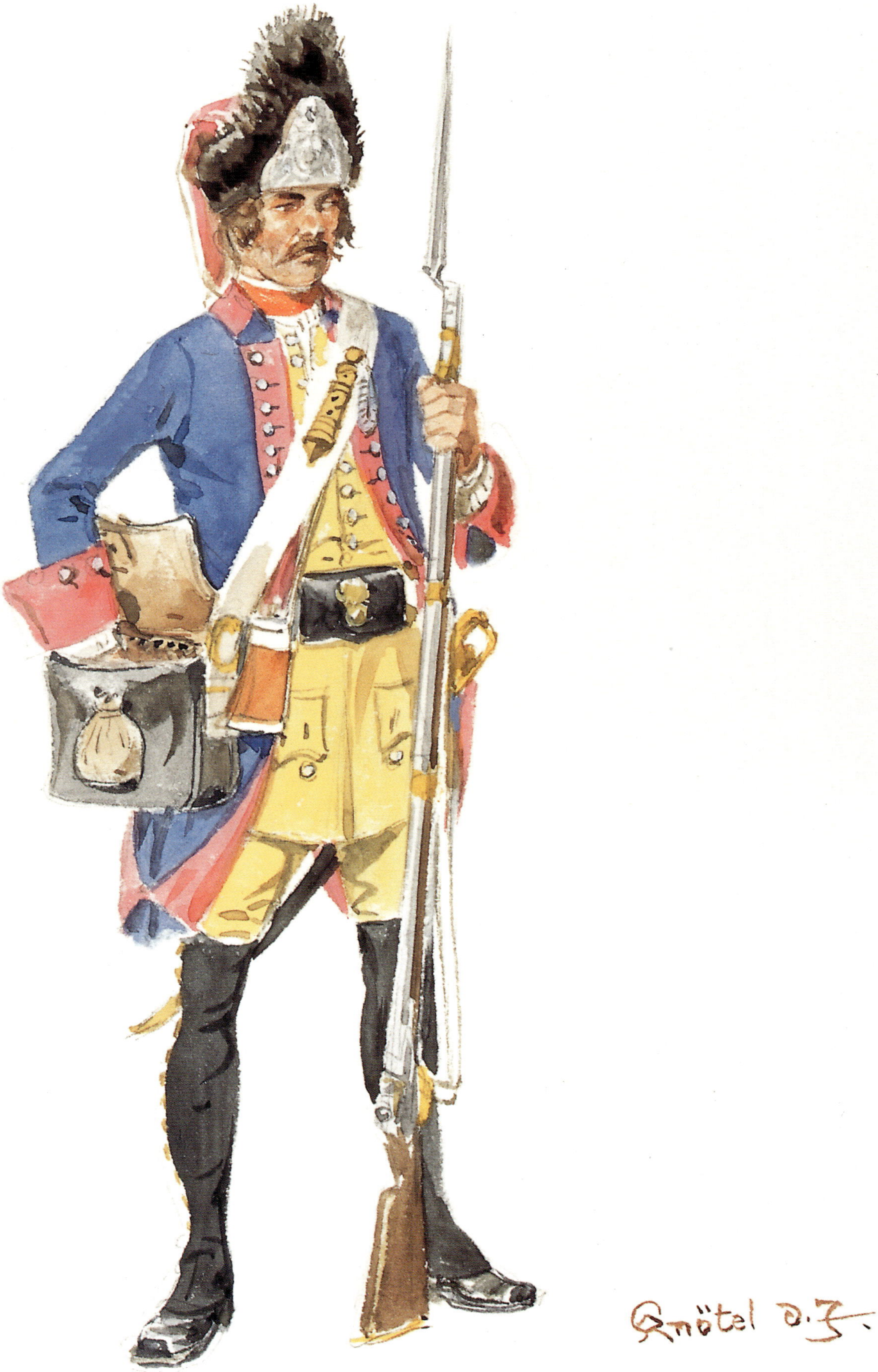

Grenadier, Holnstein Infantry Regiment, Bavaria 1755.

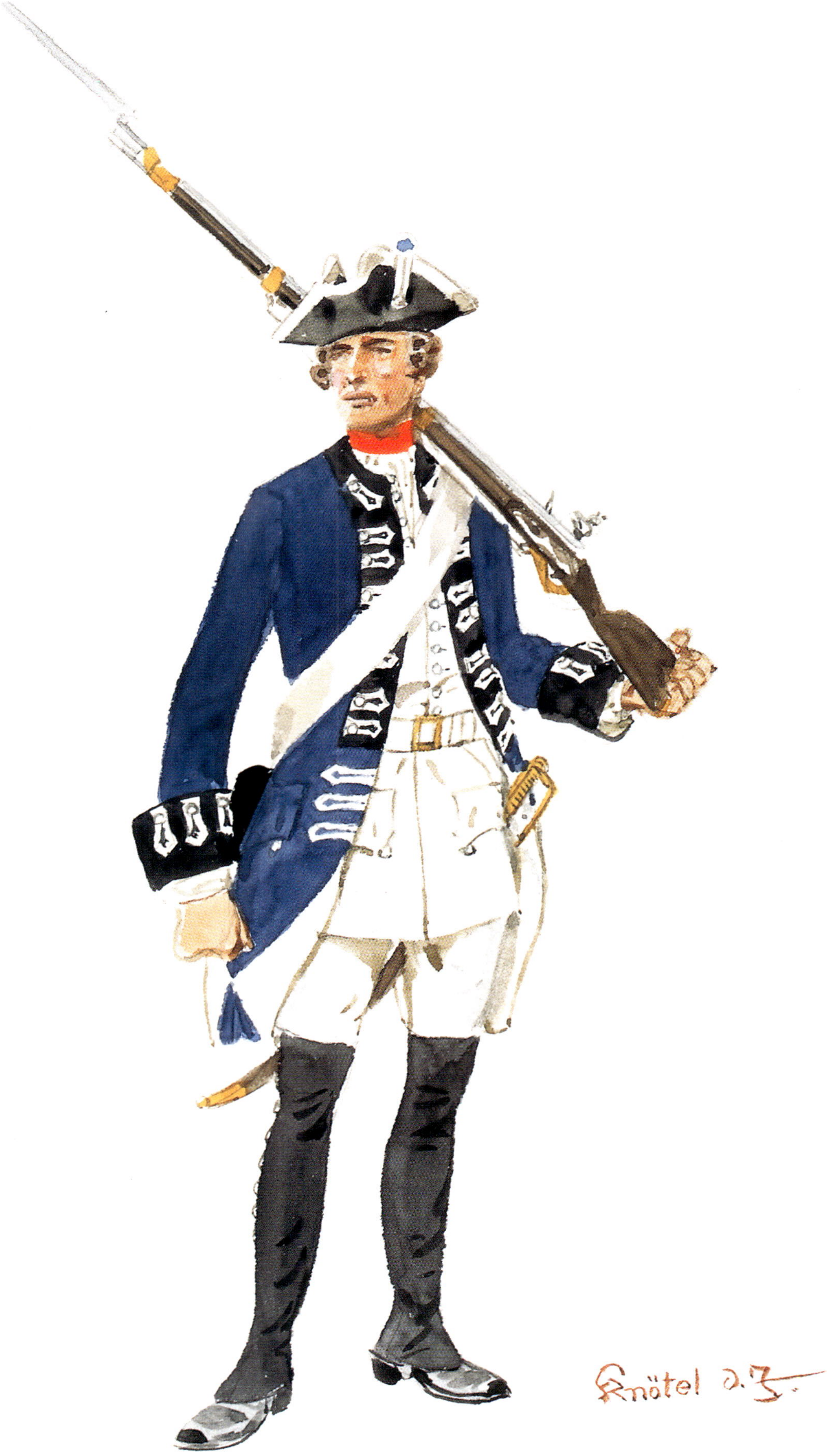

Private, Leib Regiment, Bavaria 1760.

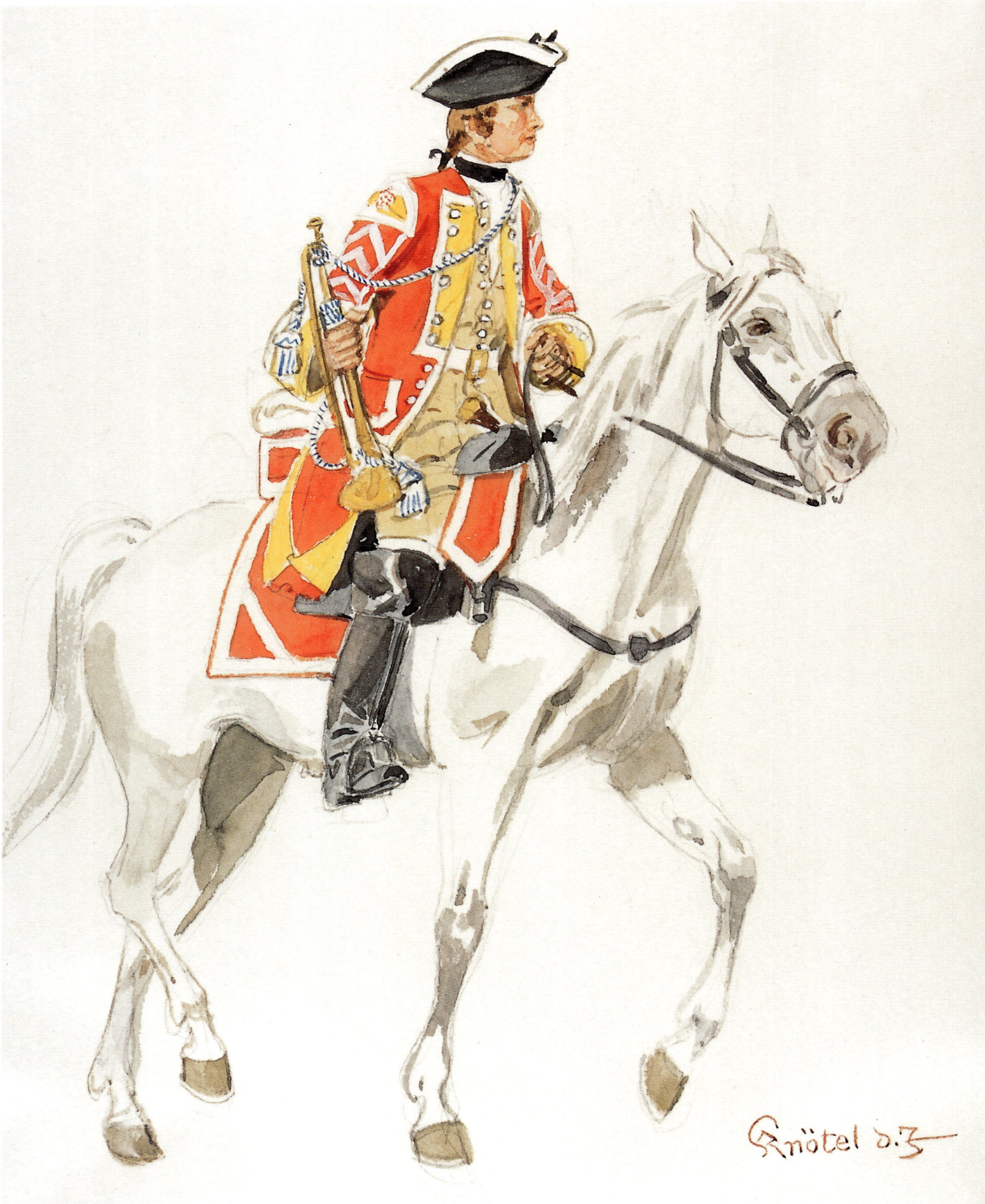

Trumpeter, Törring Cuirassier Regiment, Bavaria 1755.

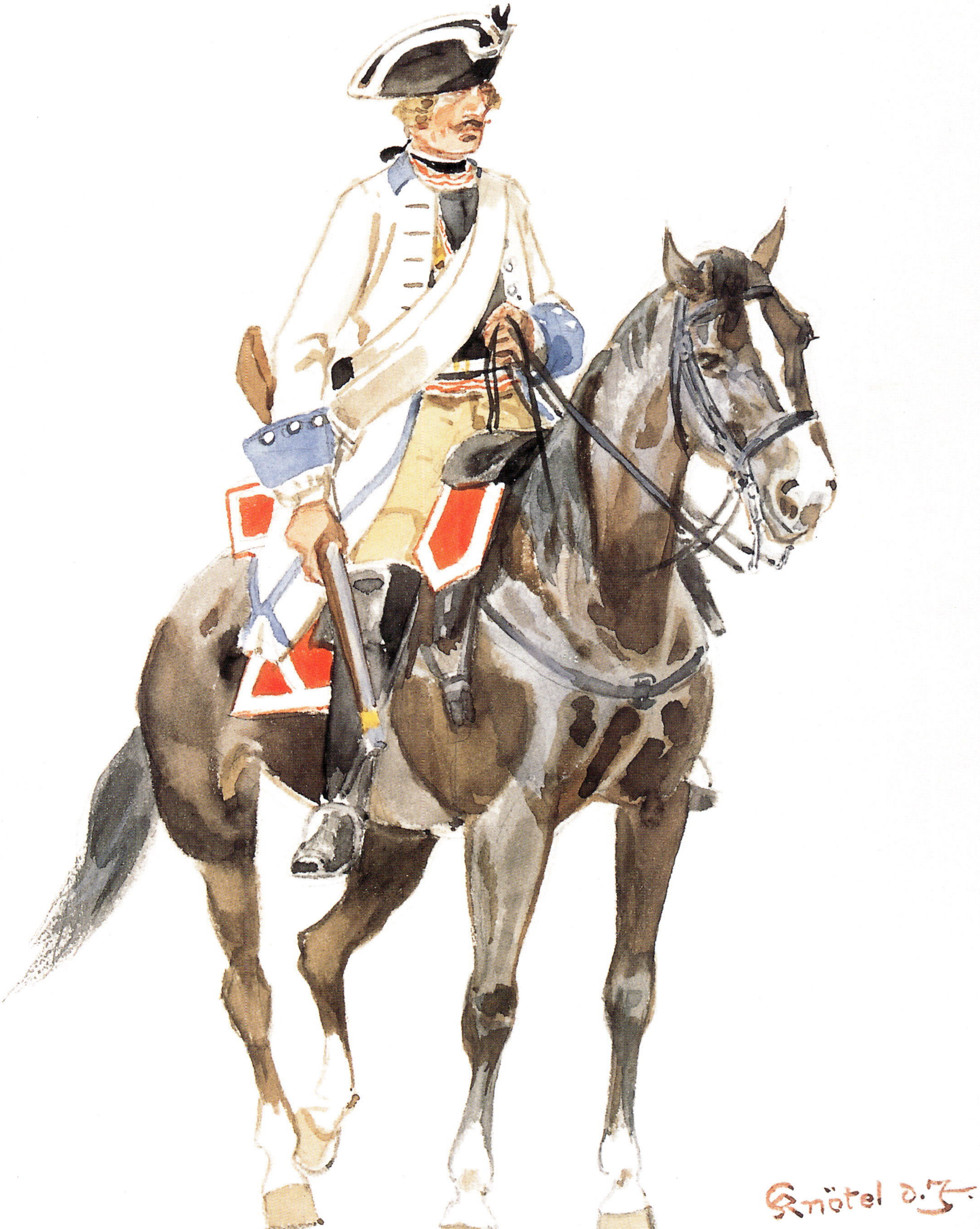

Taxis Cuirassier Regiment, Bavaria 1755.

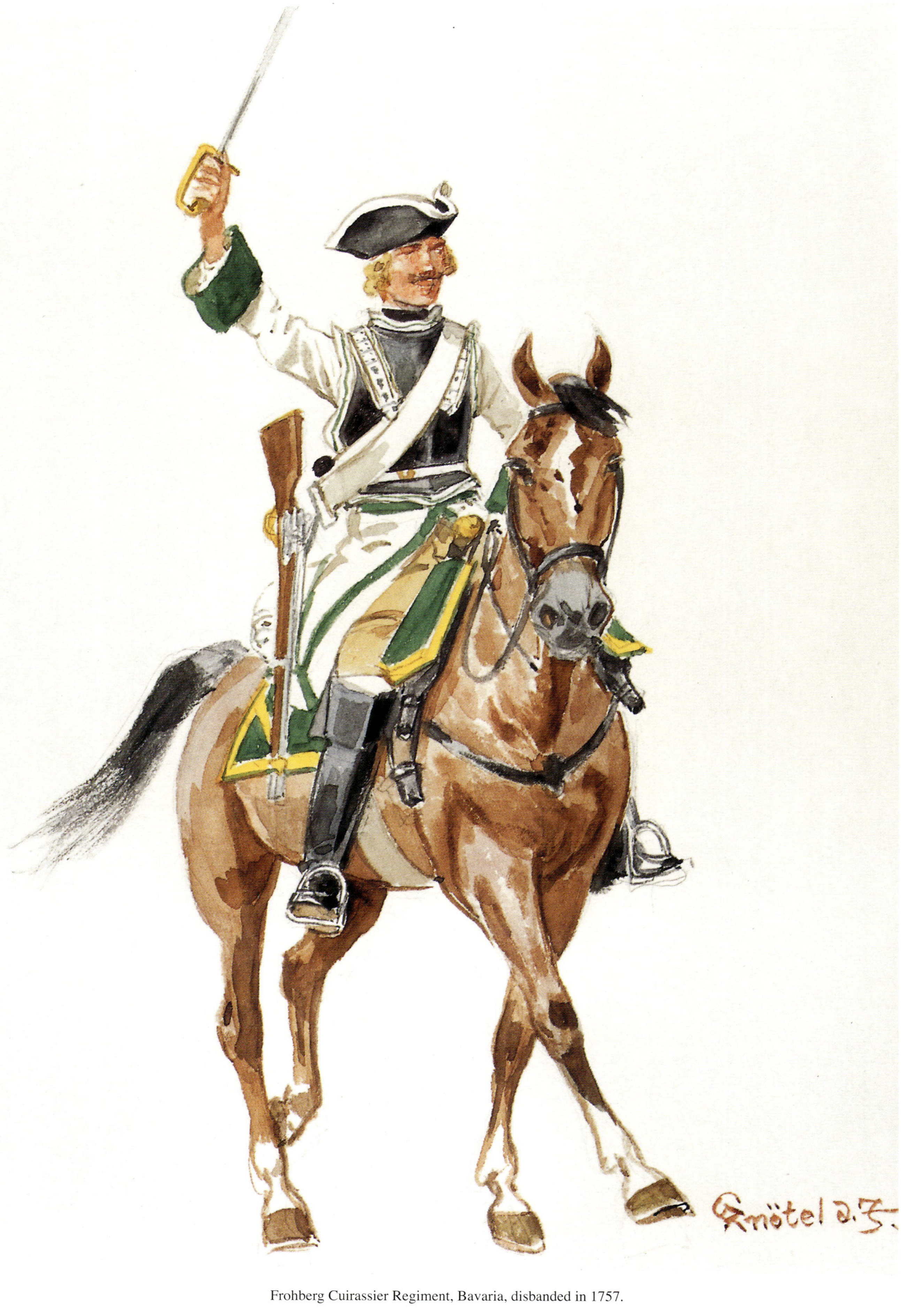

Frohberg Cuirassier Regiment, Bavaria, disbanded in 1757.

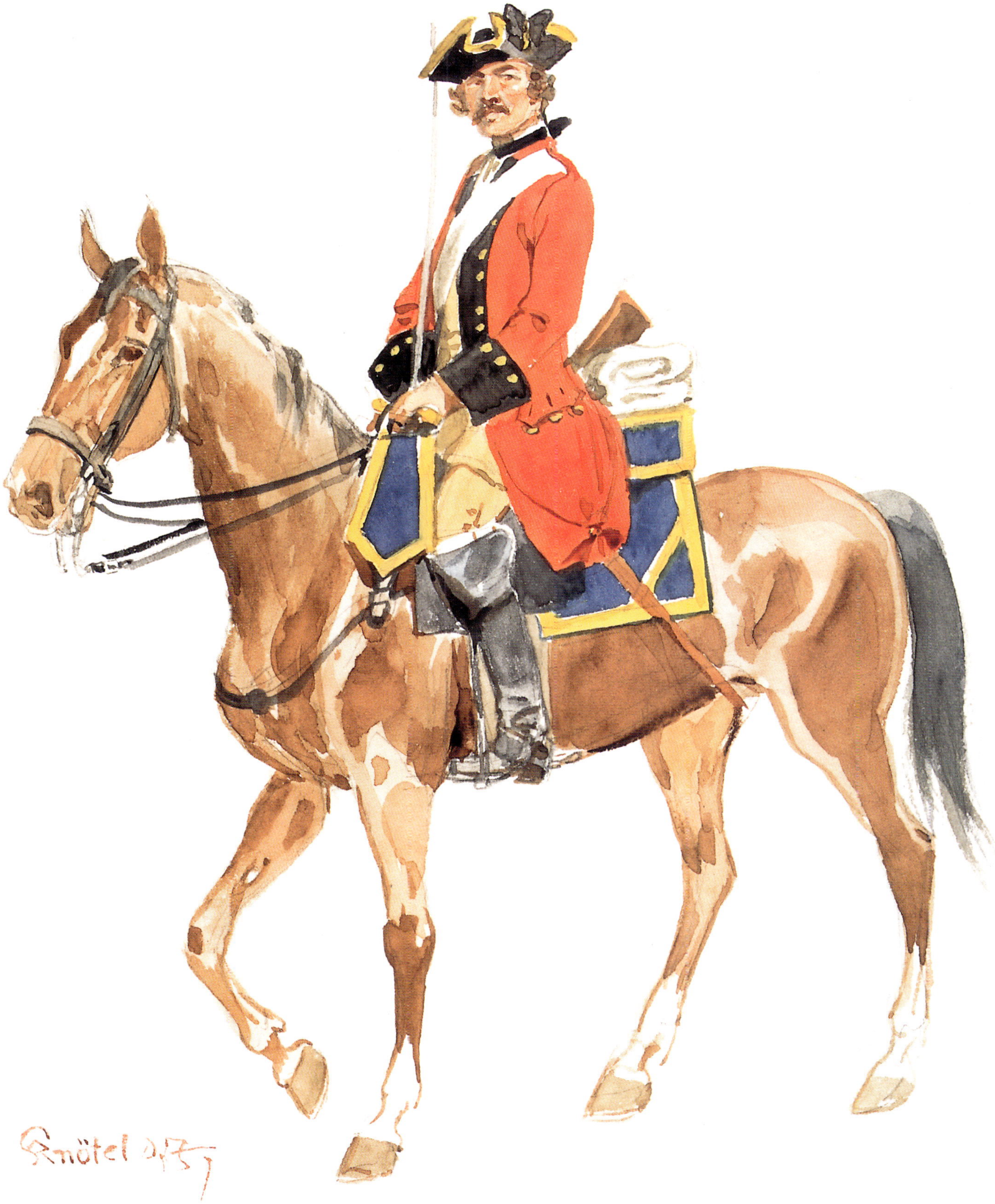

Dragoon, Preysing Regiment, Bavaria 1755.

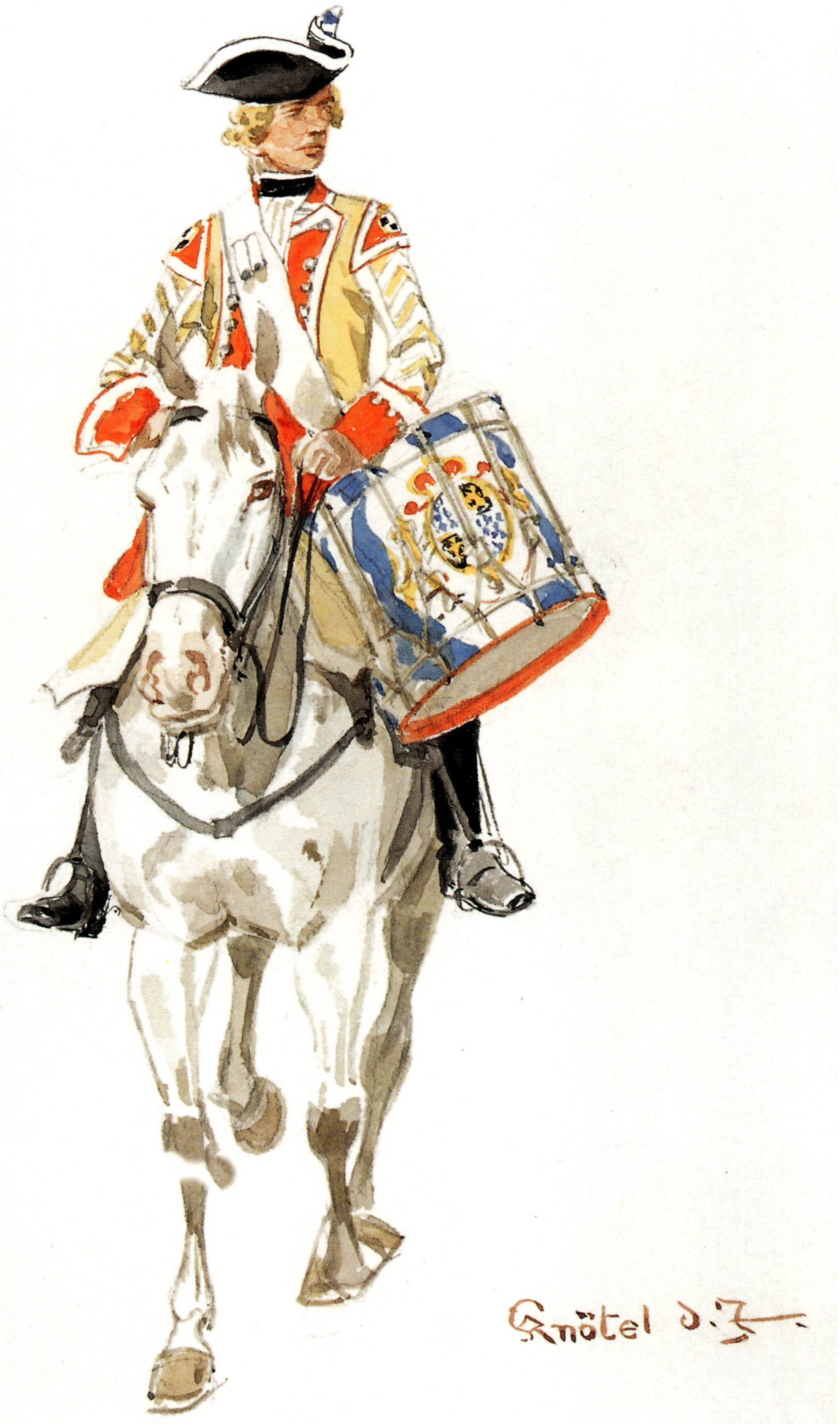

Drummer, Hohenzollern Dragoon Regiment, Bavaria.

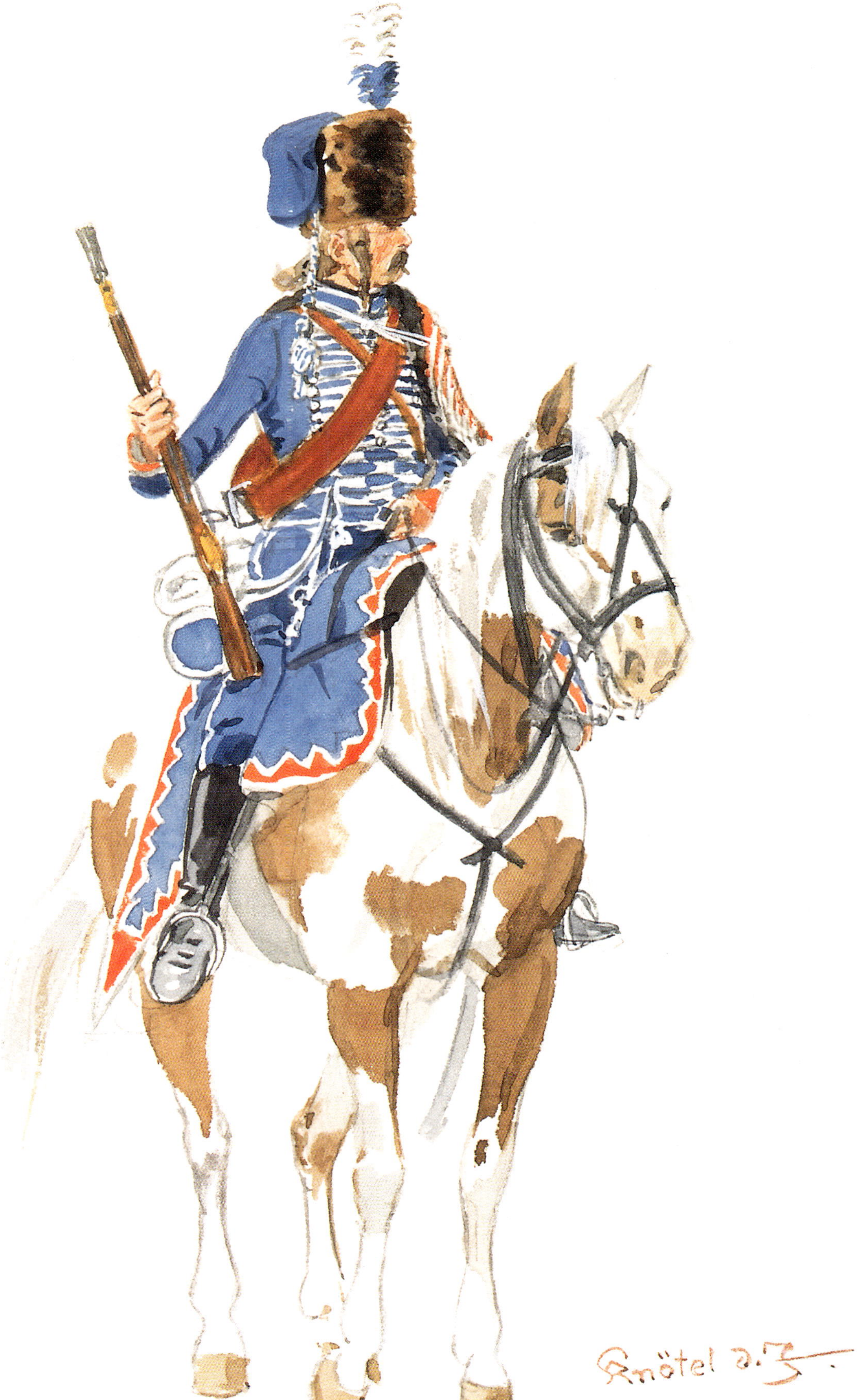

Hussar-Corps Count Piosasque, Bavaria 1755.

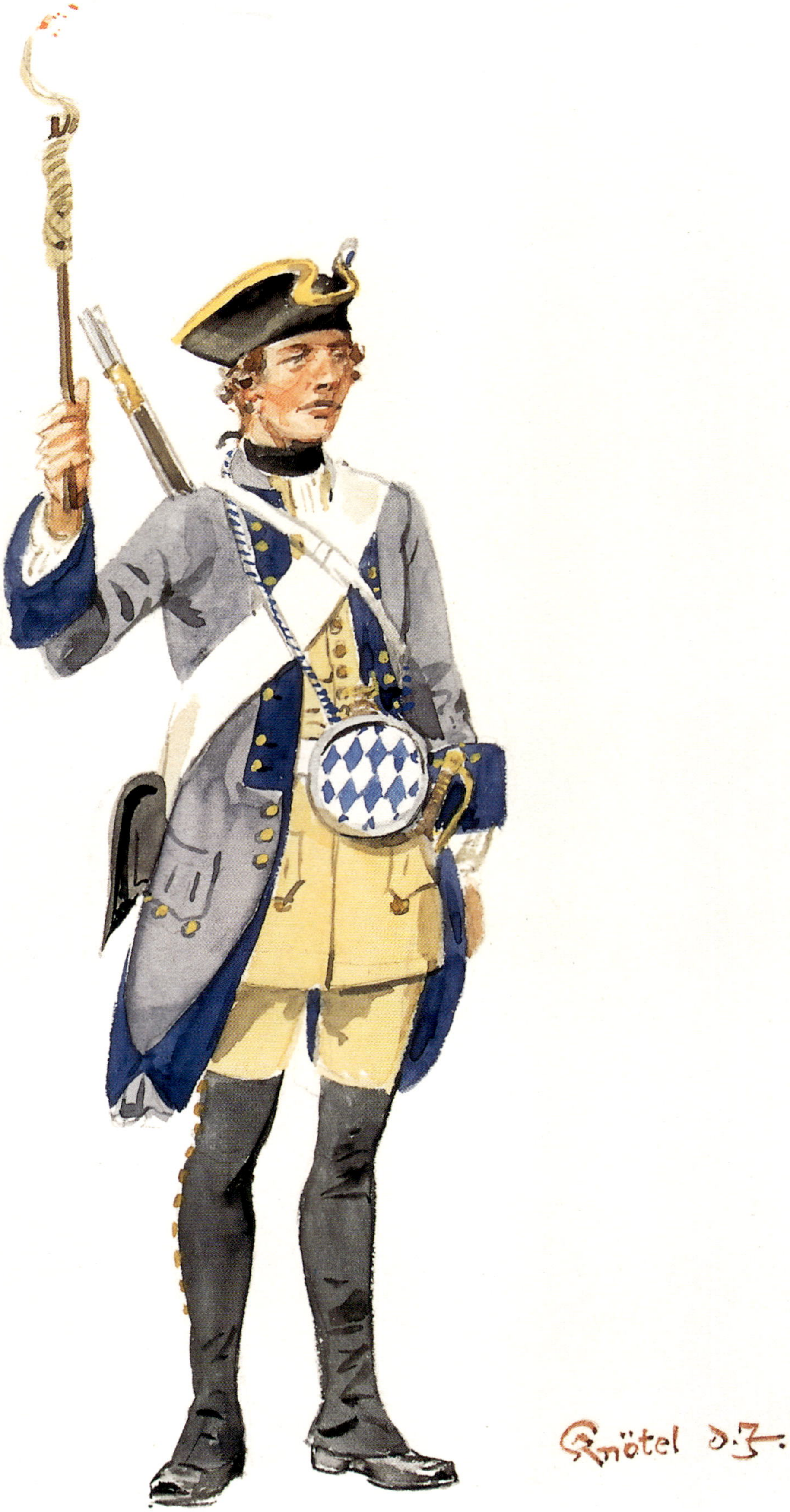

Artillery, Bavaria 1755.

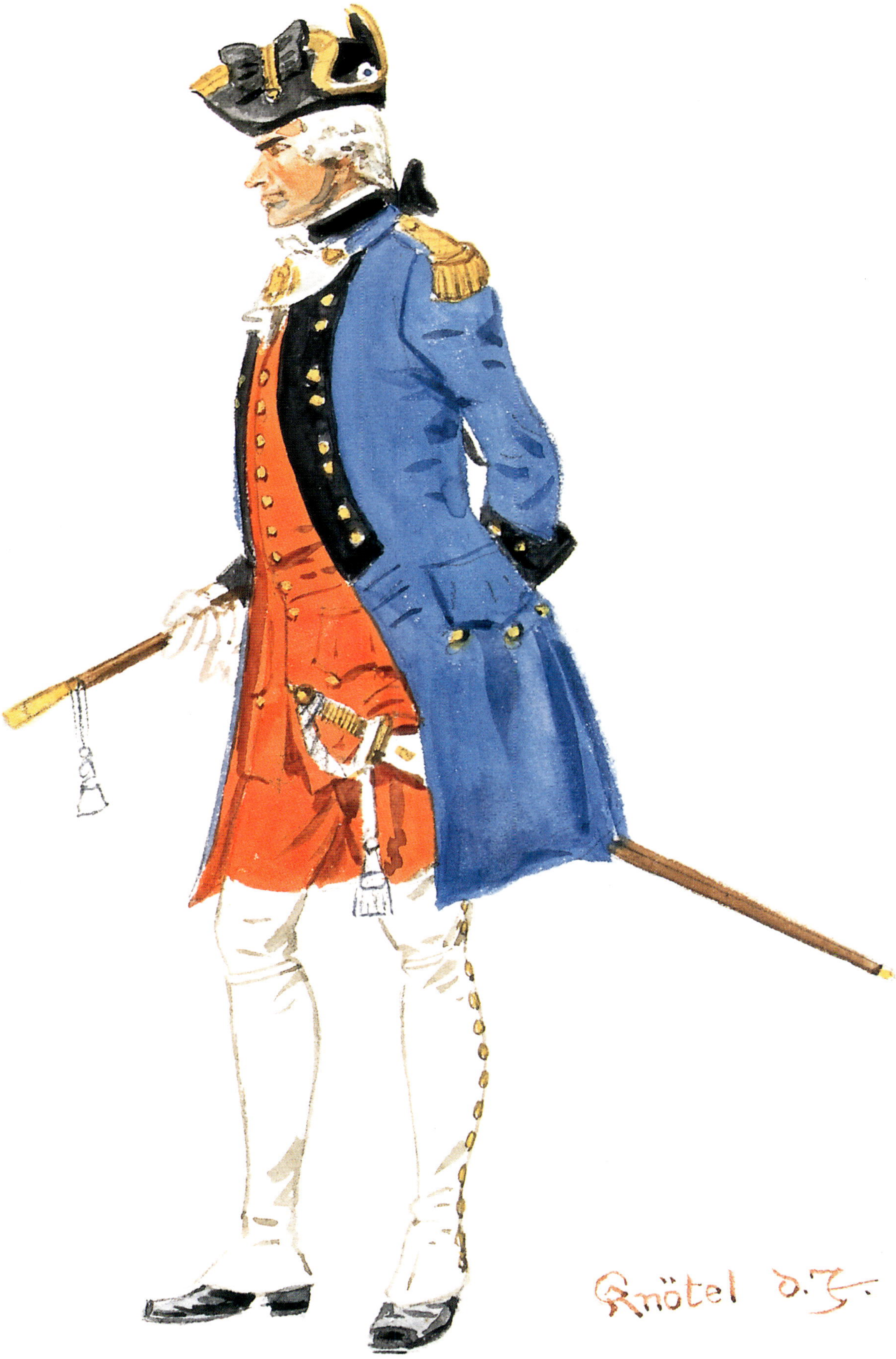

Officer, Engineer Corps, Bavaria 1755.

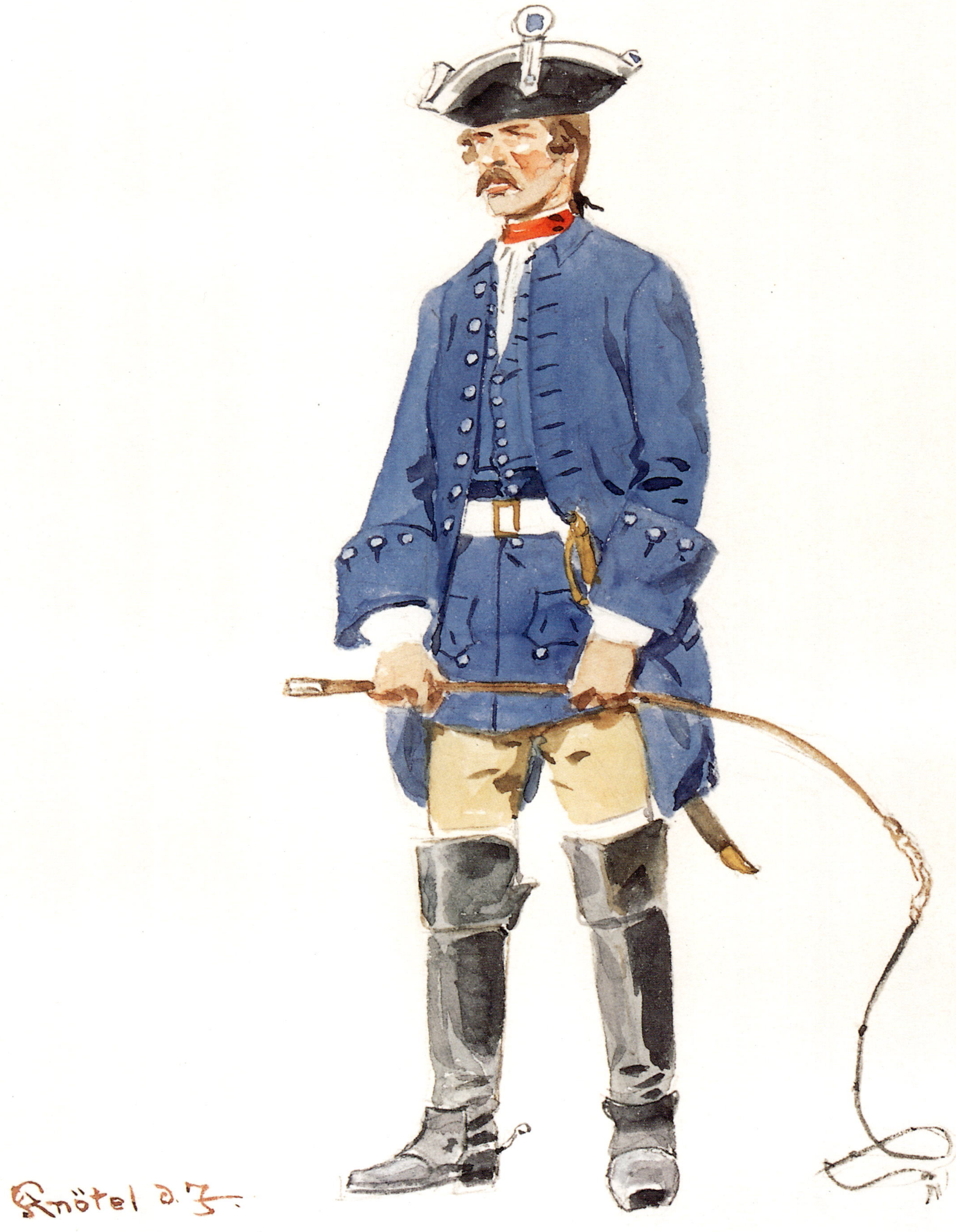

Supply train driver, Bavaria 1755.

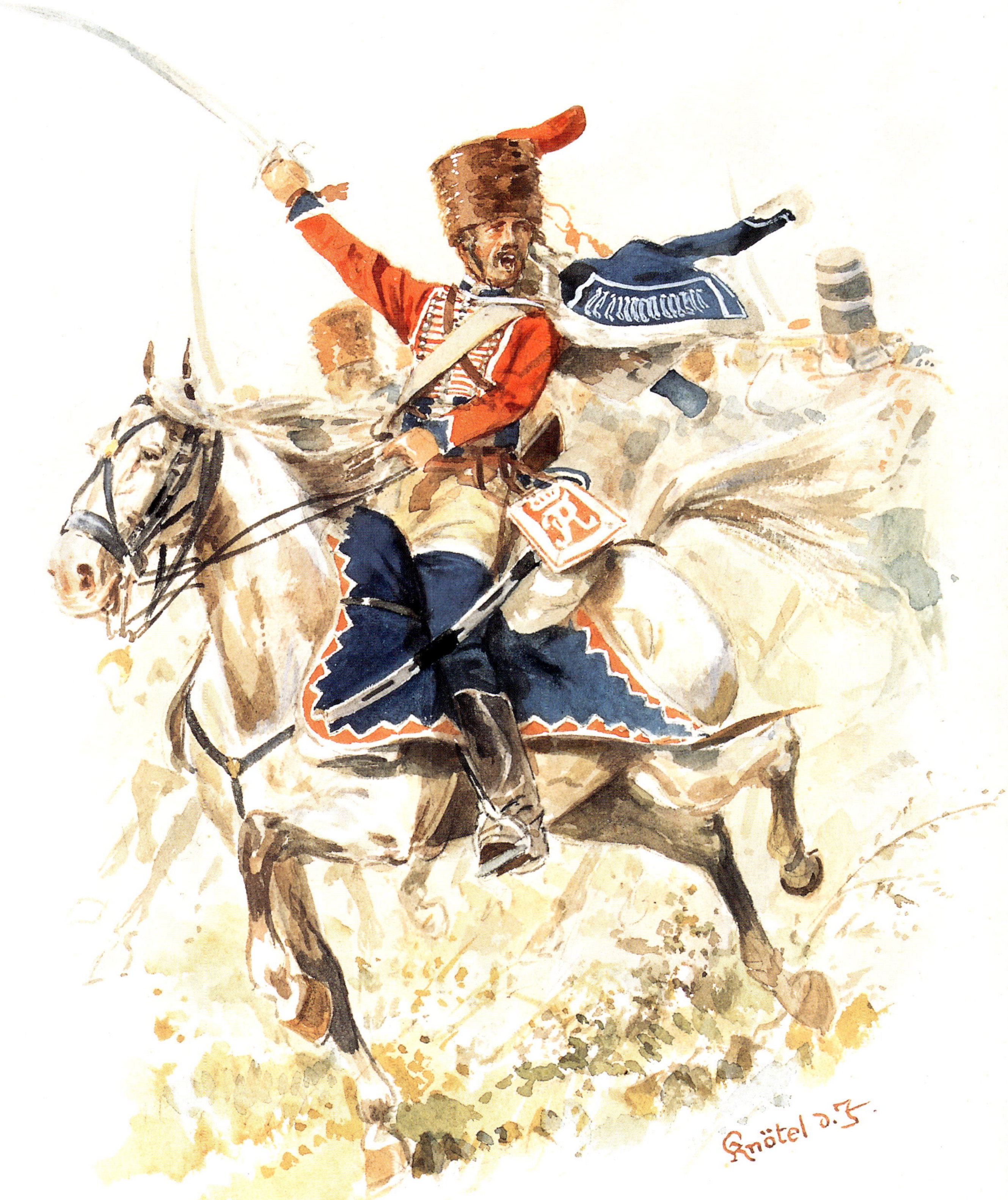

Hussar, 2nd Regiment v. Ziethen, Kingdom of Prussia 1756-1763.

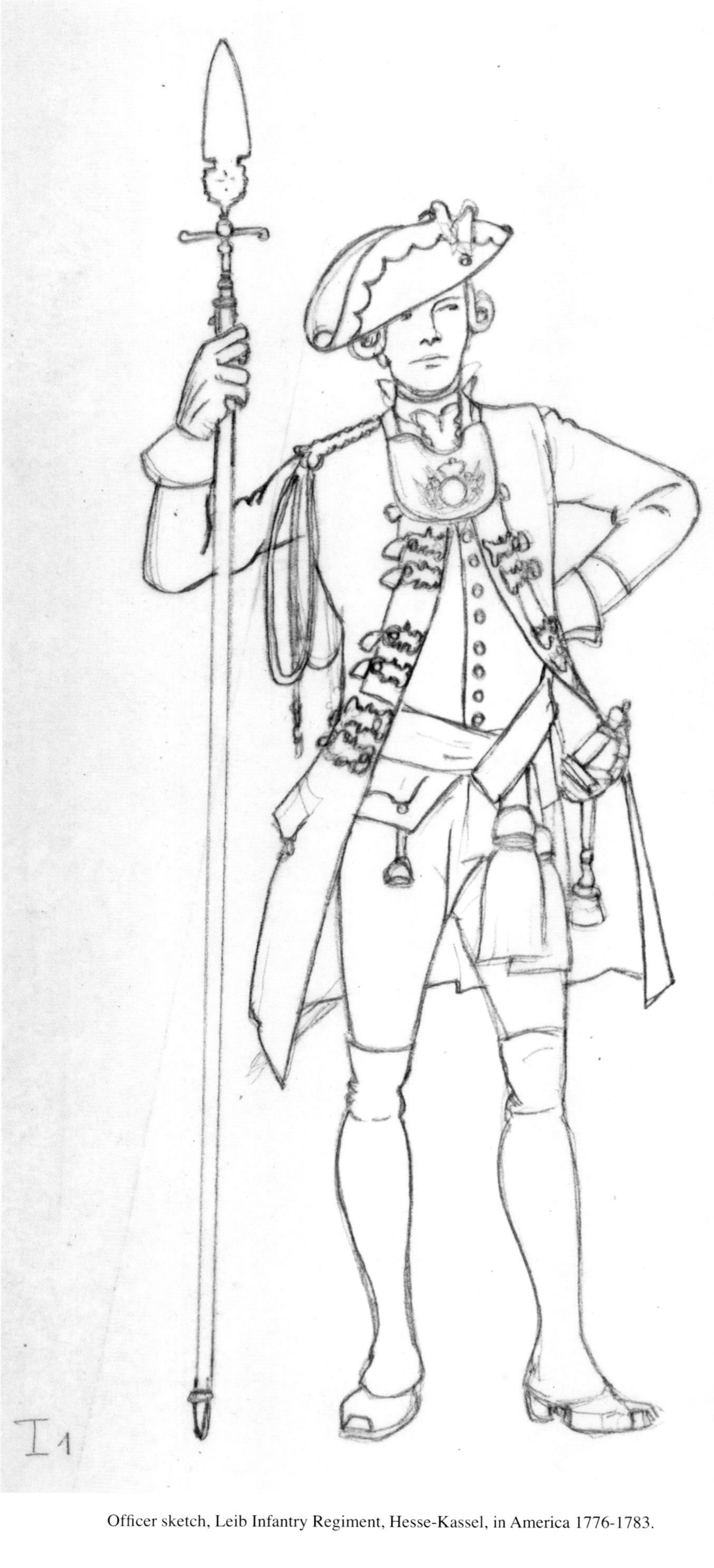

Officer sketch, Leib Infantry Regiment, Hesse-Kassel, in America 1776-1783.

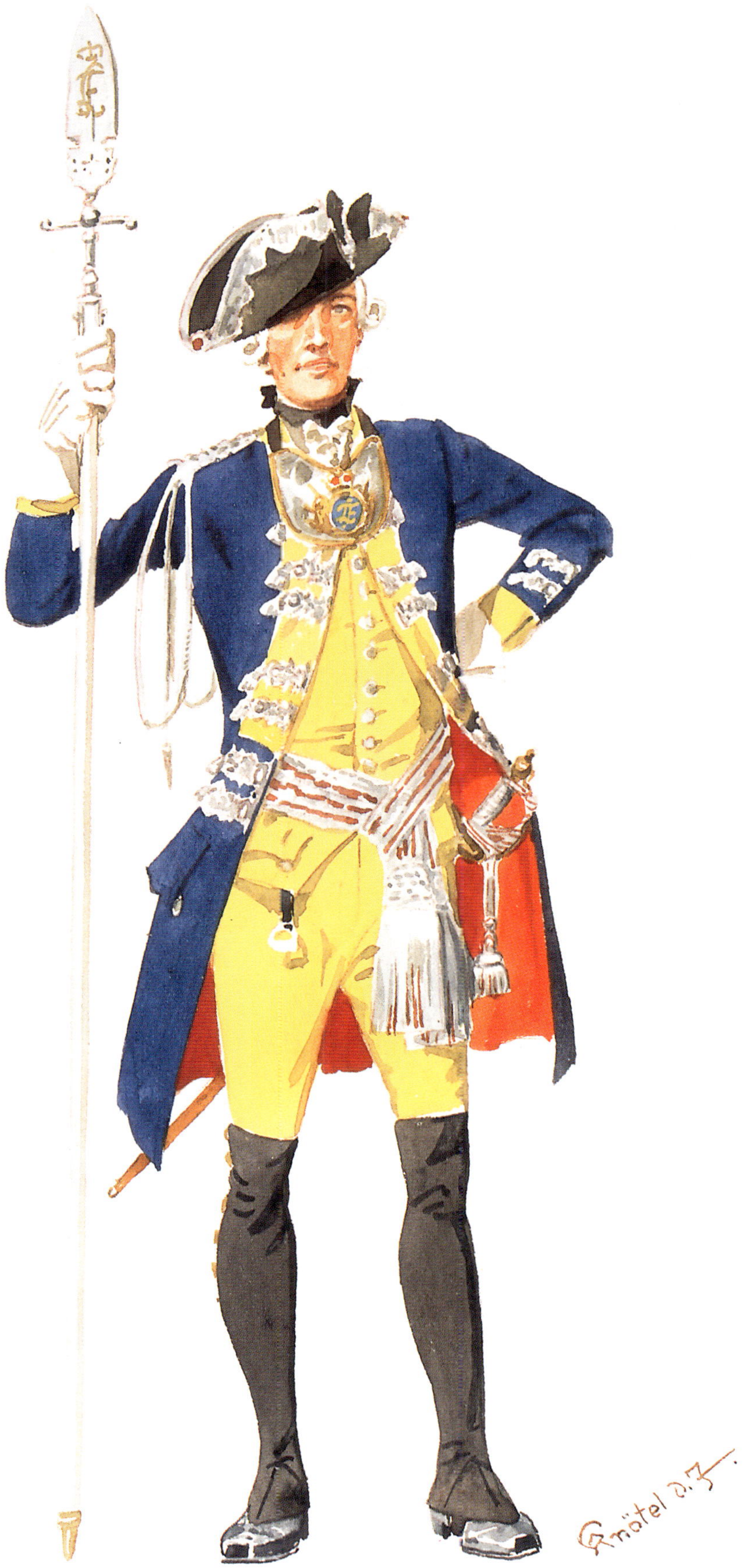

Officer, Leib Infantry Regiment, Hesse-Kassel, in America 1776-1783. The officers wore no insignia of rank due to high officer casualty rates. The field and staff officers generally wore high boots, and their distinctive embroidery was removed soon after they arrived in America.

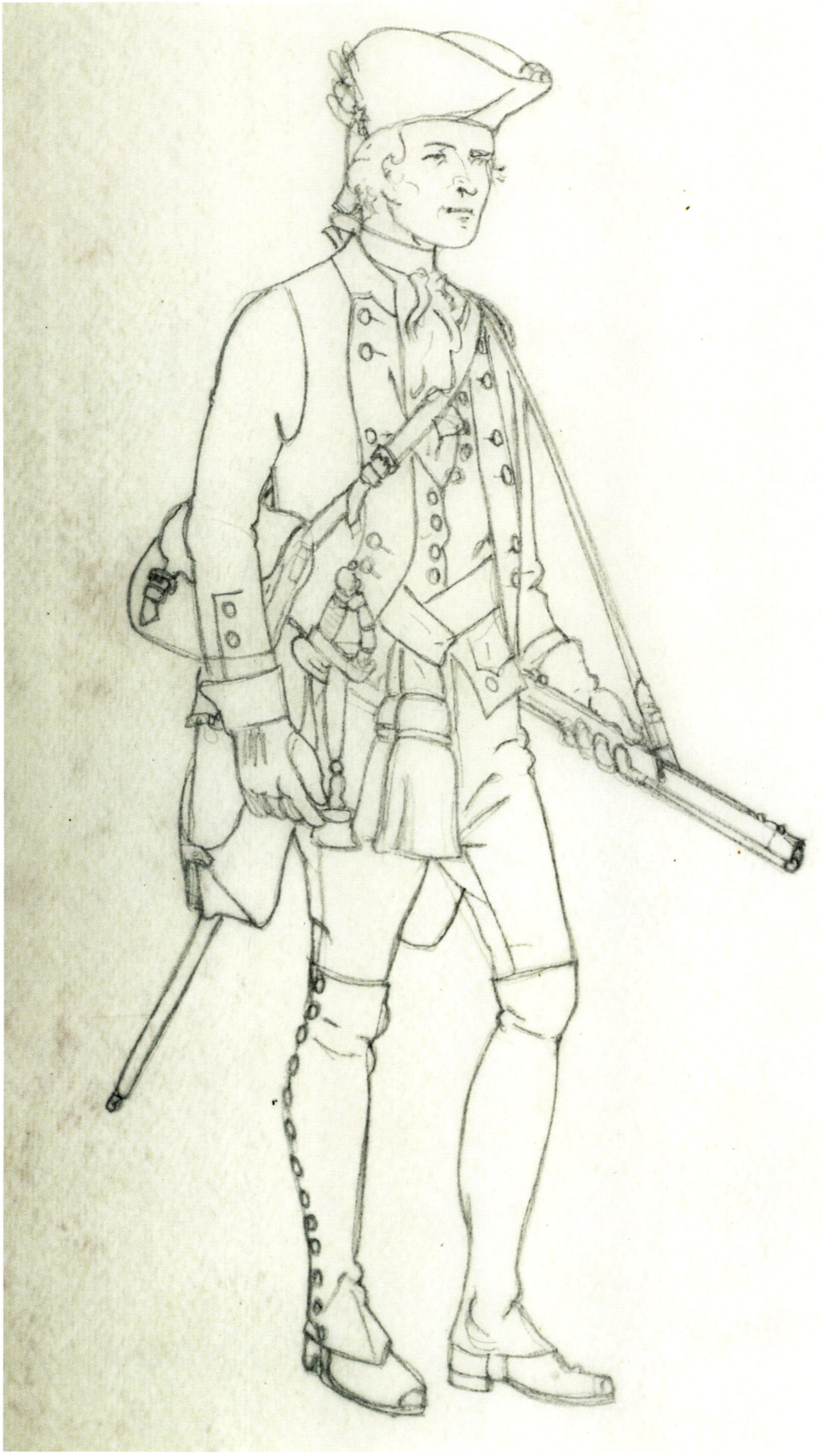

Officer sketch in field dress, Leib Infantry Regiment, Hesse-Kassel, in America 1776-1783.

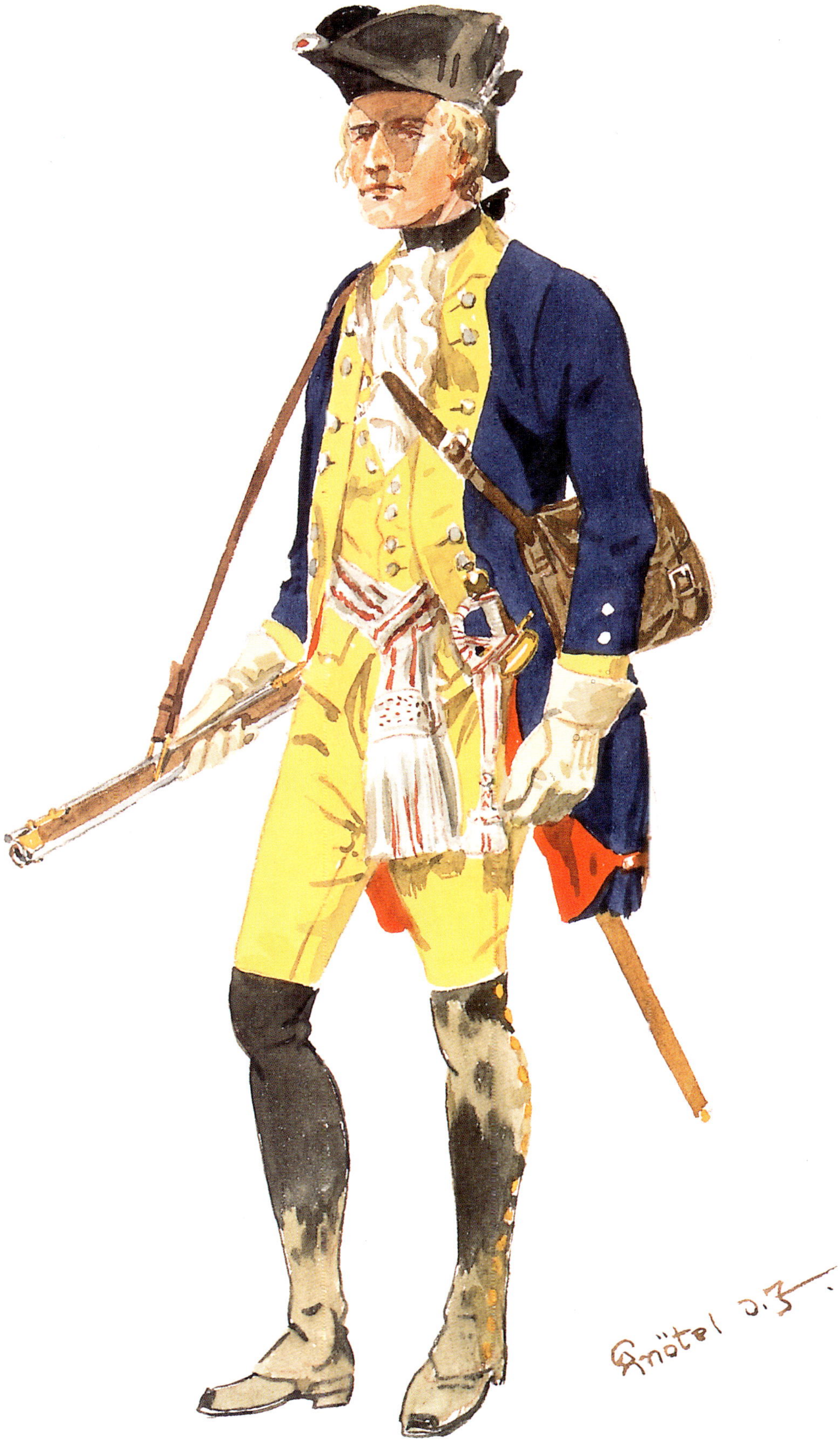

Officer in field dress, Leib Infantry Regiment, Hesse-Kassel, in America 1776–1783. Due to the high officer casualty rate in America, distinctions in dress between officers and men were soon dropped. Their armament consisted of rifles or muskets.

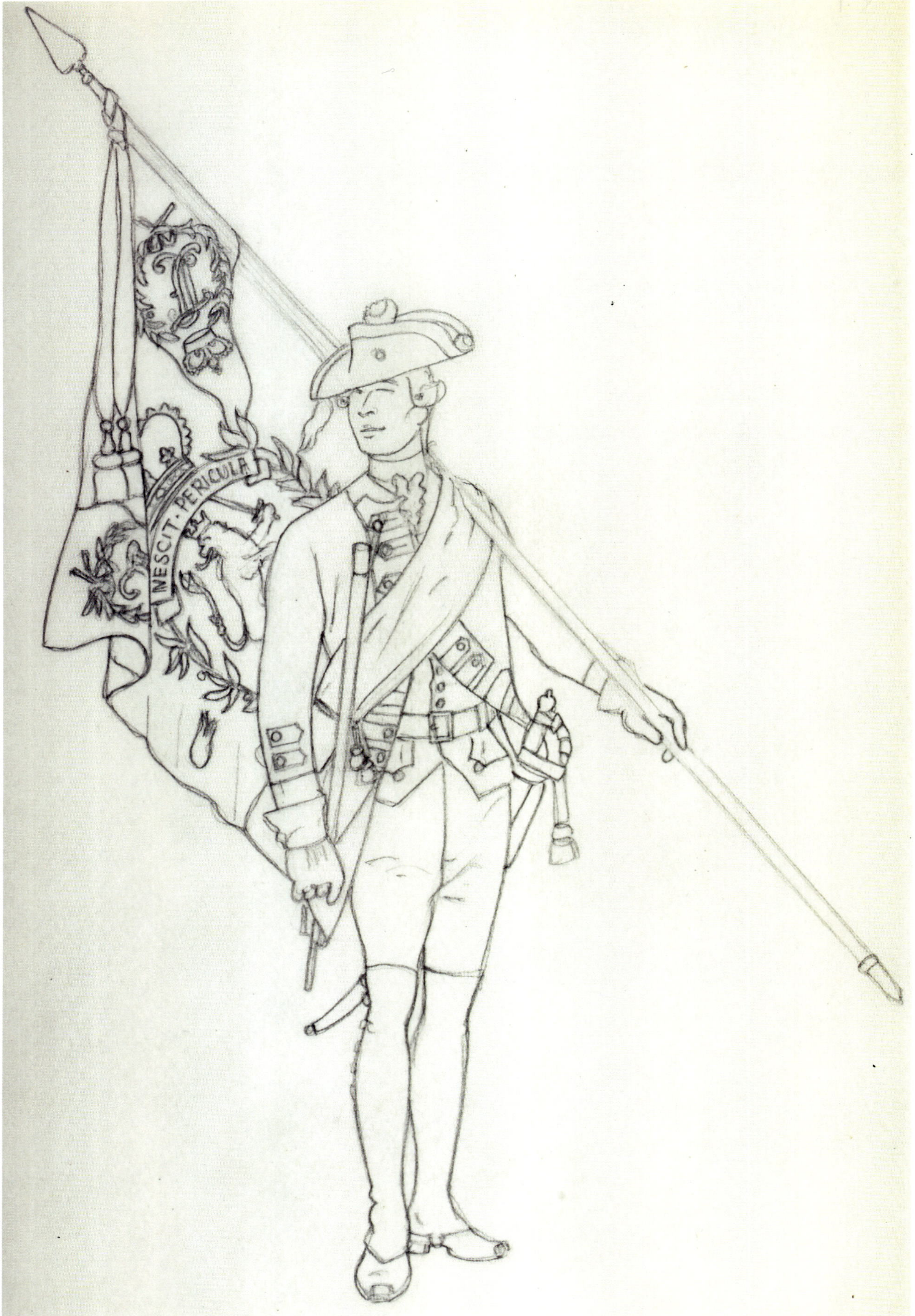

Regimental Colors sketch, Leib Infantry Regiment, Hesse-Kassel, in America 1776-1783.

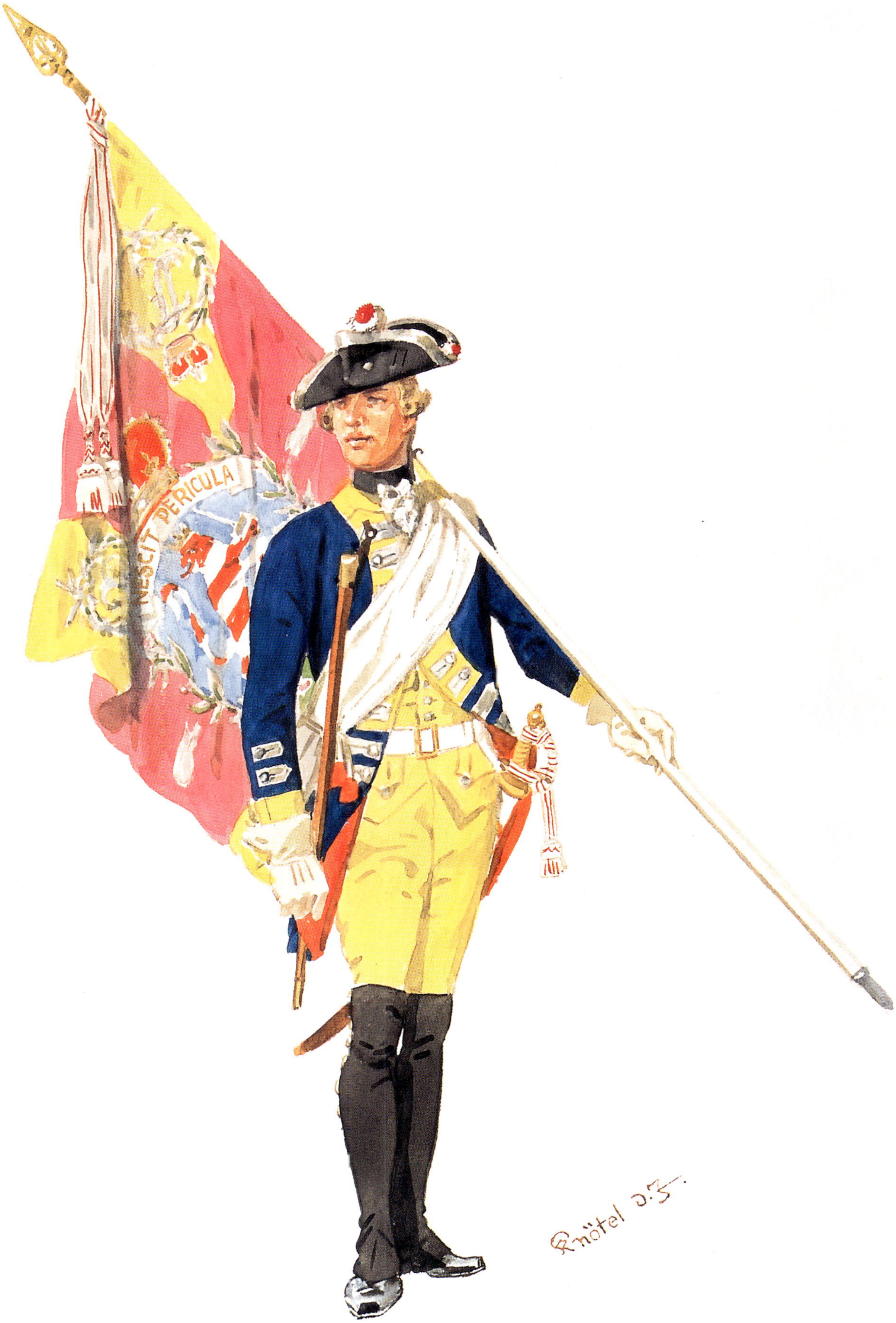

Regimental Colors, Leib Infantry Regiment, Hesse-Kassel, in America 1776-1783. Each regiment bore one Princely (Leib) color and up to four regimental colors.

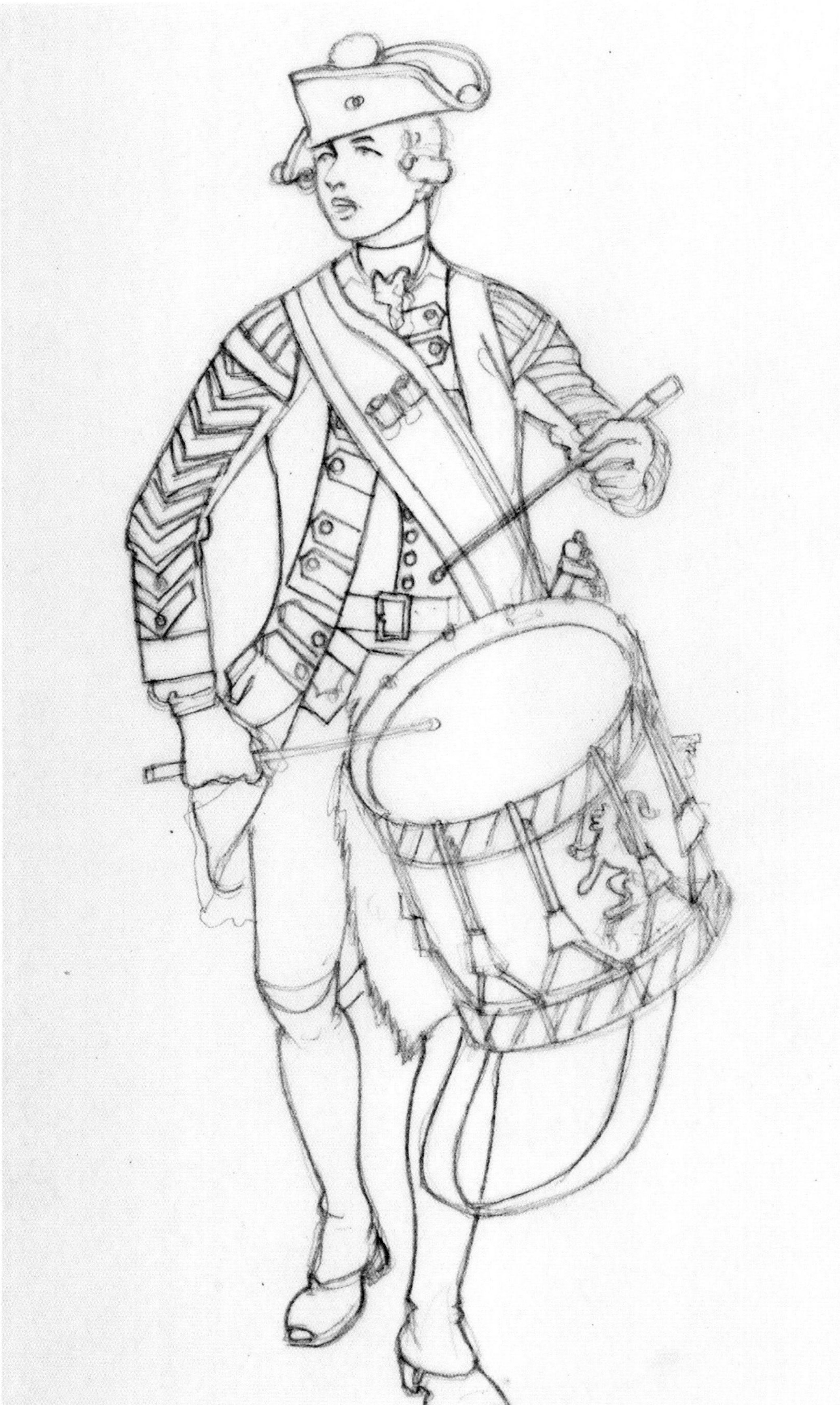

Drummer sketch, Leib Infantry Regiment, Hesse-Kassel, in America 1776-1783.

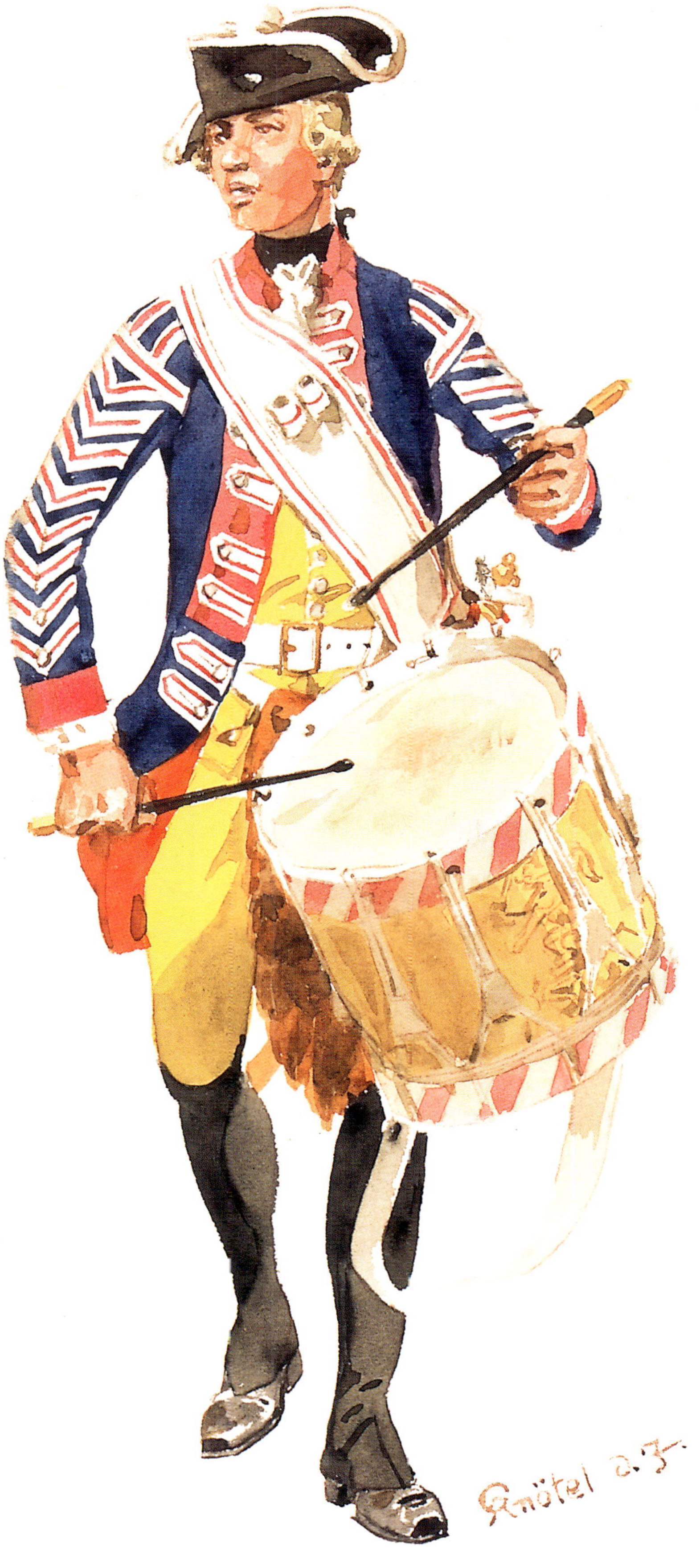

Drummer, Leib Infantry Regiment, Hesse-Kassel, in America 1776-1783. Drummers and musicians were distinguished by swallow-nest decorations on the shoulders and chevrons along the sleeves.

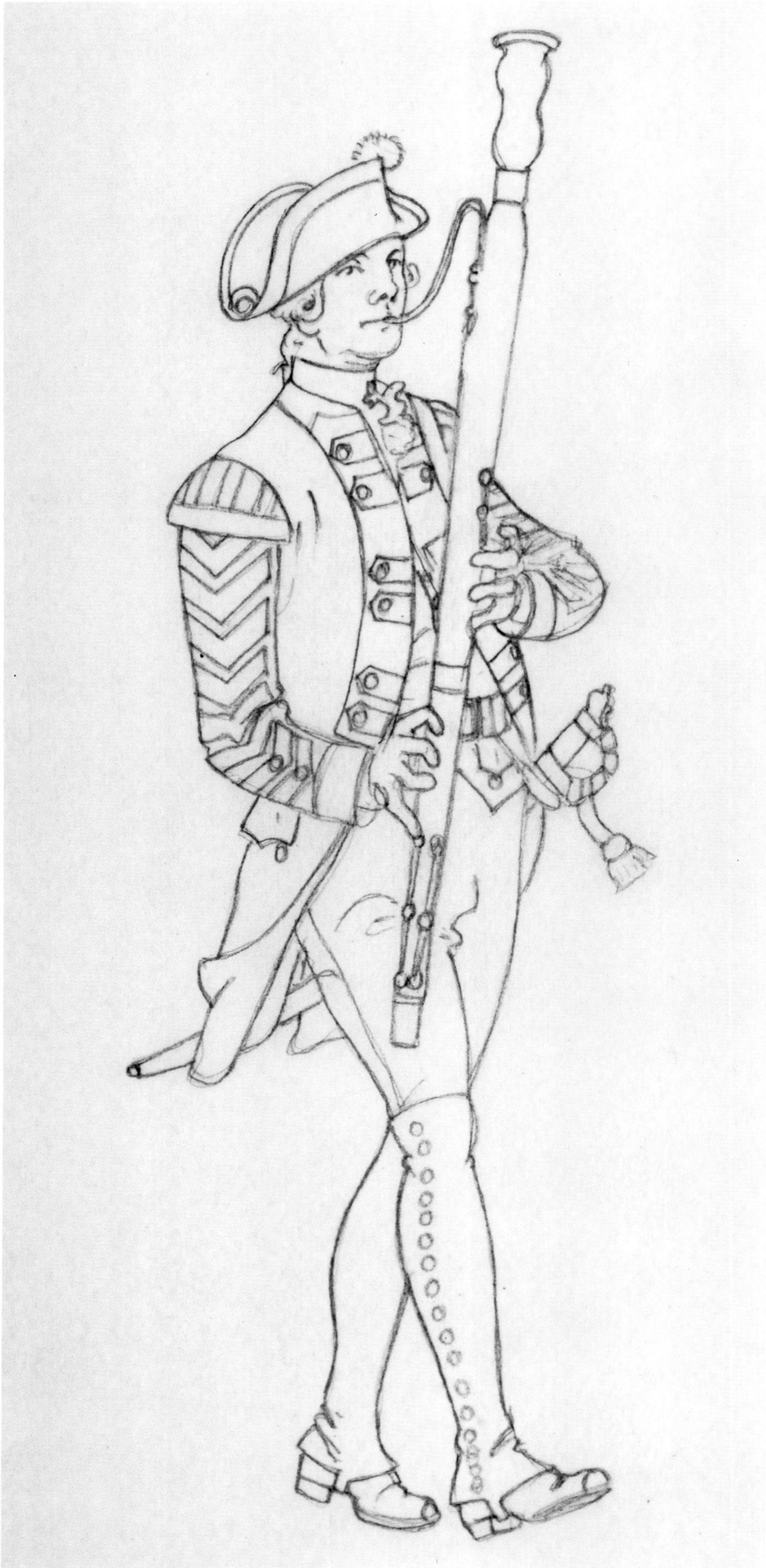

Musician sketch, Leib Infantry Regiment, Hesse-Kassel, in America 1776-1783.

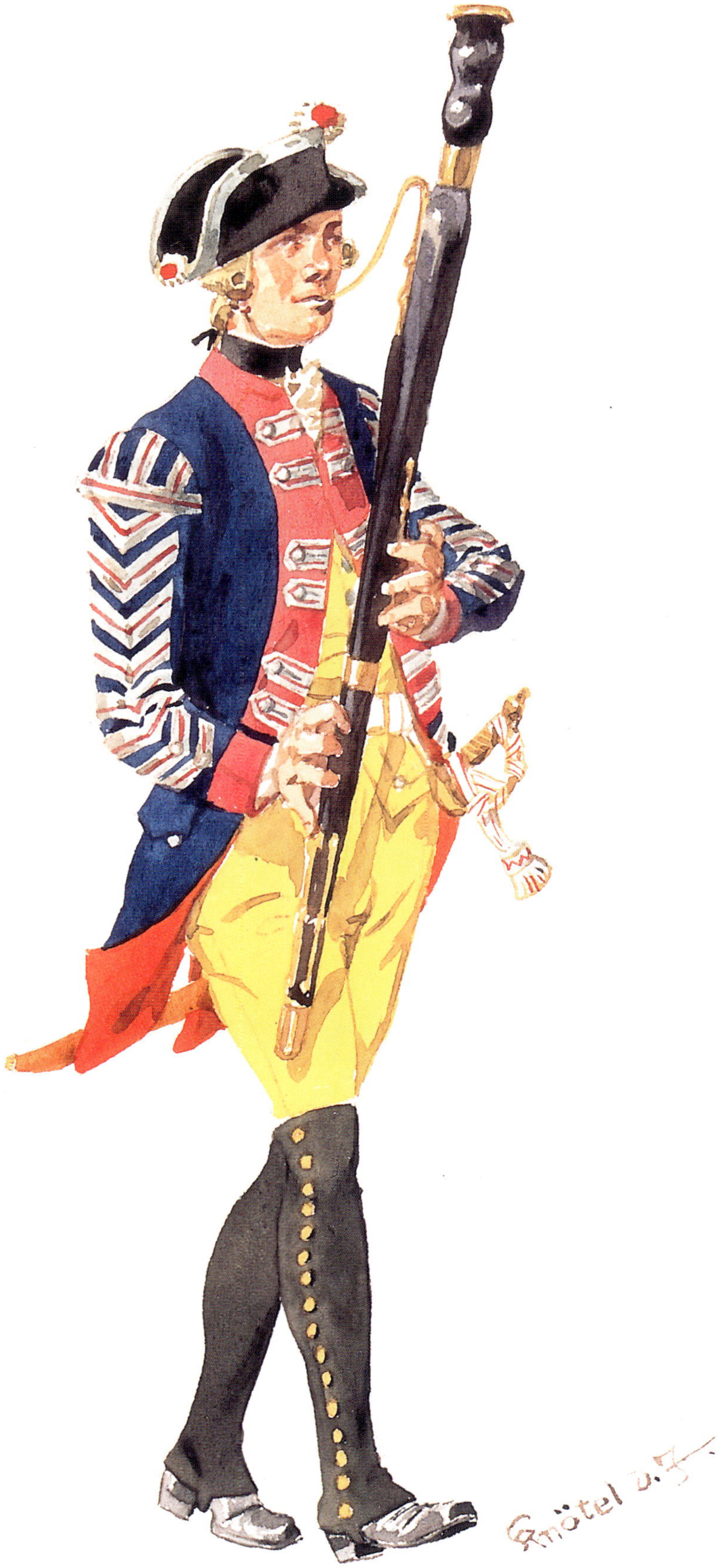

Musician, Leib Infantry Regiment, Hesse-Kassel, in America 1776-1783. 18th century regimental musicians were also called „hoboists“ from French „hautbois“ or wooden instruments. The sound was therefore more like a chamber orchestra than a modern military band. Description courtesy of Alfred Umhey

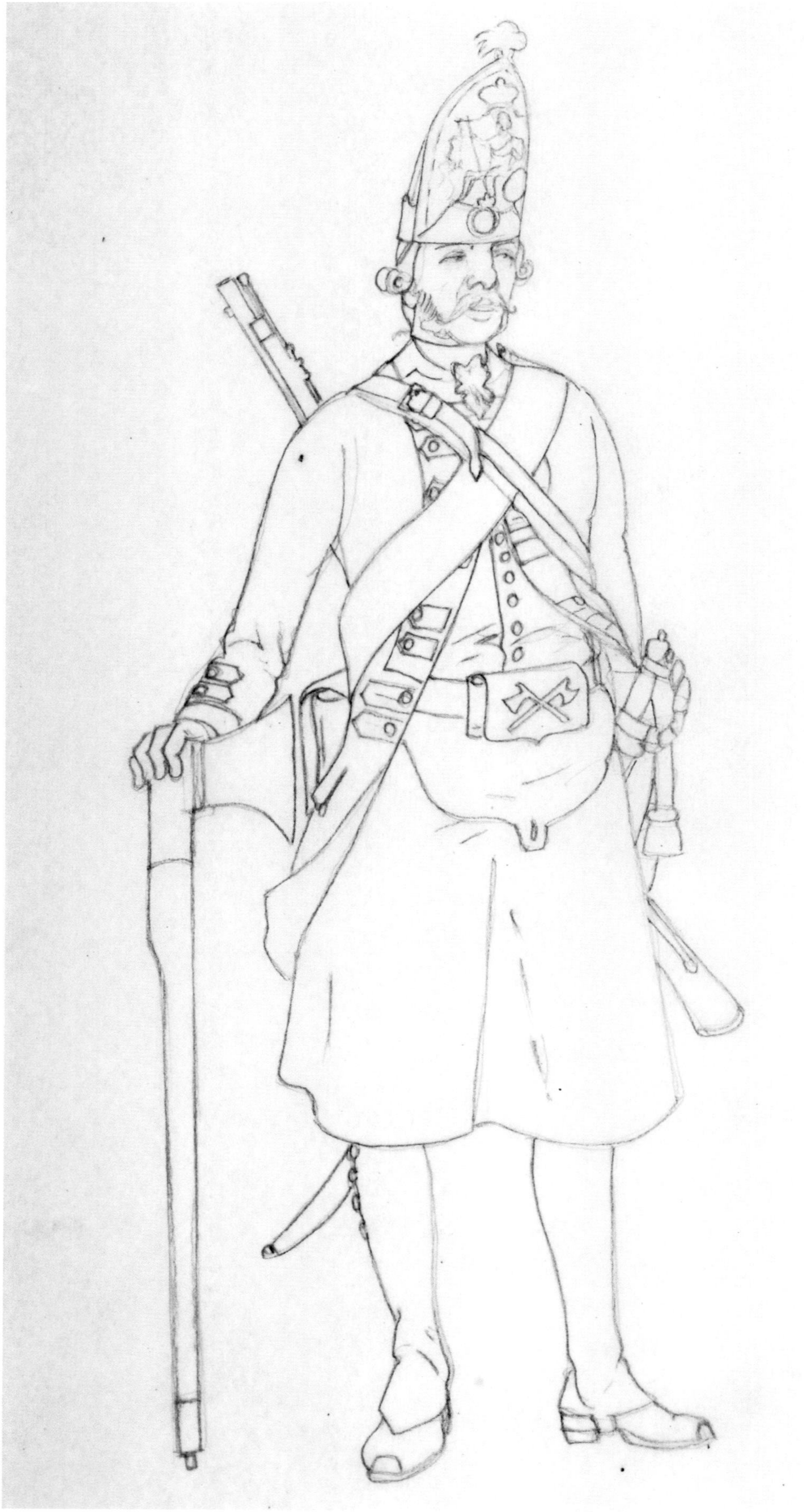

Sapper sketch, Leib Infantry Regiment, Hesse-Kassel, in America 1776-1783.

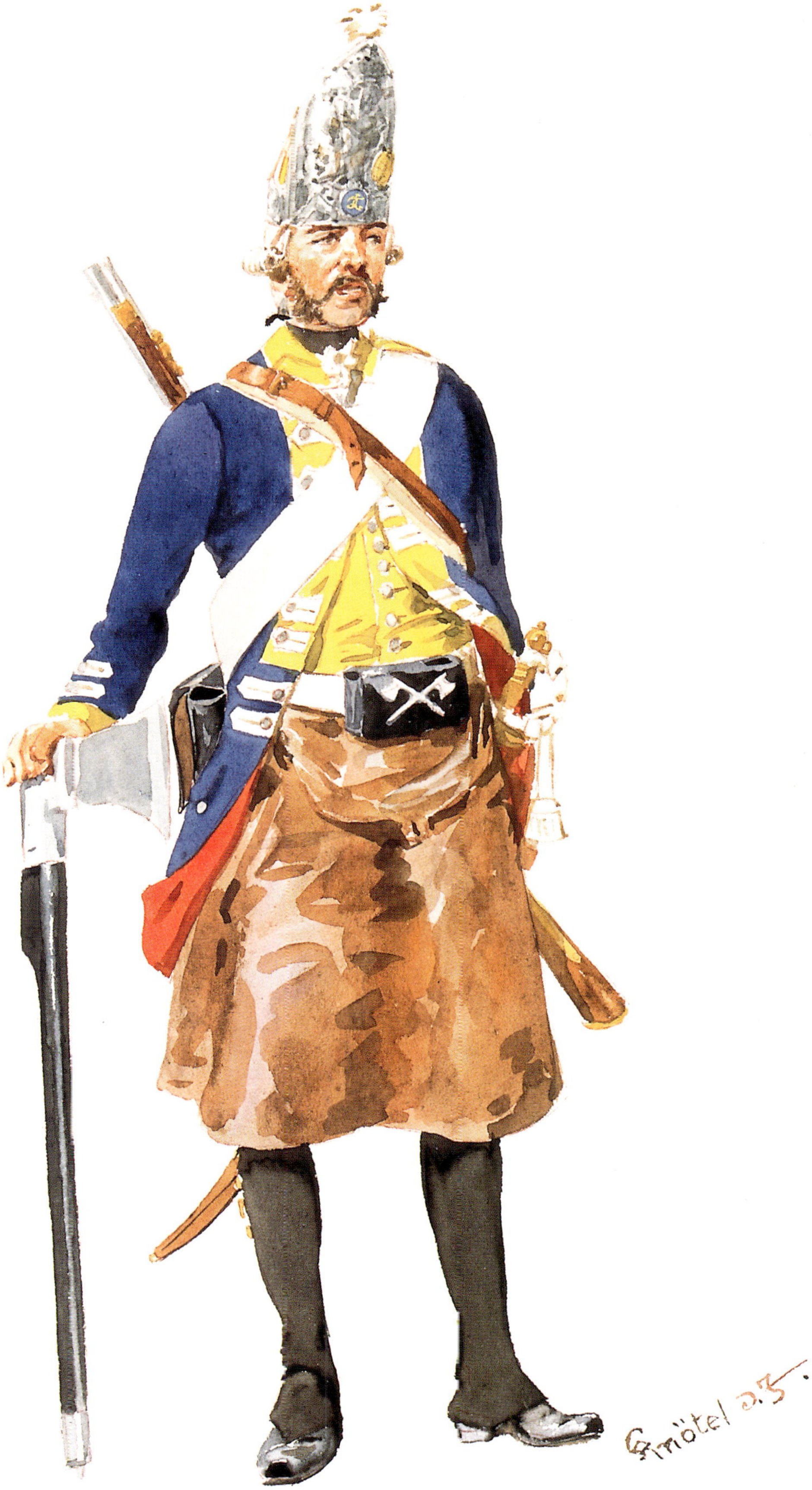

Sapper, Leib Infantry Regiment, Hesse-Kassel, in America 1776-1783. The regimental sappers were in fact carpenters. In combat they cleared obstacles or built barricades. The leather apron was worn for protection and as a distinction of their profession.

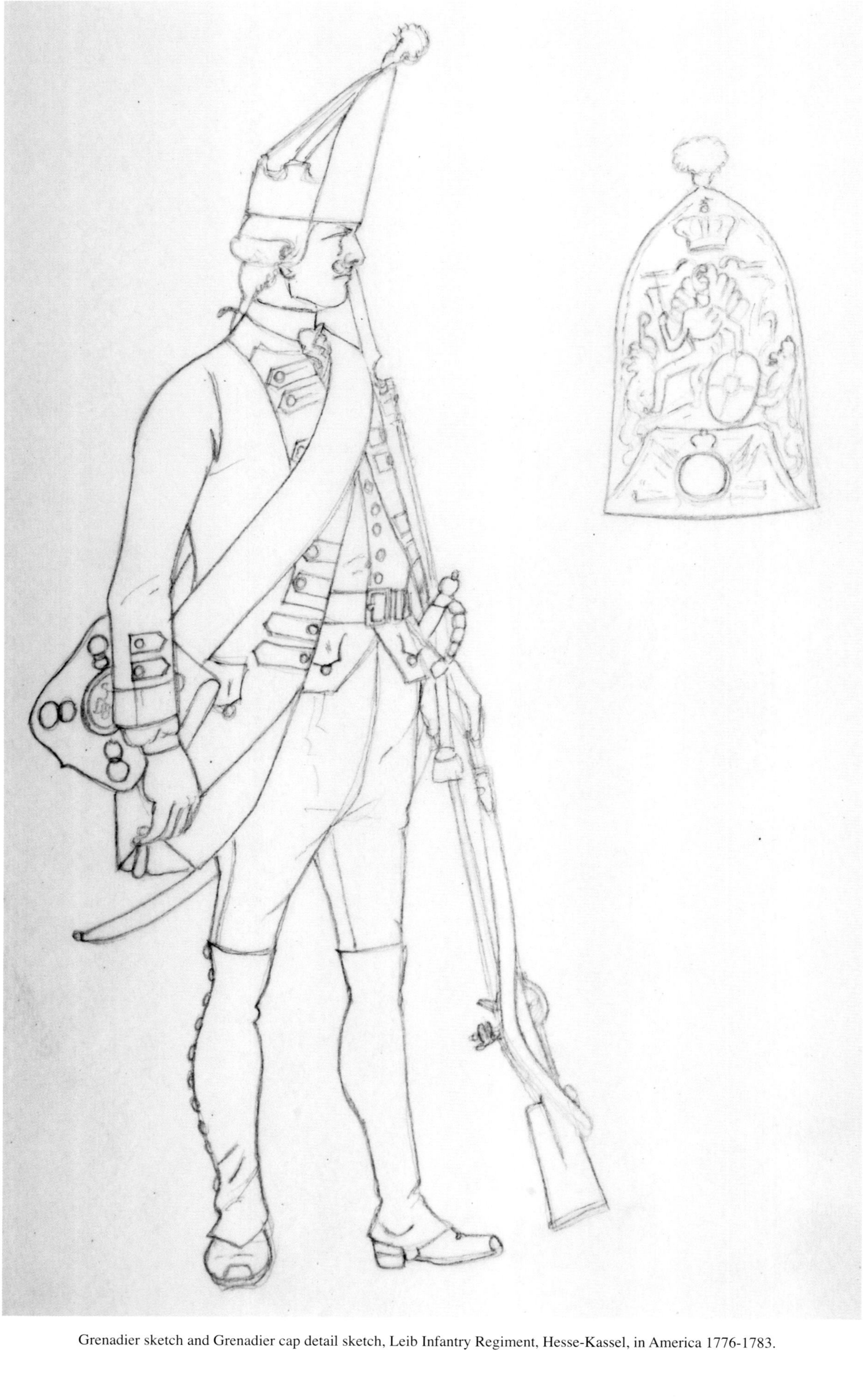

Grenadier sketch and Grenadier cap detail sketch, Leib Infantry Regiment, Hesse-Kassel, in America 1776-1783.

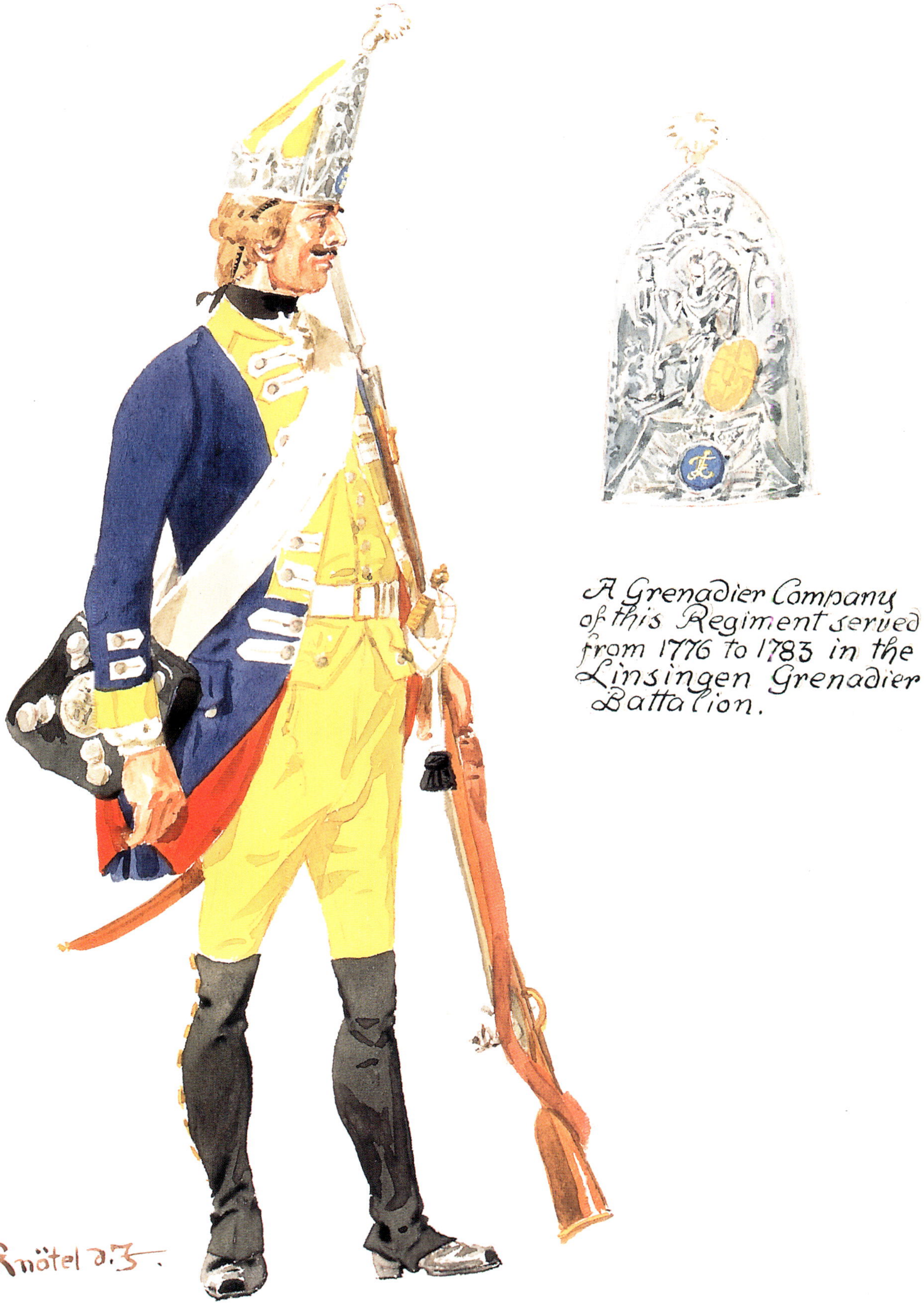

Grenadier and Grenadier cap detail, Leib Infantry Regiment, Hesse-Kassel, in America 1776-1783. A Grenadier Company of this Regiment served from 1776-1783 in the Linsingen Grenadier Battalion.

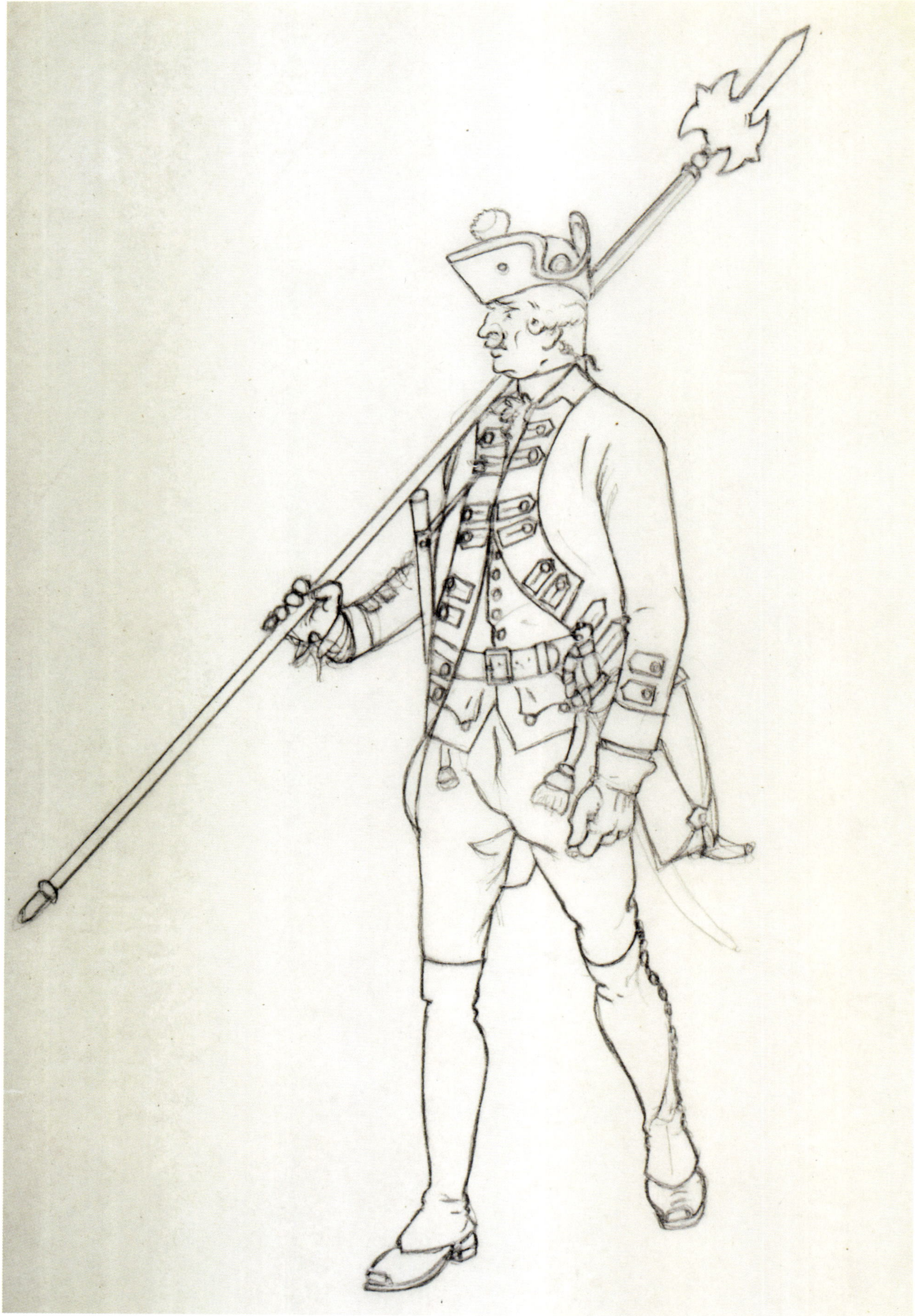

Musketeer Noncommissioned Officer sketch, Leib Infantry Regiment, Hesse-Kassel, in America 1776-1783.

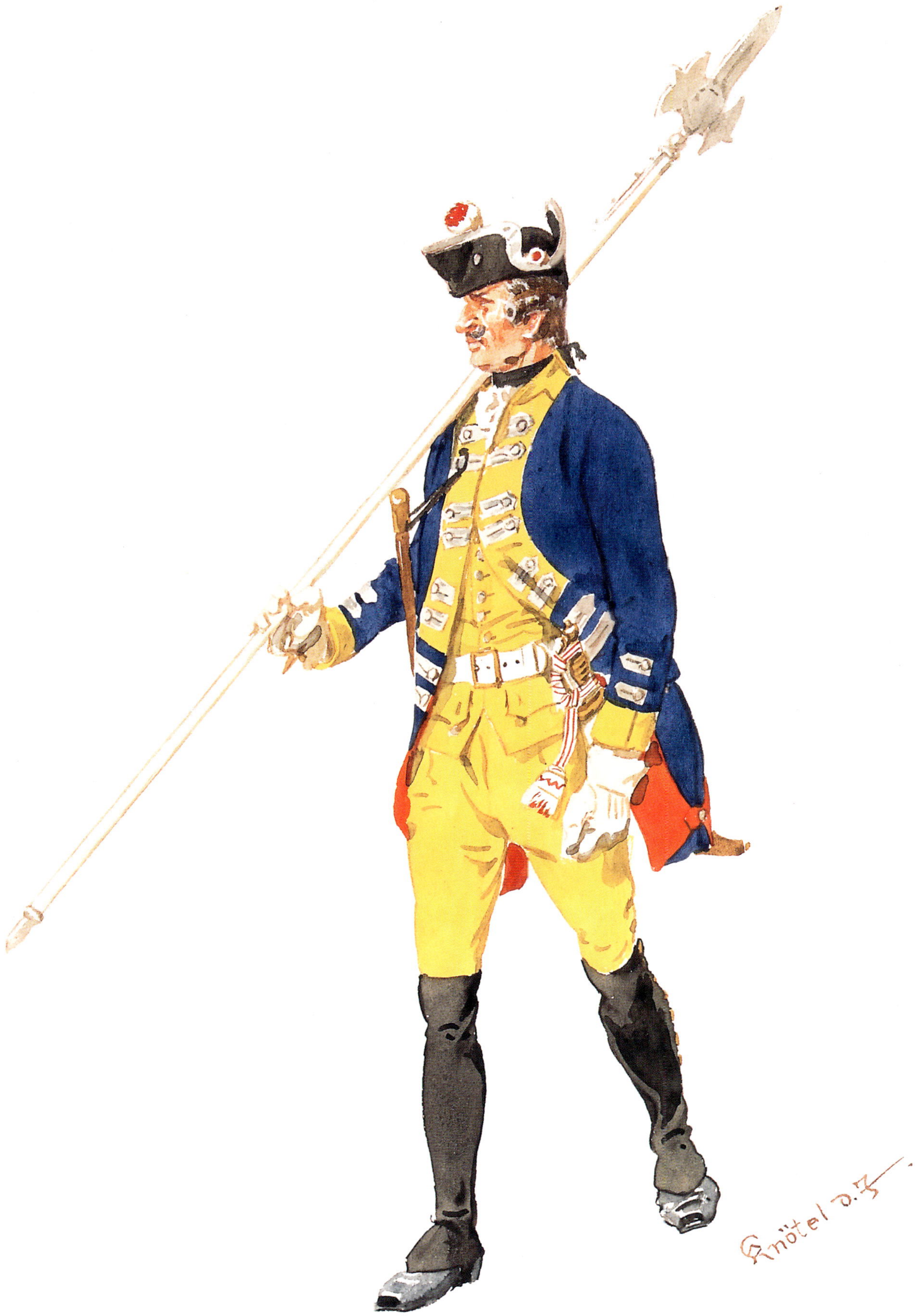

Musketeer Noncommissioned Officer, Leib Infantry Regiment, Hesse-Kassel, in America 1776-1783. The NCO is armed with a halberd and carries a stick, fixed to one of the buttonholes, which was used for punishment.

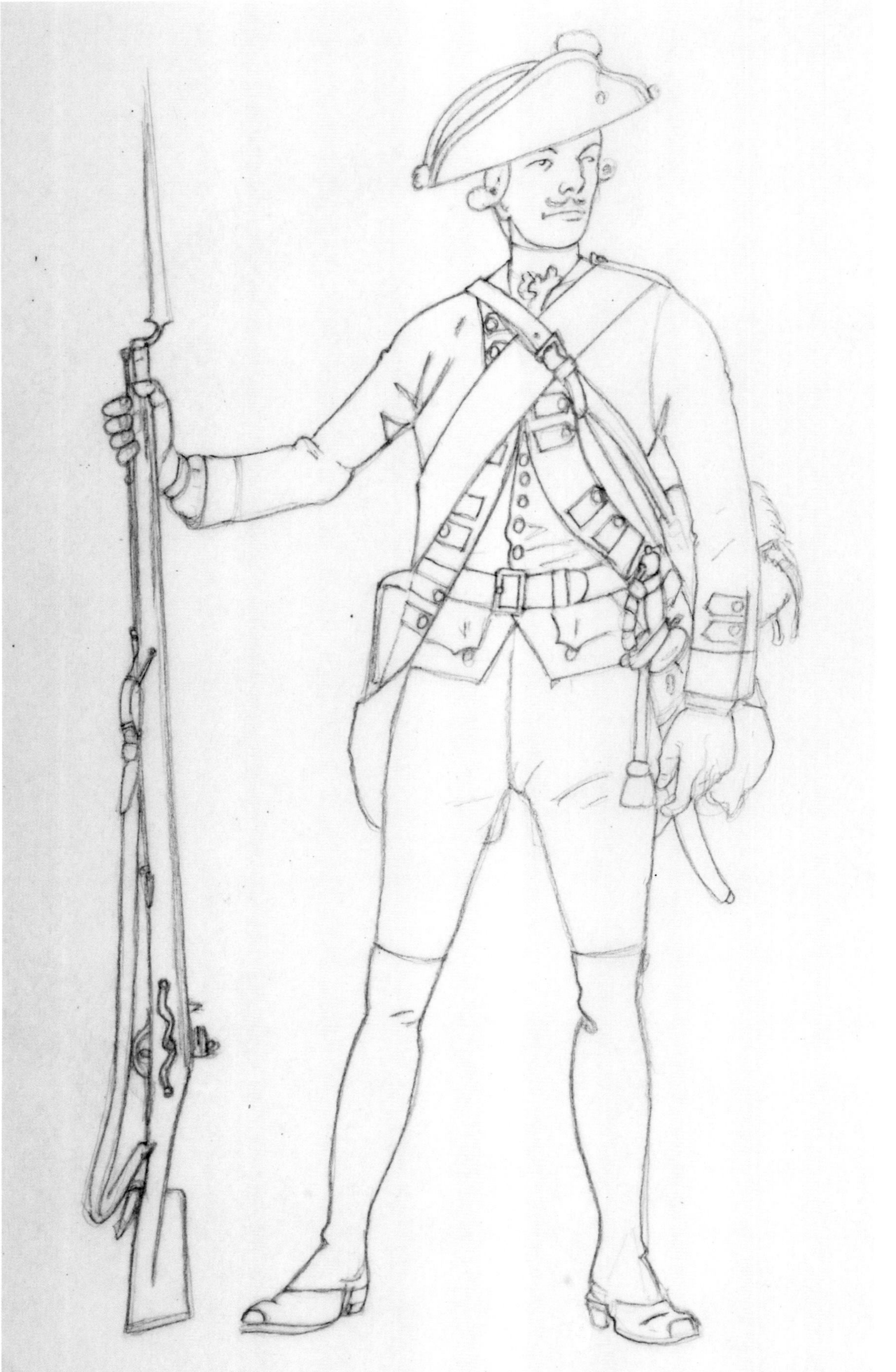

Musketeer sketch, Leib Infantry Regiment, Hesse-Kassel, in America 1776-1783.

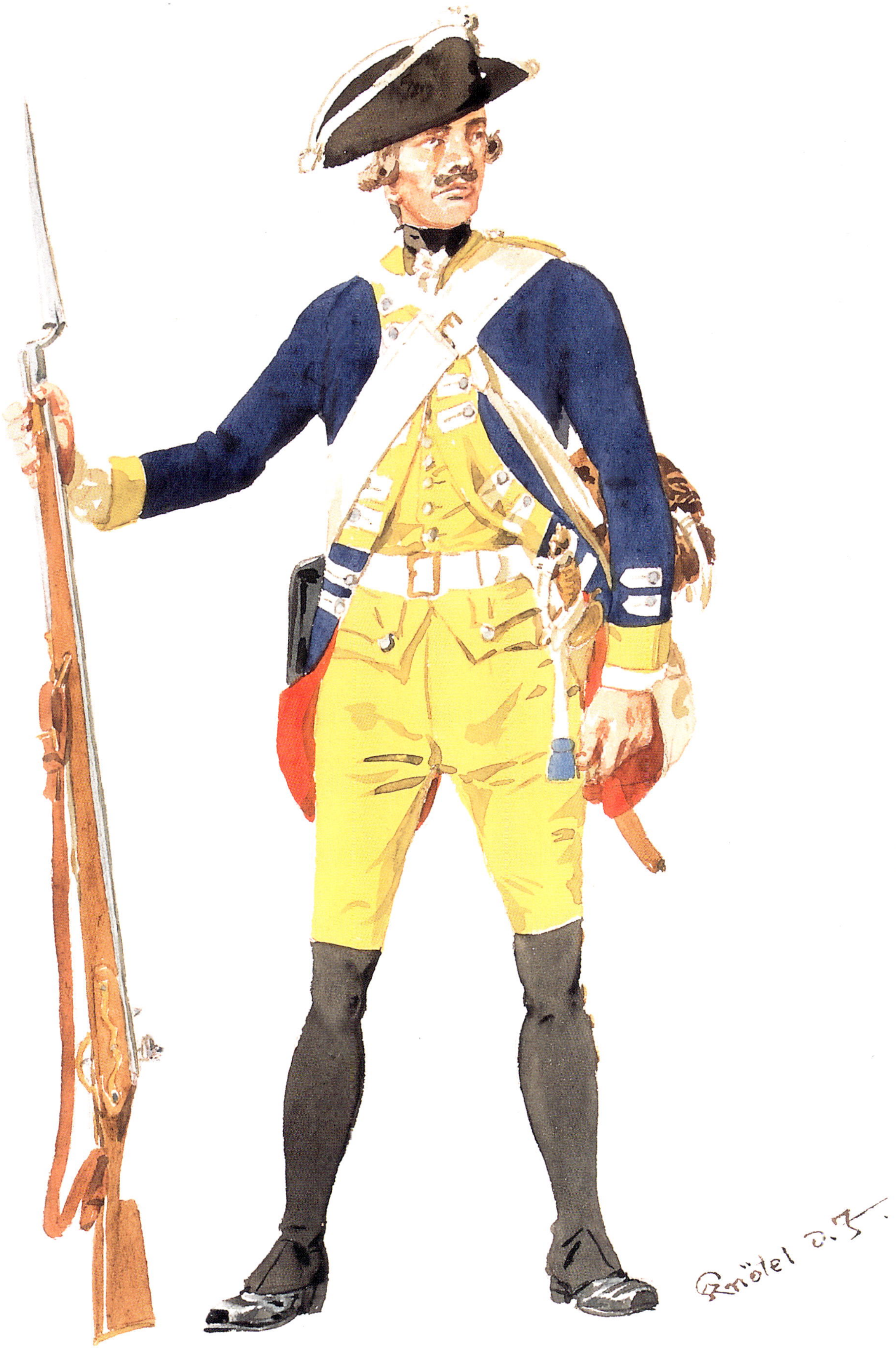

Musketeer, Leib Infantry Regiment, Hesse-Kassel, in America 1776-1783.

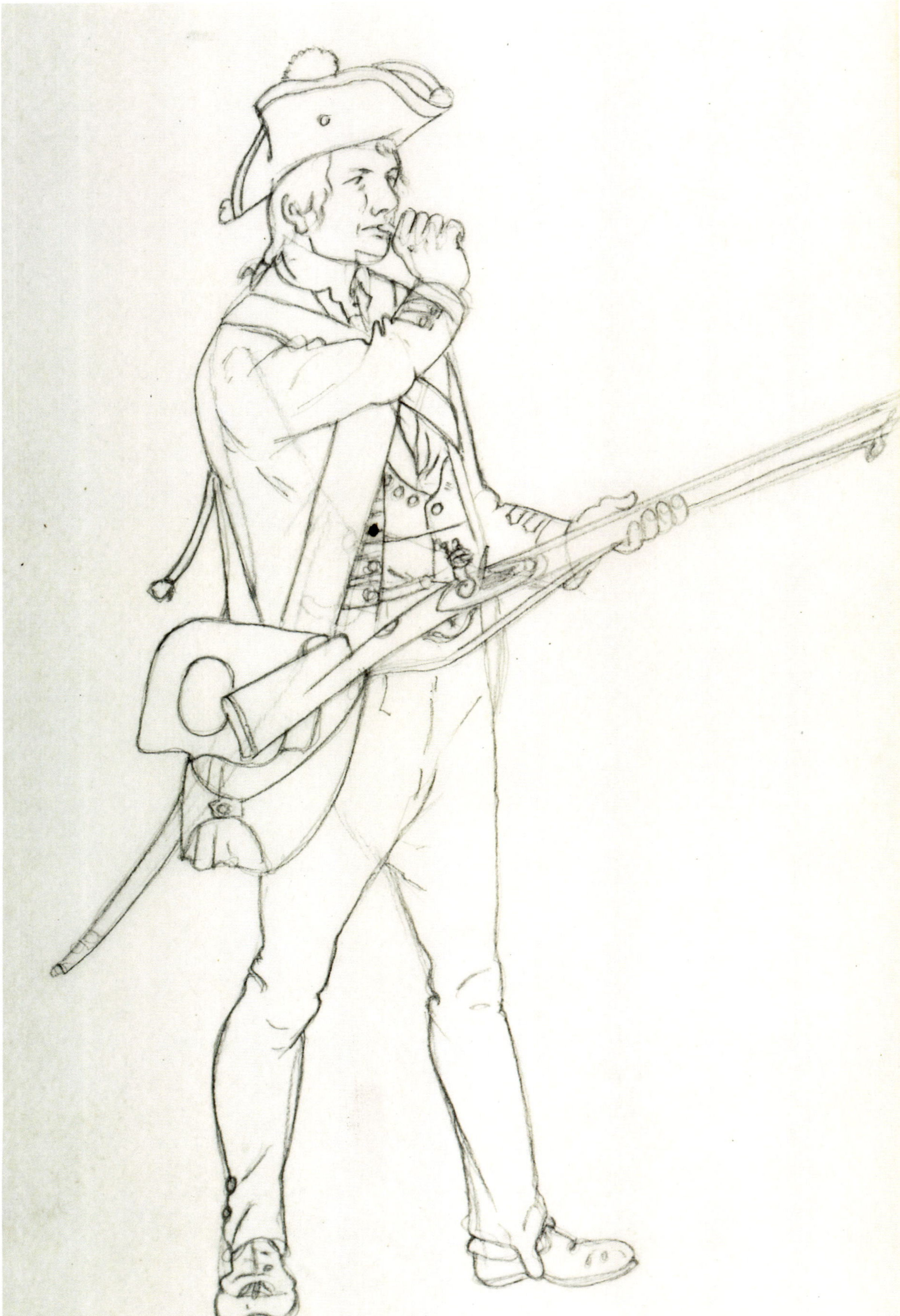

Musketeer in field dress sketch, Leib Infantry Regiment, Hesse-Kassel, in America 1776-1783.

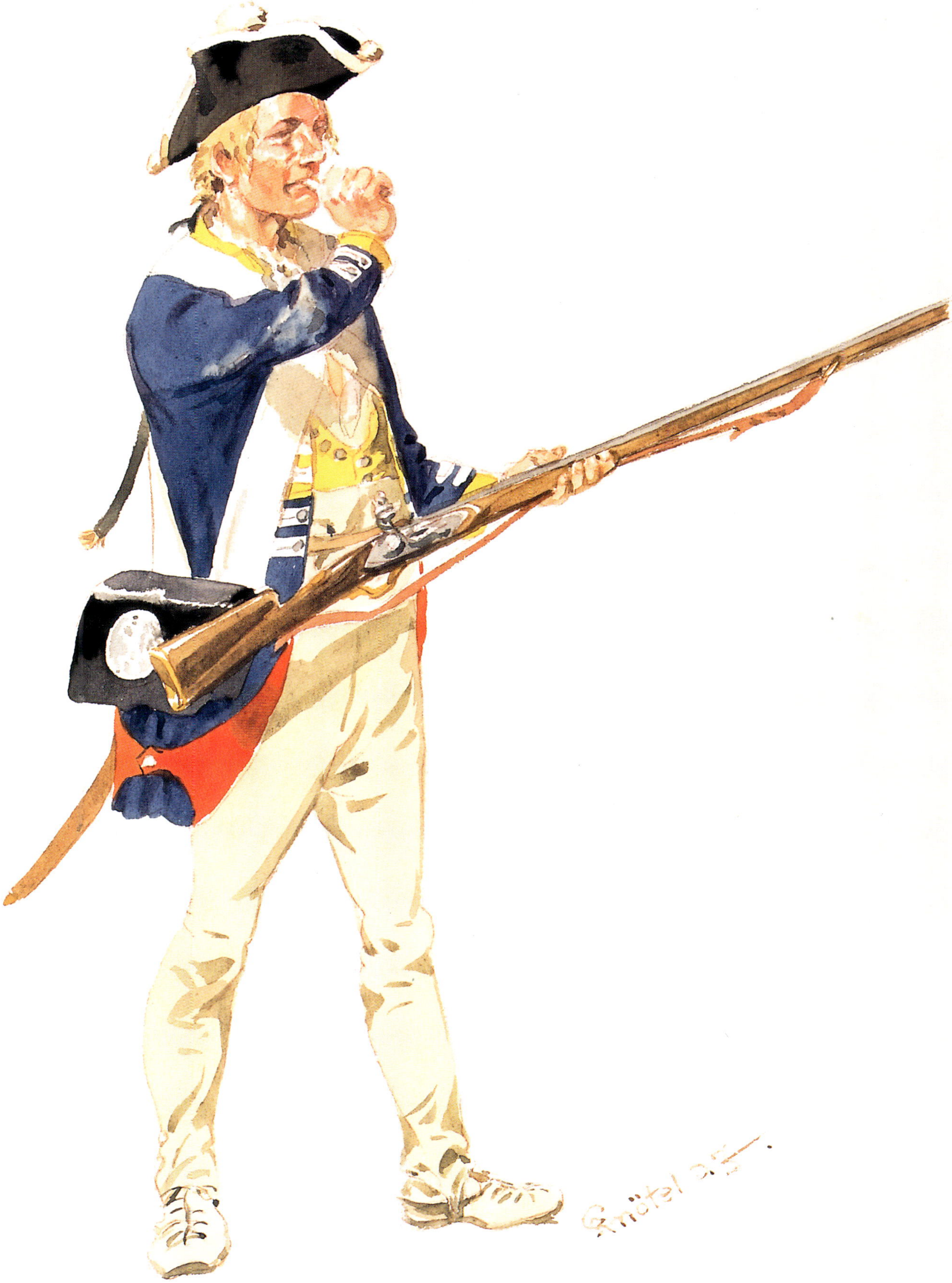

Musketeer in field dress, Leib Infantry Regiment, Hesse-Kassel. in America 1776-1783. The difference to the full dress seen previously is obvious. Moccasins replaced the shoes, linen trousers were worn for comfort and the hair was no longer curled.

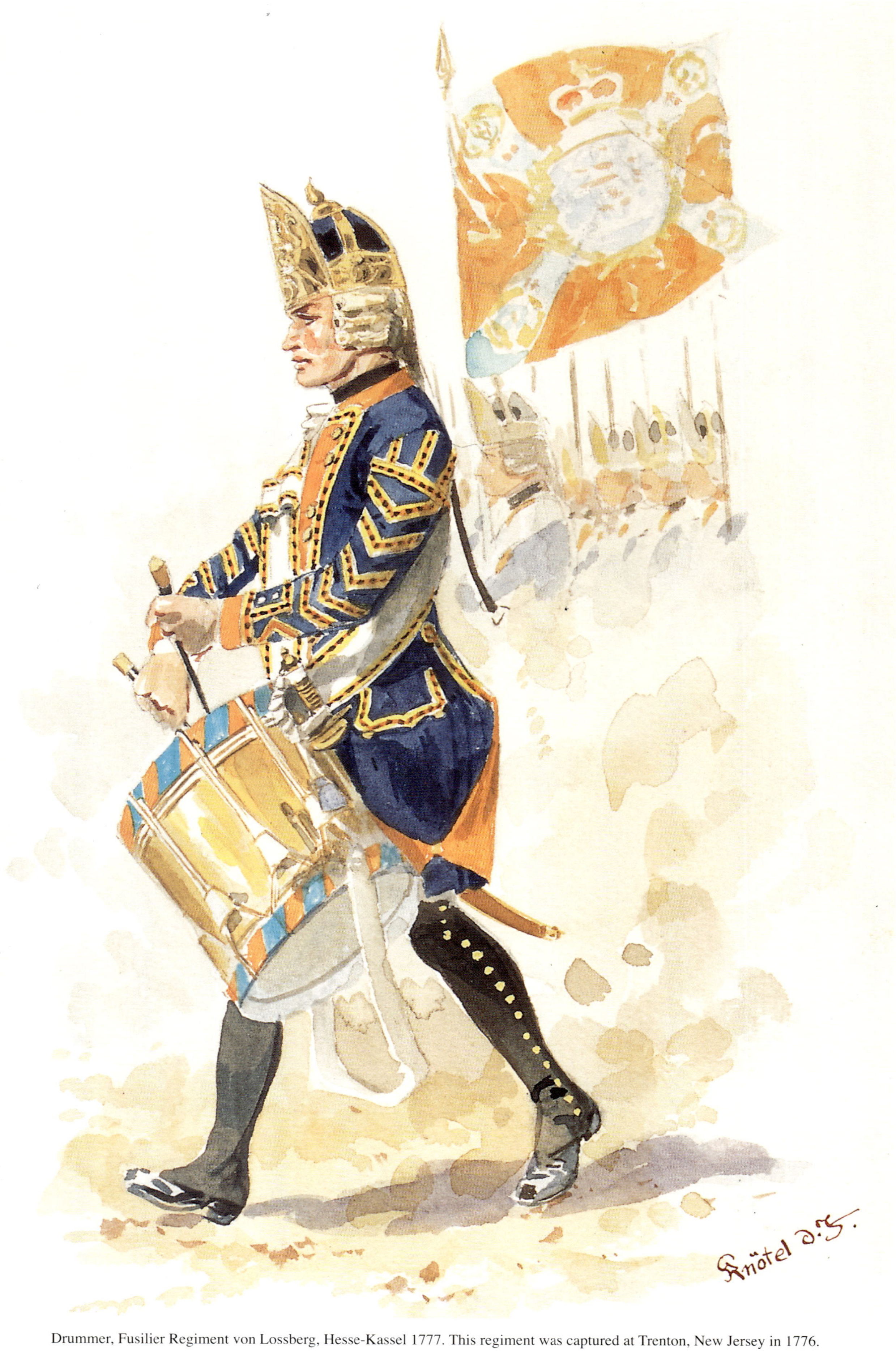

Drummer, Fusilier Regiment von Lossberg, Hesse-Kassel 1777. This regiment was captured at Trenton, New Jersey in 1776.

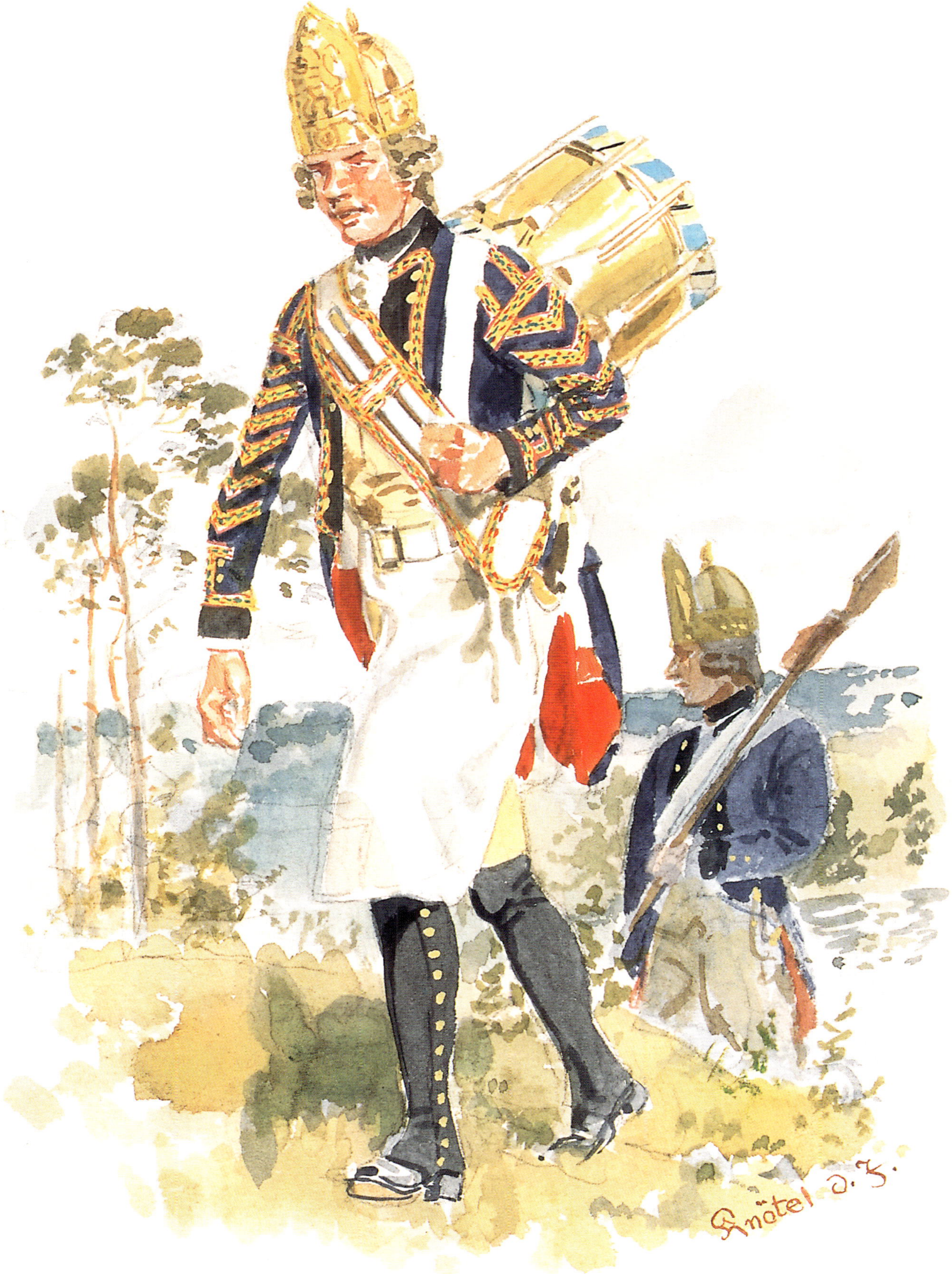

Drummer, Fusilier Regiment von Knyphausen, Hesse-Kassel 1777. This regiment was also captured at Trenton, New Jersey in 1776.

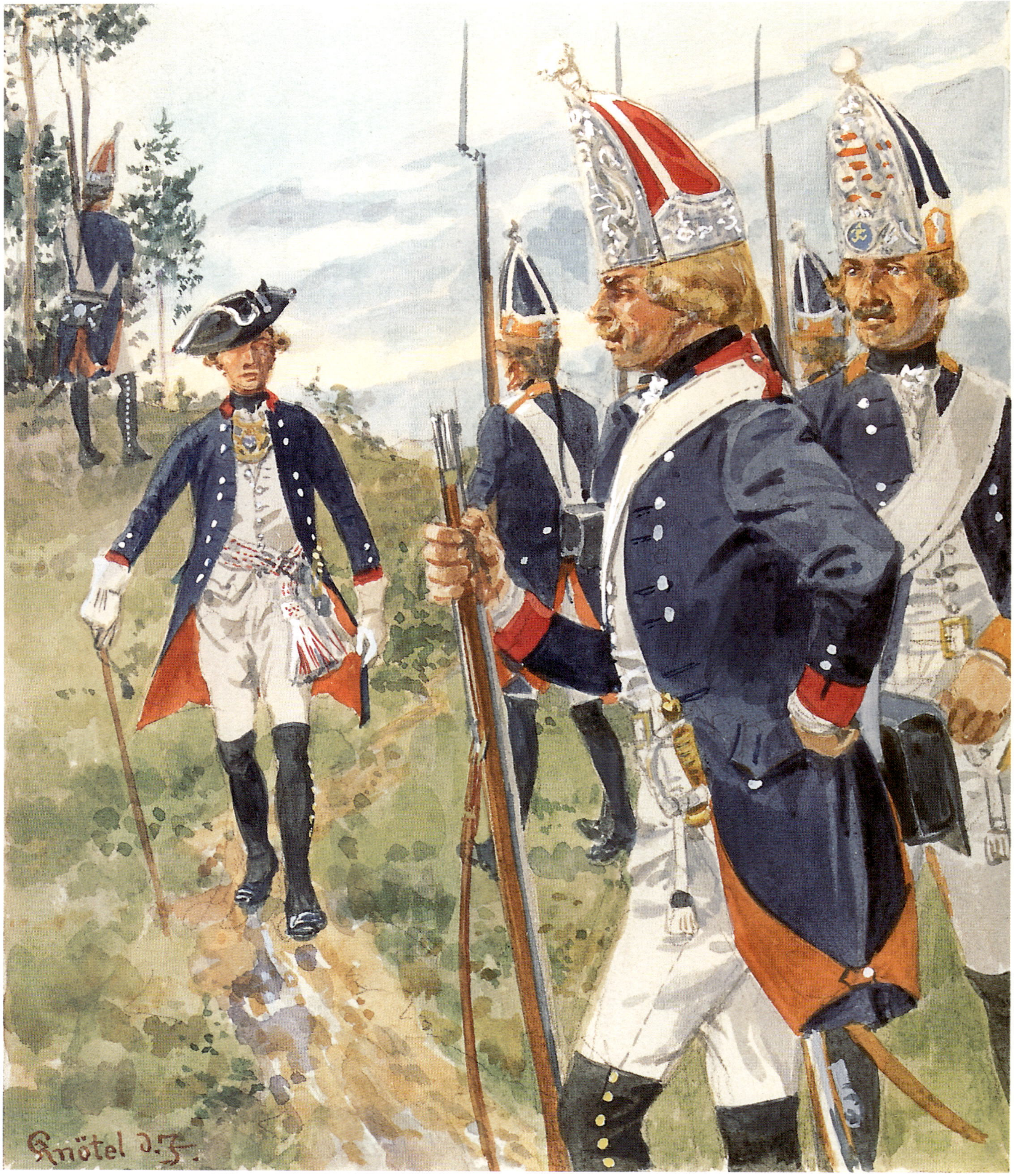

Grenadier Battalion Graf., Hesse-Kassel 1778. The 4th Grenadier Battalion was a provisional, composite unit formed in 1776 from grenadier companies of the Grenadier Regiment Rall and Garrison Regiments Wissenbach, Stein and Bünau.

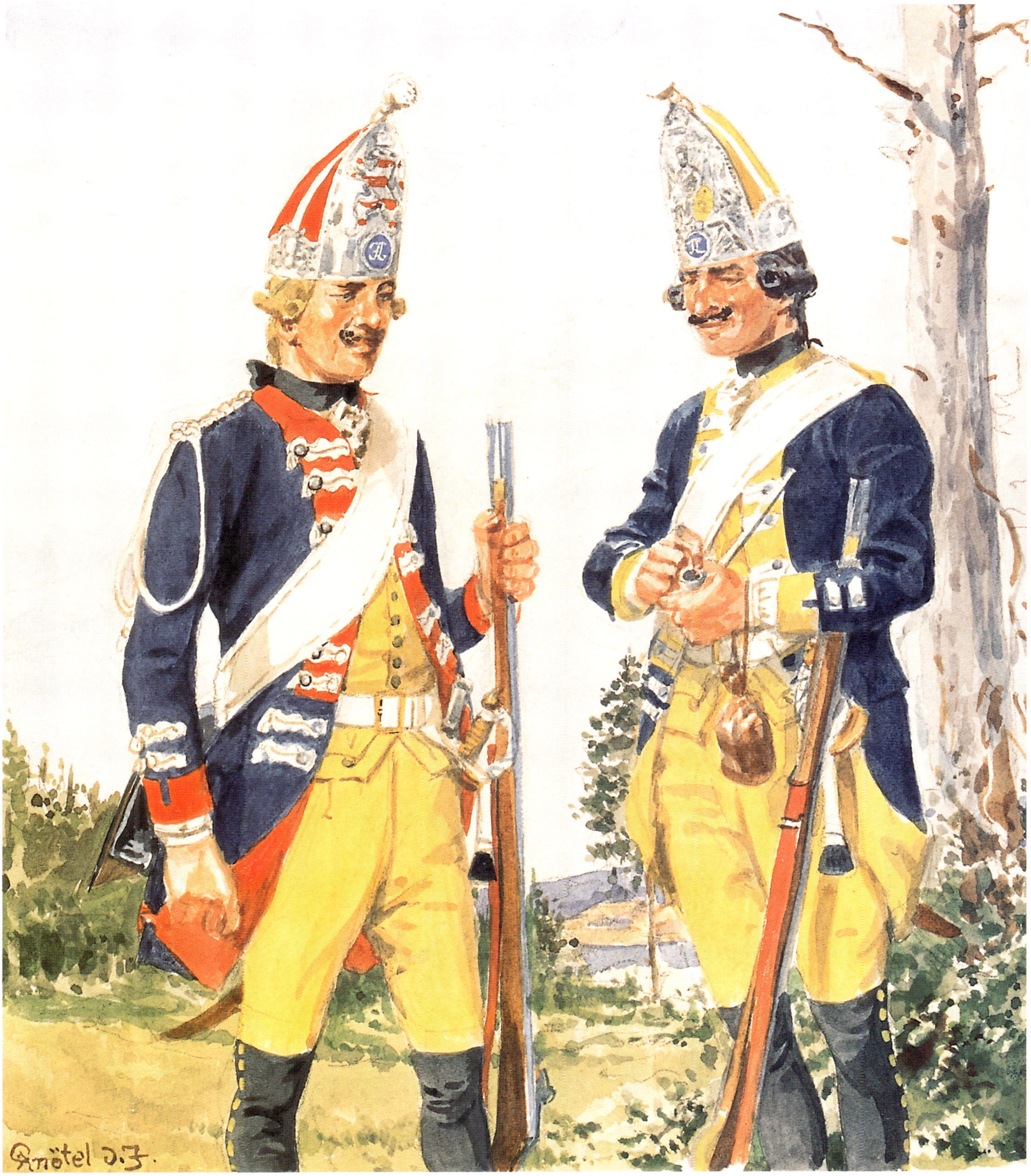

Smoking break, Grenadier Battalion v. Linsingen, Hesse-Kassel, 1778. A provisional, composite unit formed in 1776 from grenadier companies of the Guard Regiment, Leib Infantry Regiment and Mirbach Infantry Regiment. Served in North America.

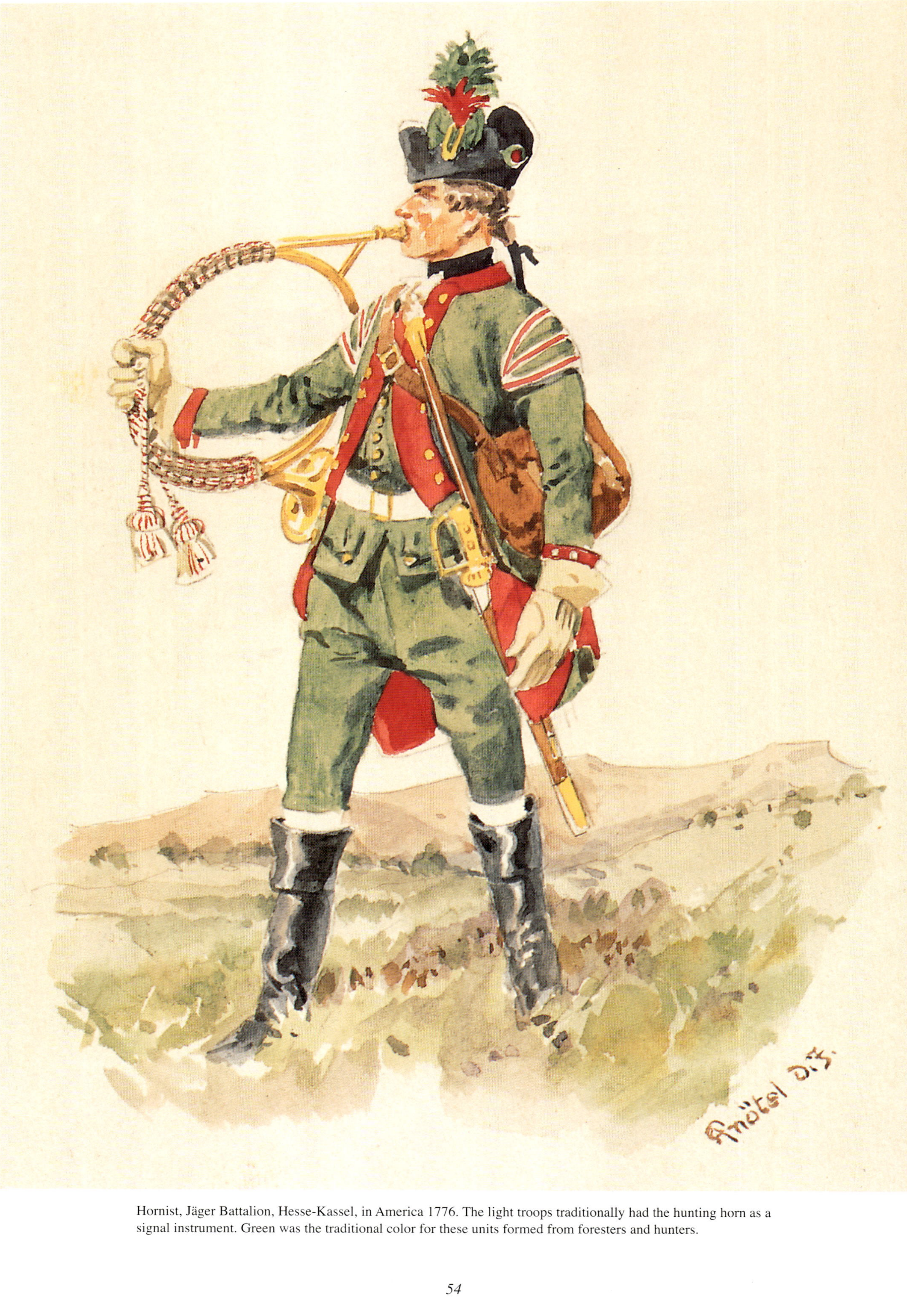

Hornist, Jäger Battalion, Hesse-Kassel, in America 1776. The light troops traditionally had the hunting horn as a signal instrument. Green was the traditional color for these units formed from foresters and hunters.

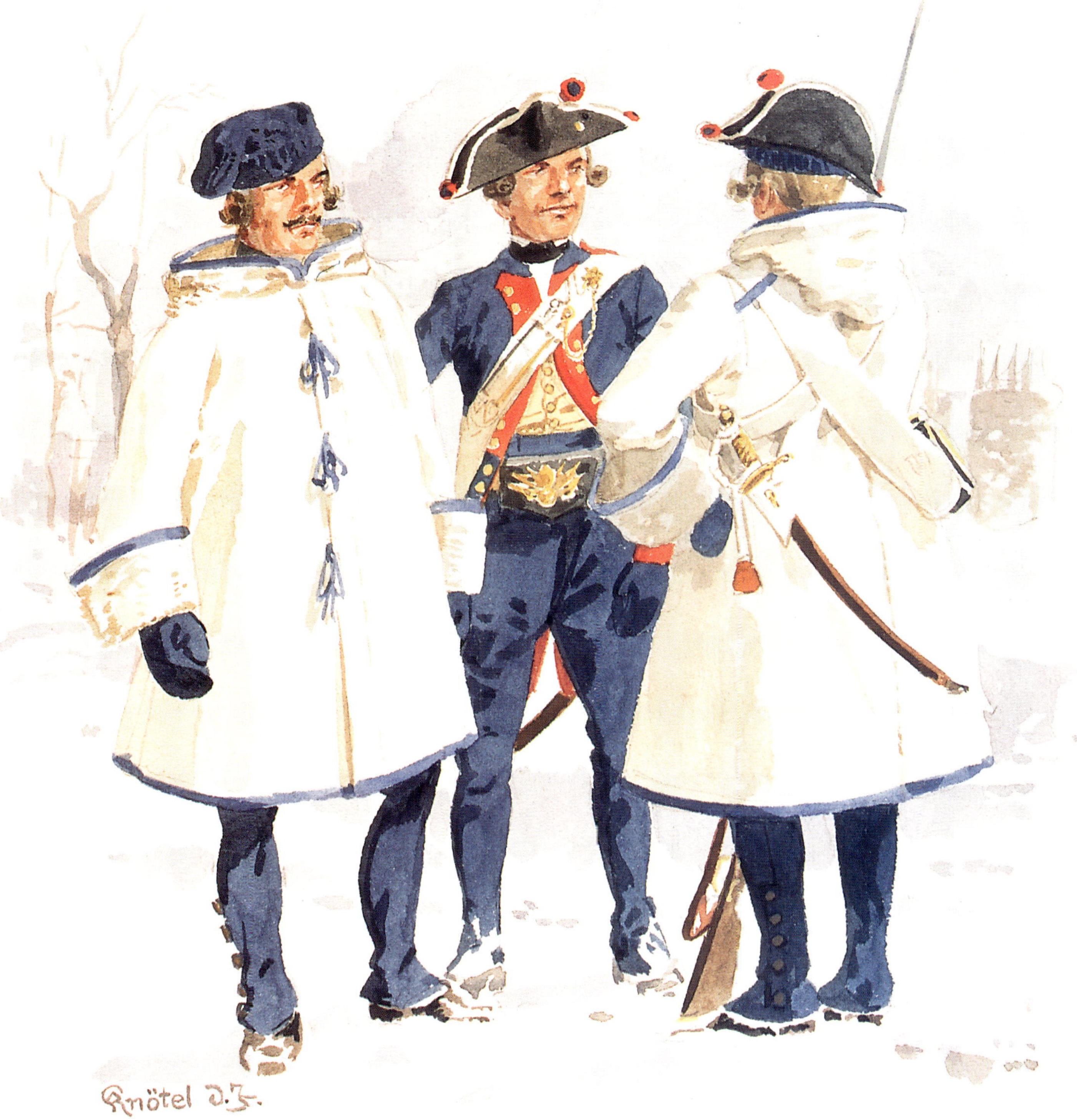

Artillery Company, Hesse-Hanau, in America December 1776. Hanau was a small principality in which the crown Prince of Hesse-Kassel ruled before he inherited the throne in Kassel.

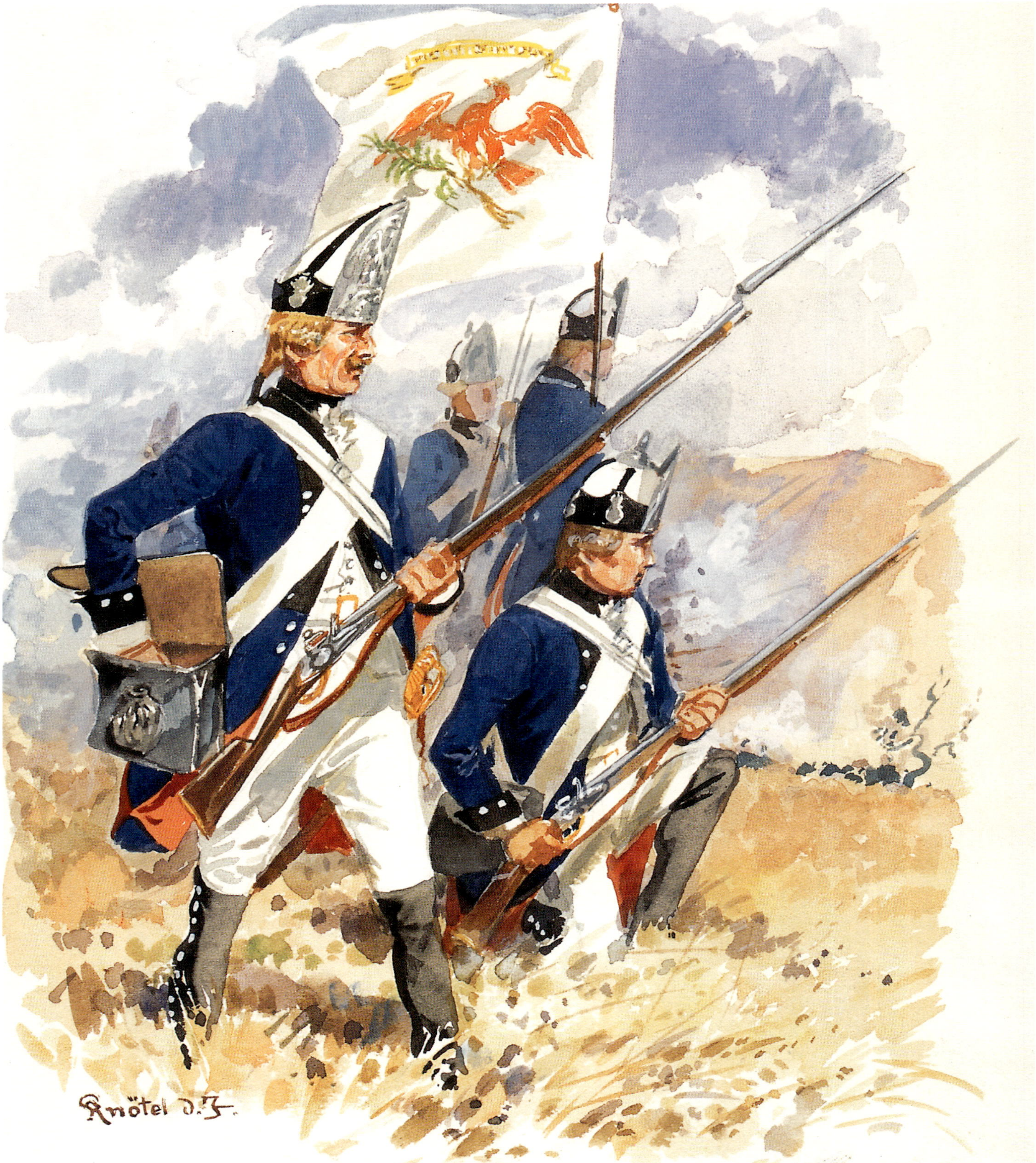

Grenadier and Fusilier, 2nd Regiment v.Voit, Anspach-Bayreuth 1777-1779. In America.

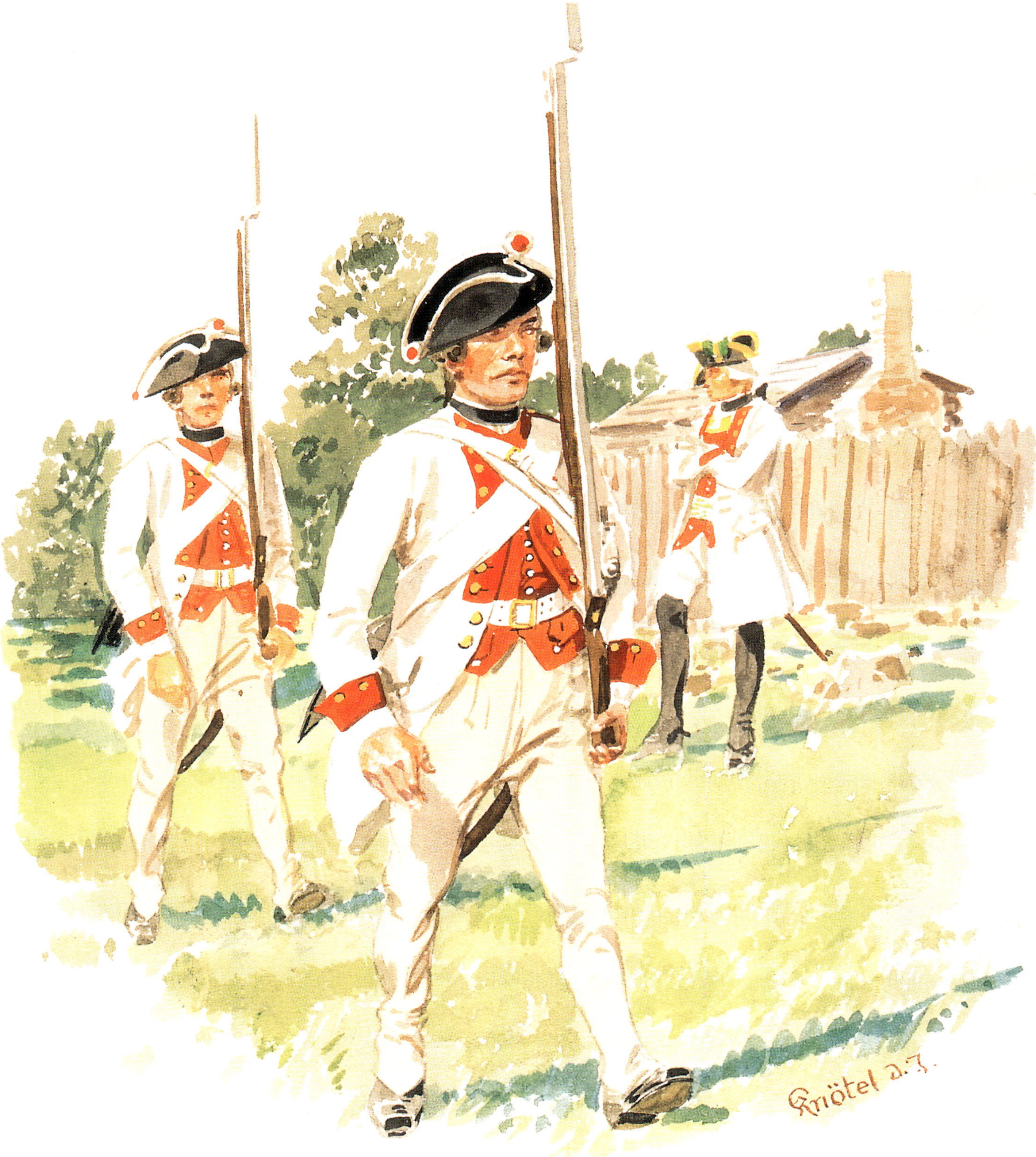

Anhalt-Zerbster Corps, in America. Musketeers and officer of the Infantry Regiment in field uniform 1778. The tiny state of Anhalt-Zerbst, ruled by the brother of Catherine the Great, was one of the smallest in Germany. Despite its small size, a regiment of 1,119 men organized in two battalions was sent to America.

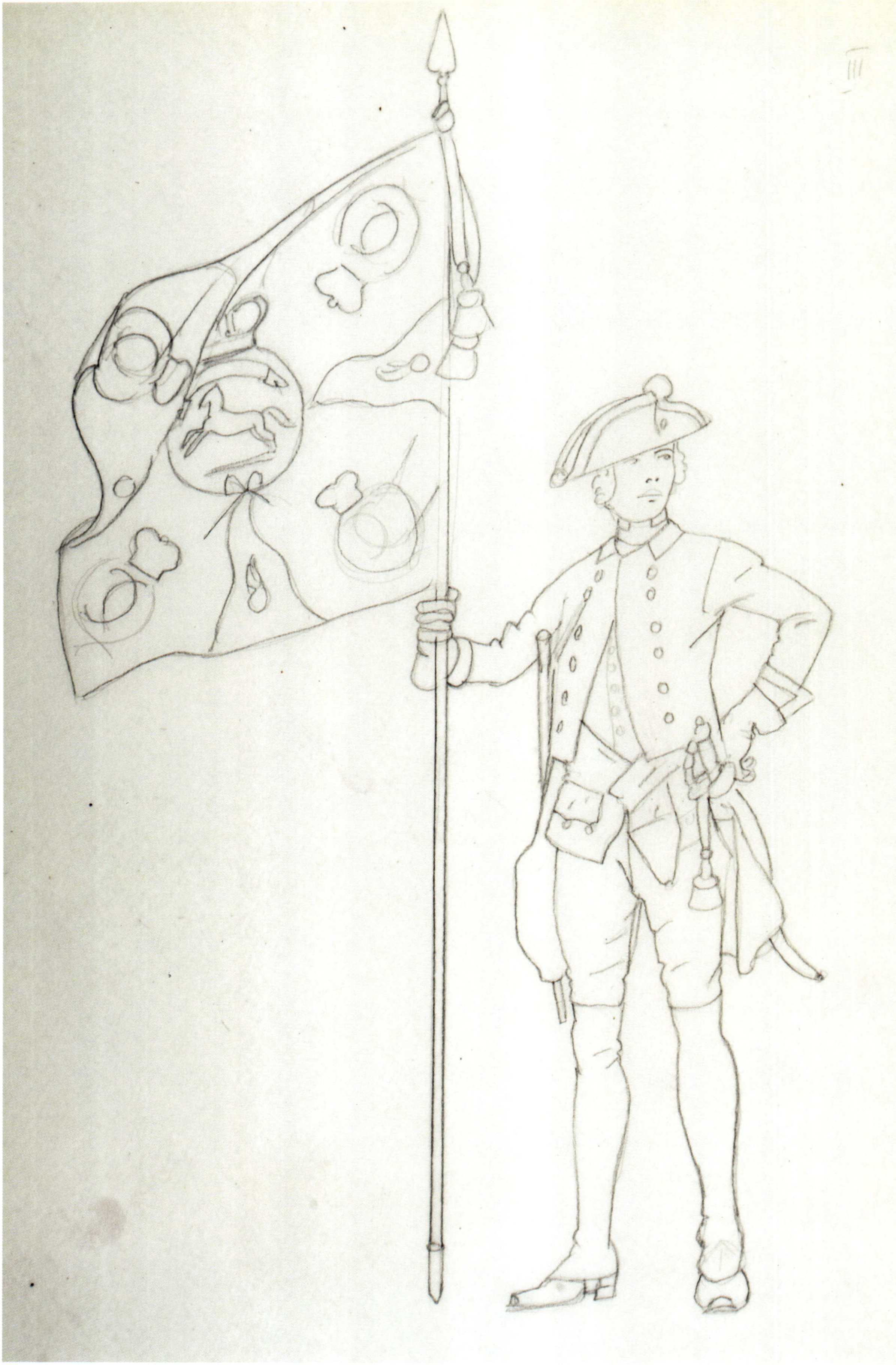

Regimental standard sketch, Prince Friedrich Infantry Regiment, Brunswick troops in Canada 1776.

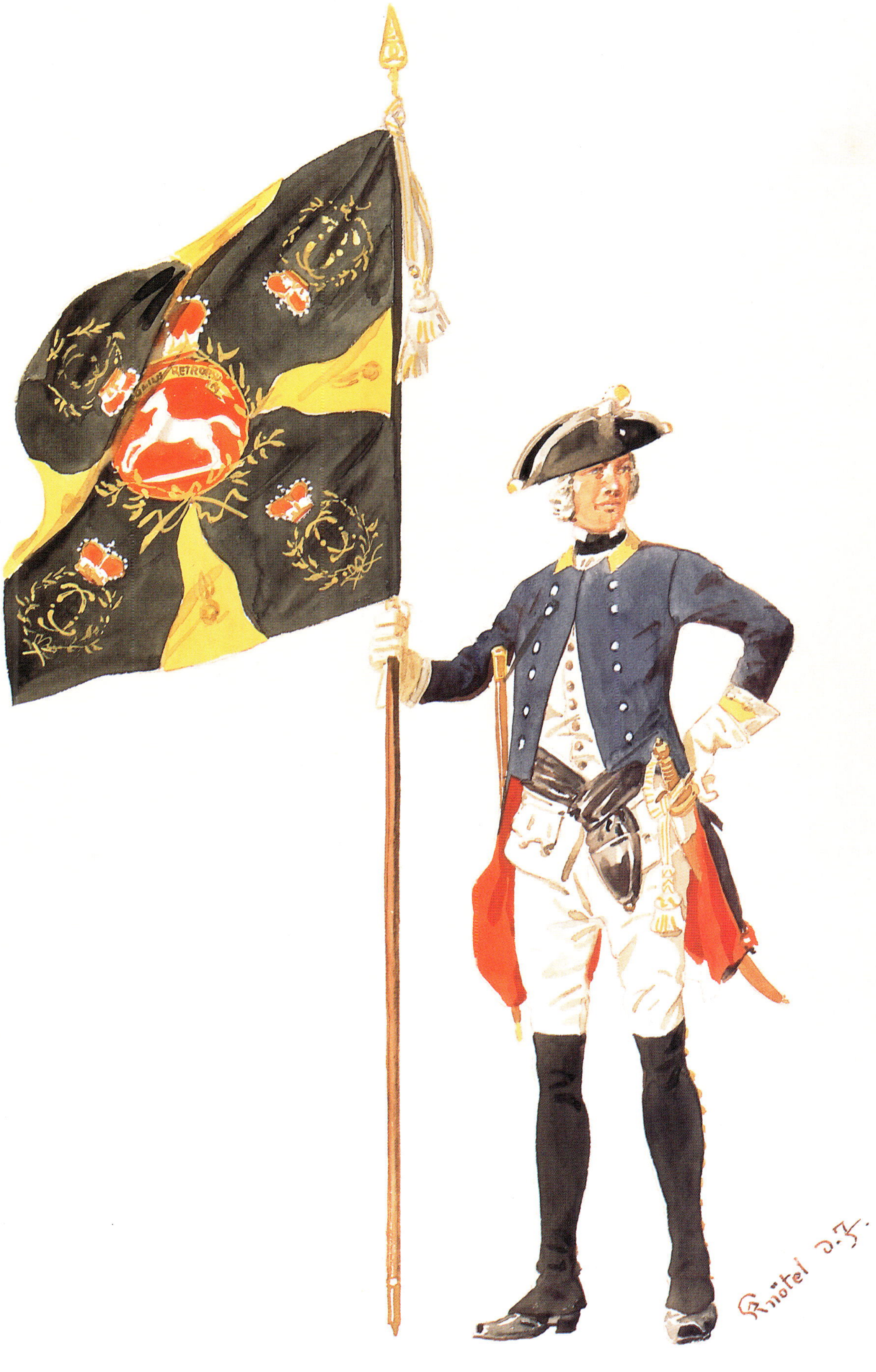

Regimental standard, Prince Friedrich Infantry Regiment, Brunswick troops in Canada 1776. This NCO carries the oilskin cover for the flag around his waist.

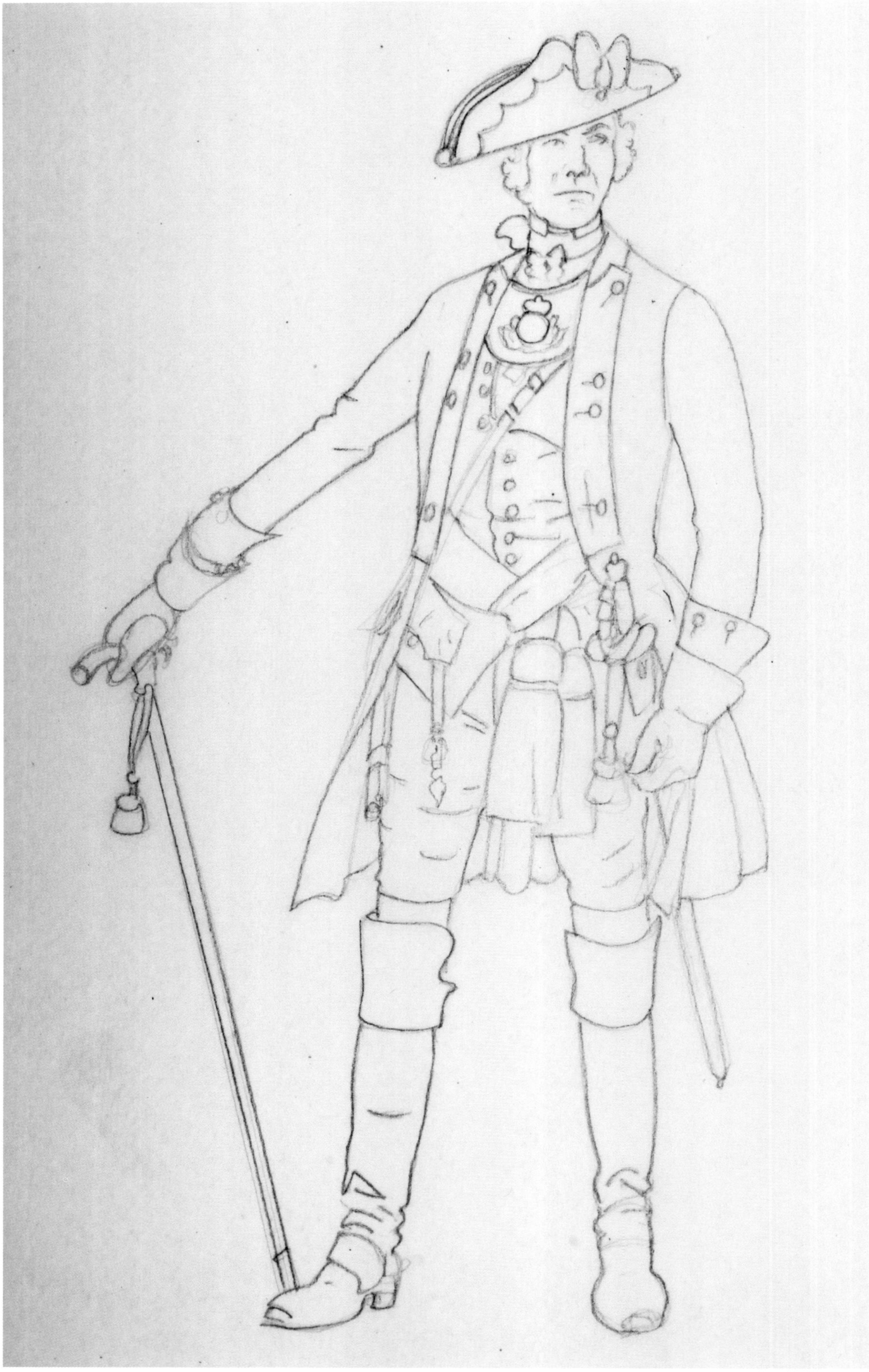

Field Officer sketch, von Rhetz Infantry Regiment, Brunswick troops in Canada 1777.

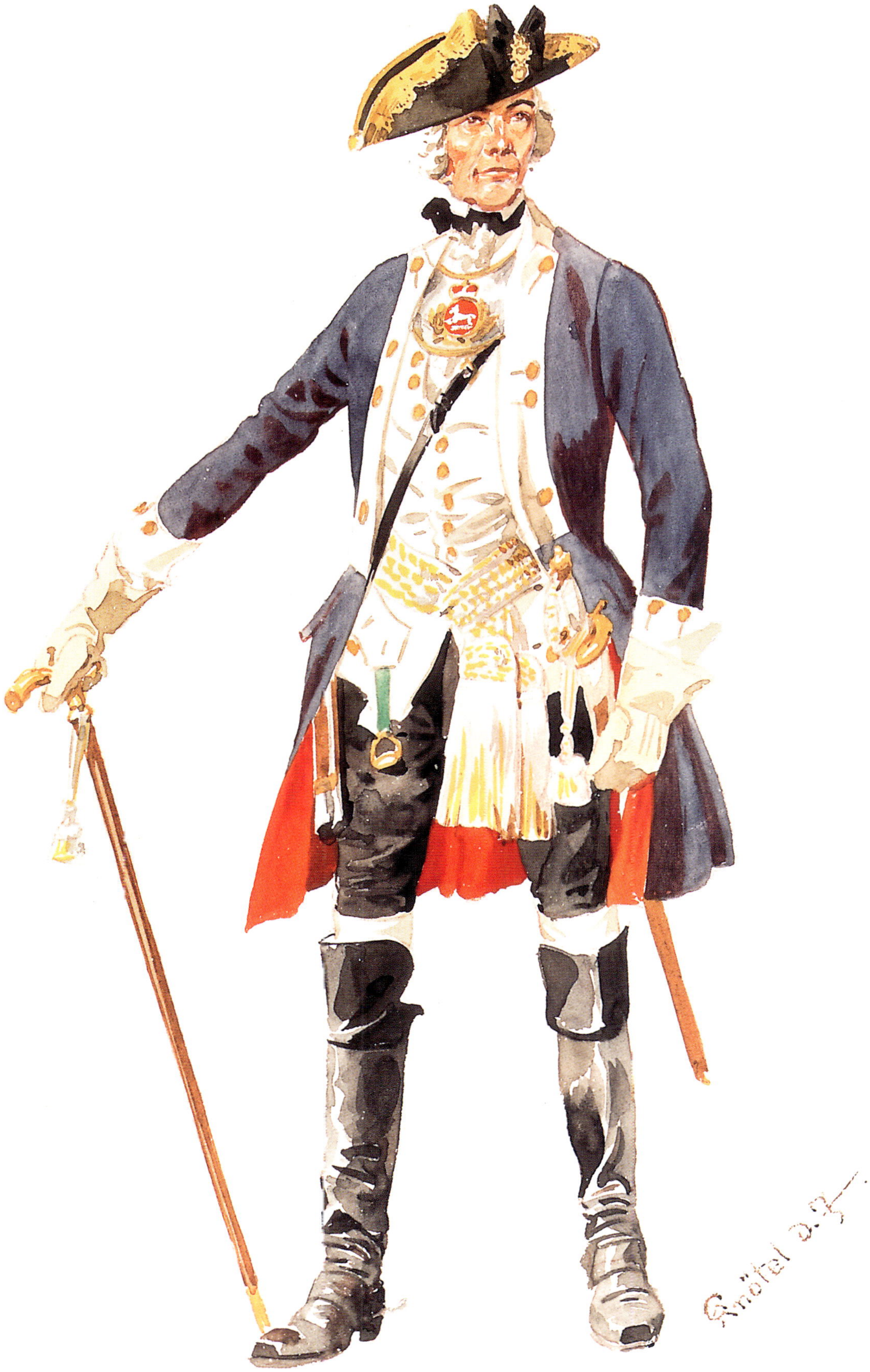

Field Officer, von Rhetz Infantry Regiment, Brunswick troops in Canada 1777. While still in full dress, this Officer is equipped with a pistol worn attached to a thin black leather strap which hangs on his right hip. The green ribbon of his pocket-watch hangs from his pocket. Note the personal seal or signet ring attached to the watch ribbon.

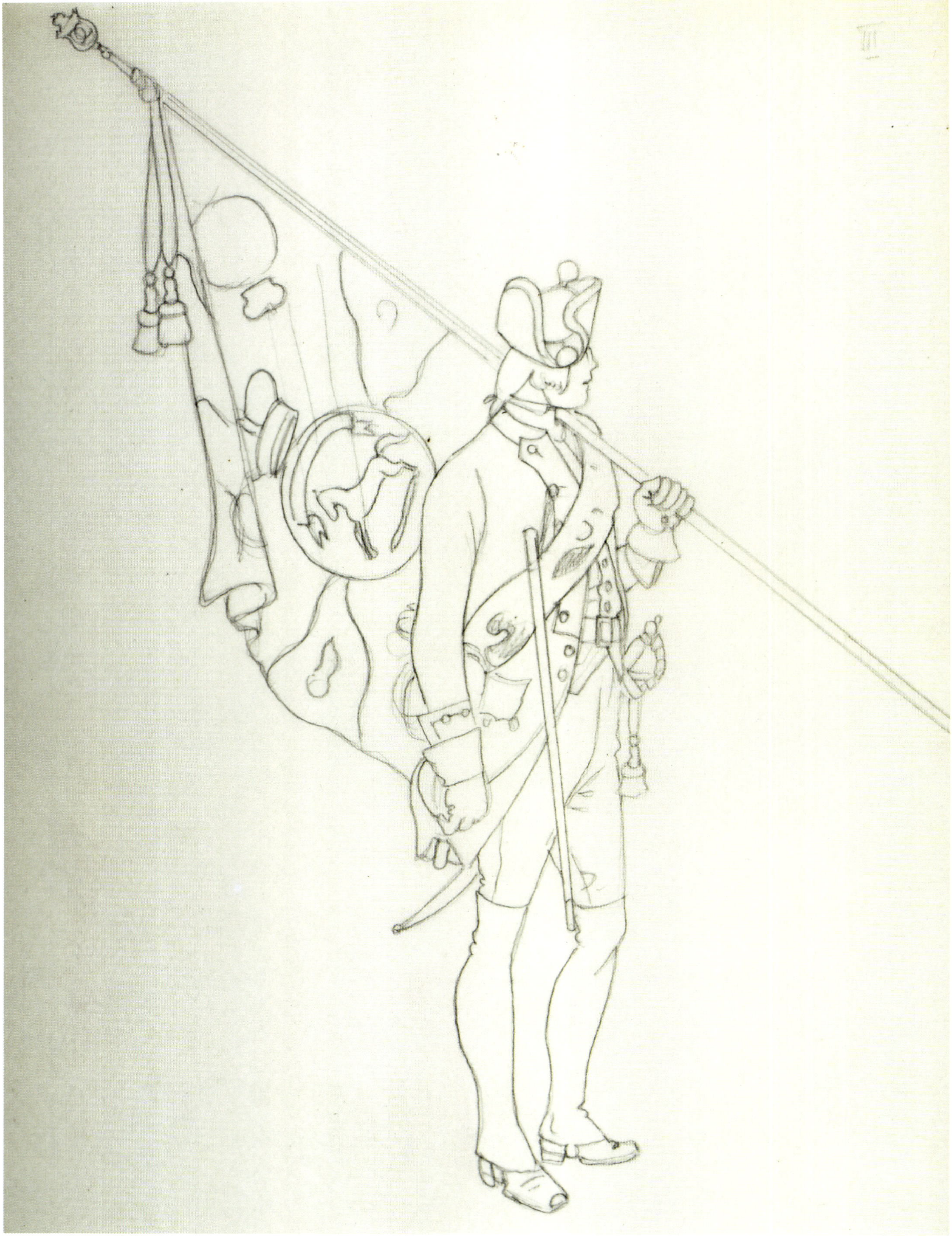

Regimental standard sketch, von Rhetz Infantry Regiment, Brunswick troops in Canada 1776.

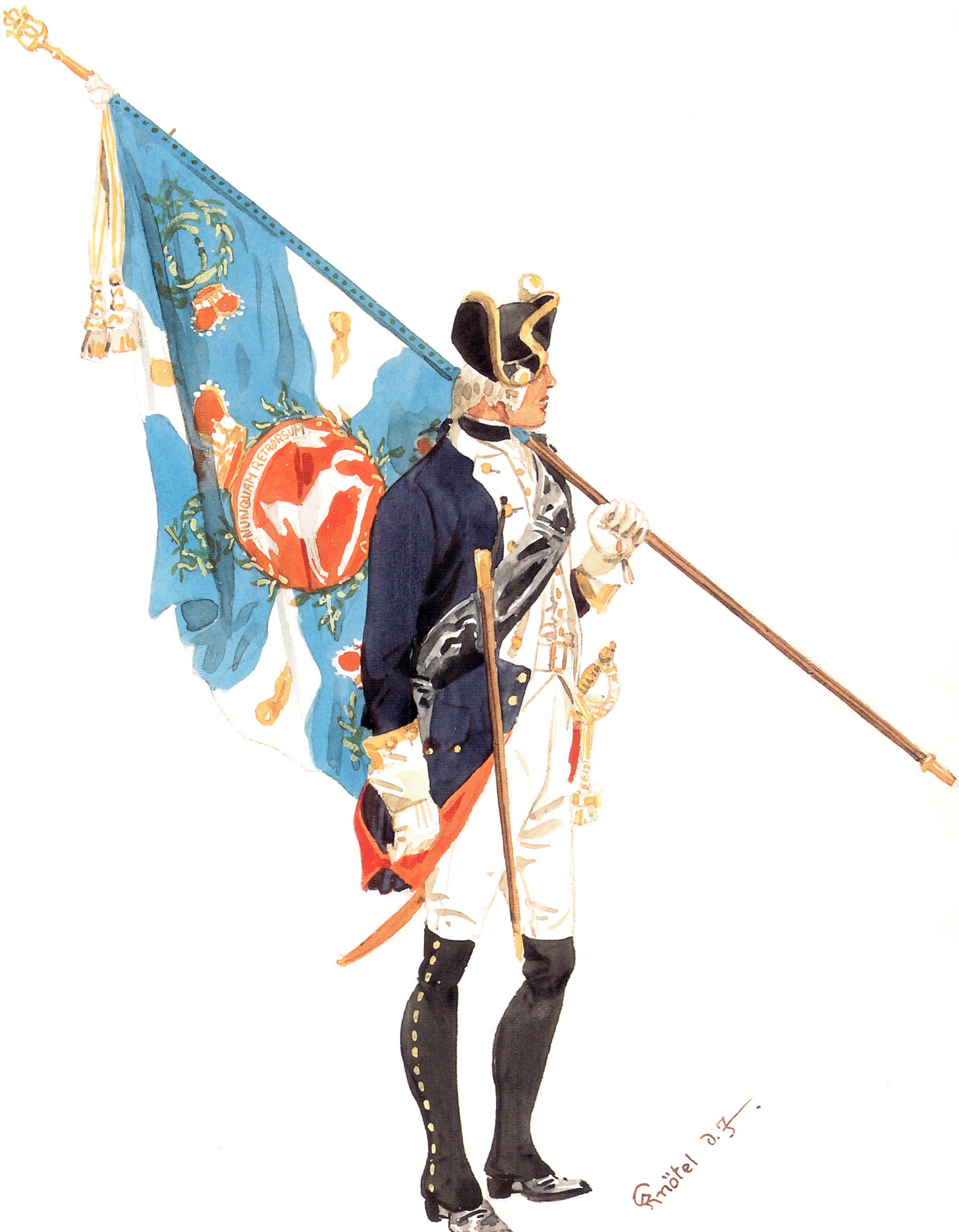

Regimental standard, von Rhetz Infantry Regiment, Brunswick troops in Canada 1776. Here the black oilskin flag cover is carried over the shoulder.

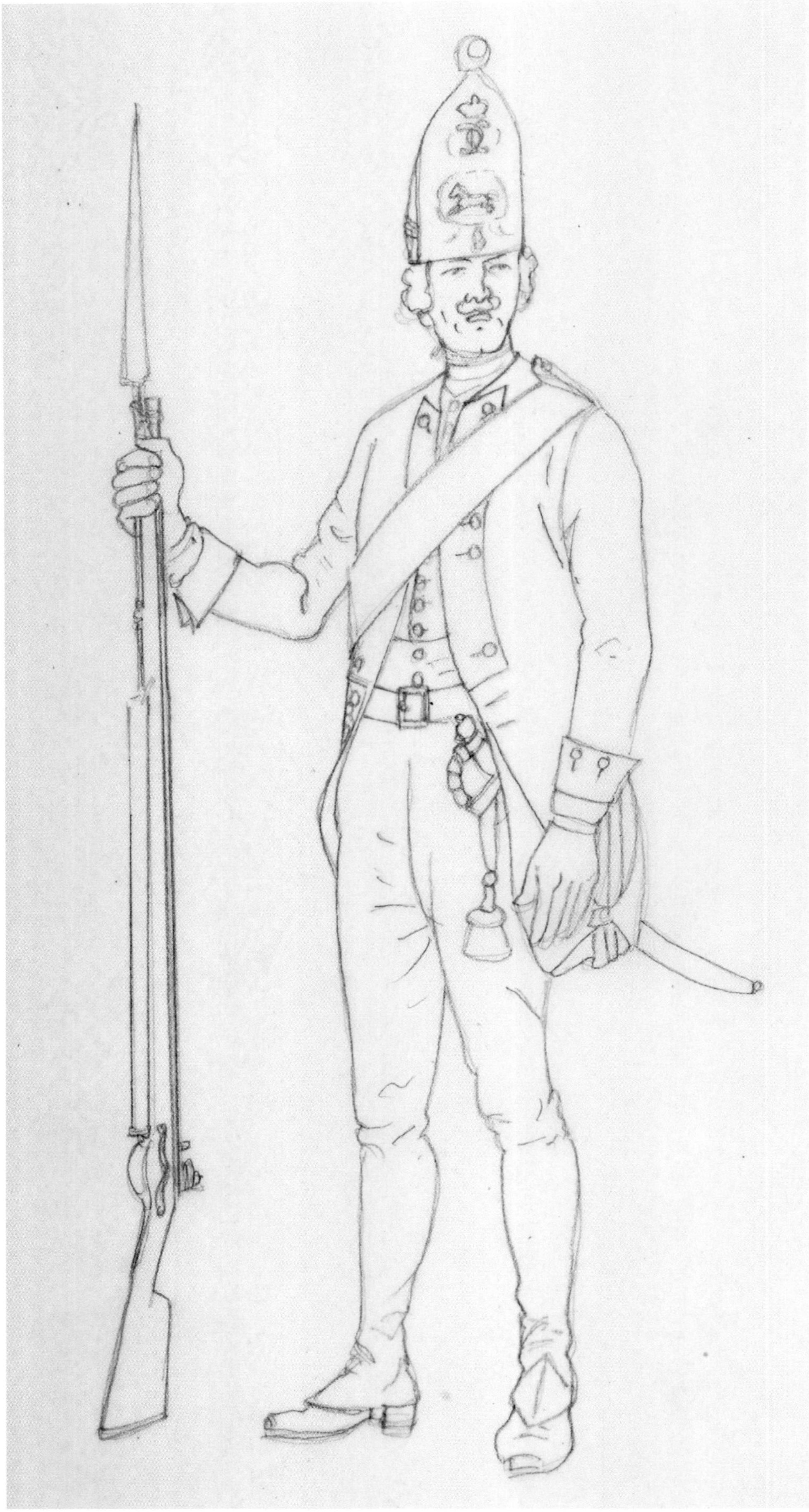

Grenadier sketch, von Riedesel Infantry Regiment, Brunswick troops in Canada 1778.

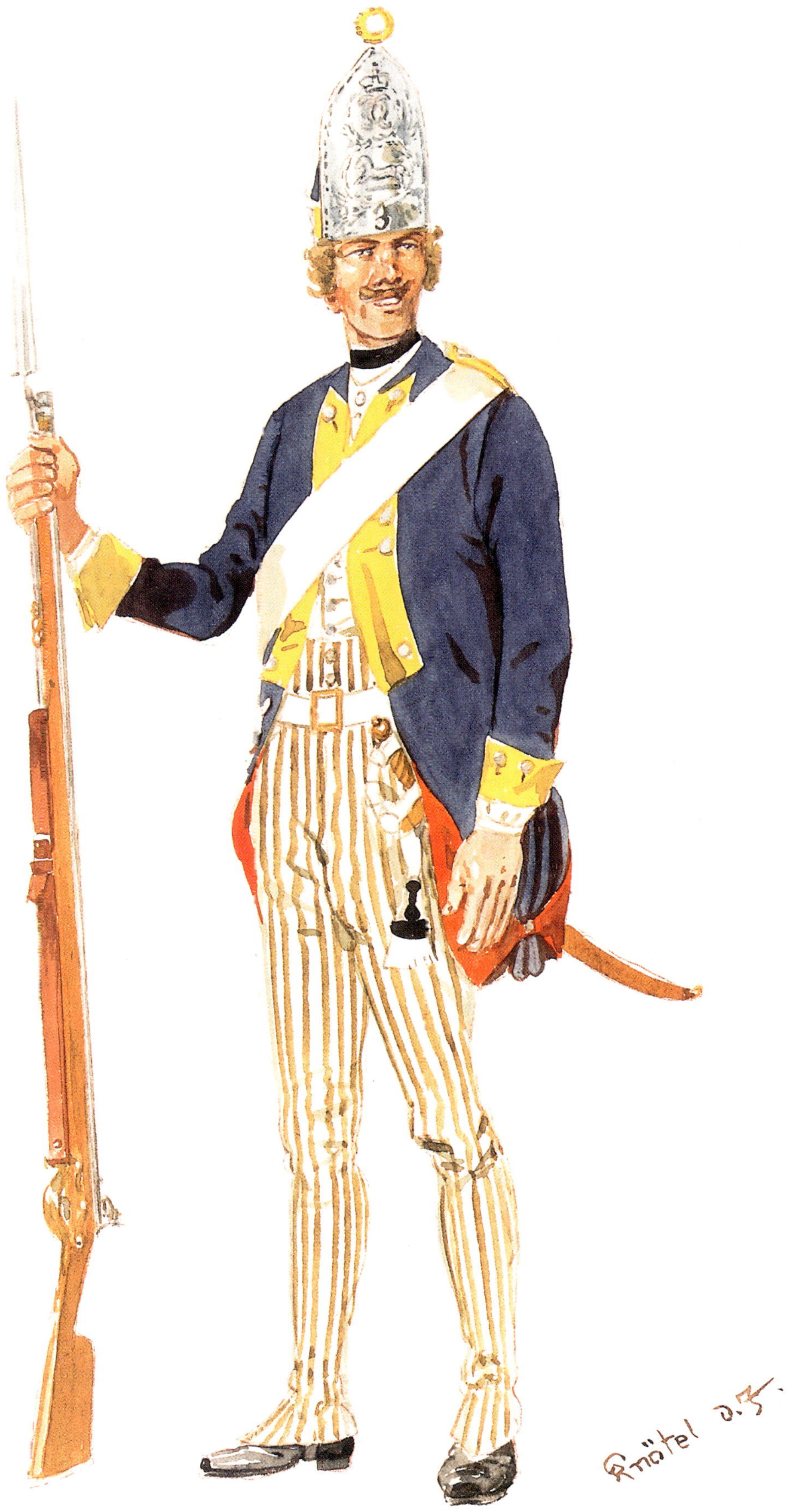

Grenadier, von Riedesel Infantry Regiment, Brunswick troops in Canada 1778.

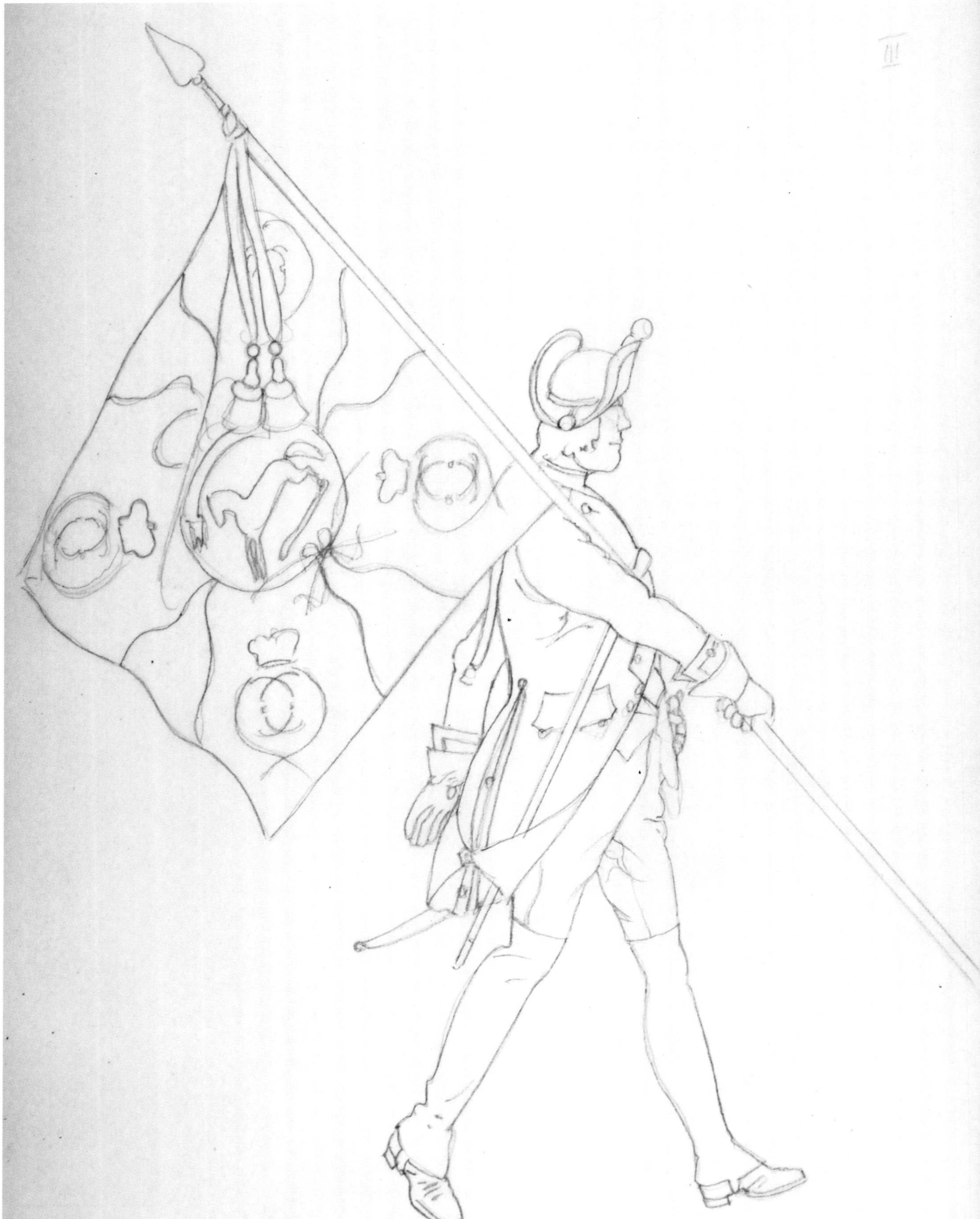

Princely standard sketch, von Specht Infantry Regiment, Brunswick troops in Canada 1776.

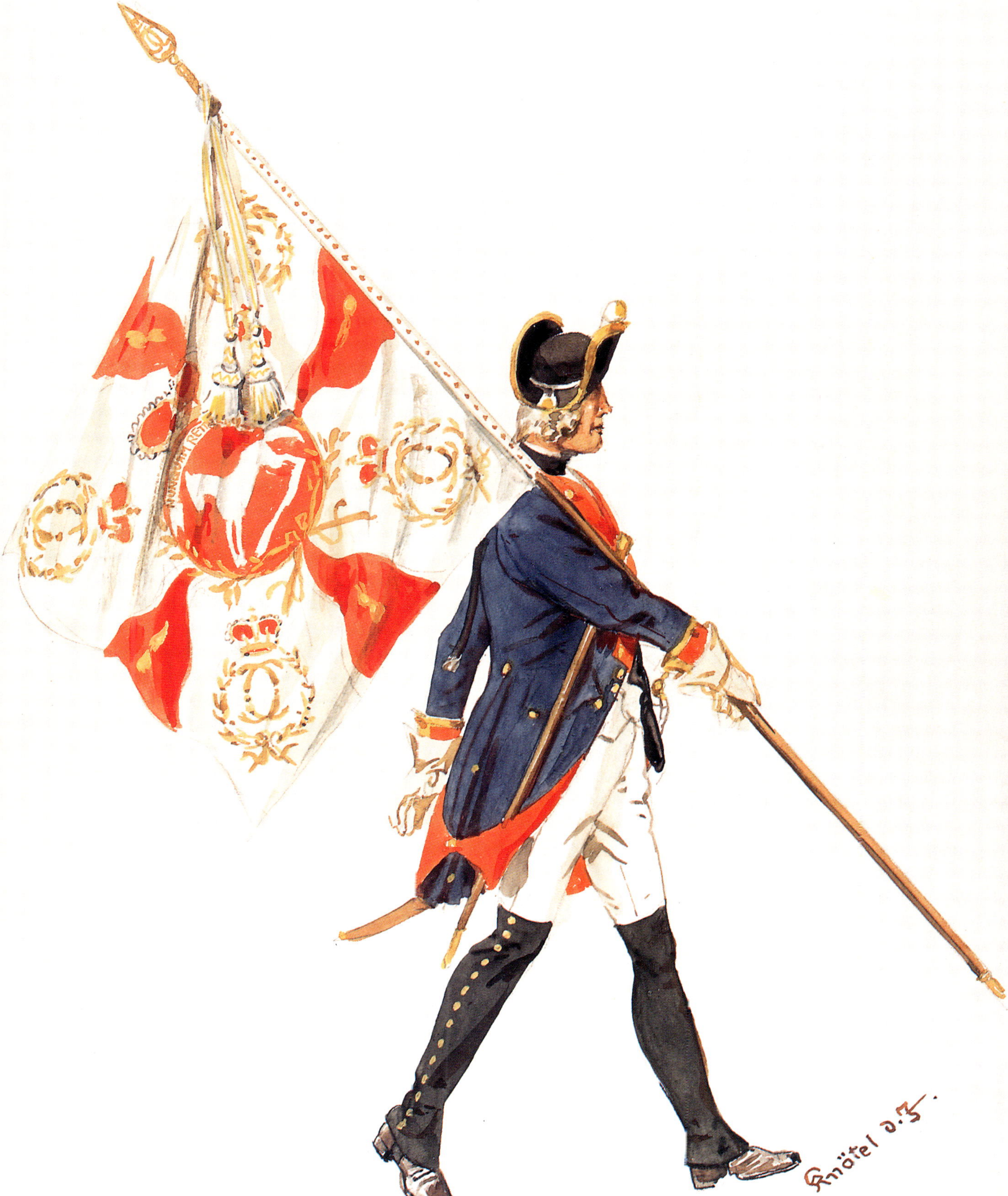

Princely standard, von Specht Infantry Regiment, Brunswick troops in Canada 1776. The Princely (Leib) flags were always white, as opposed to the colored regimental flags.

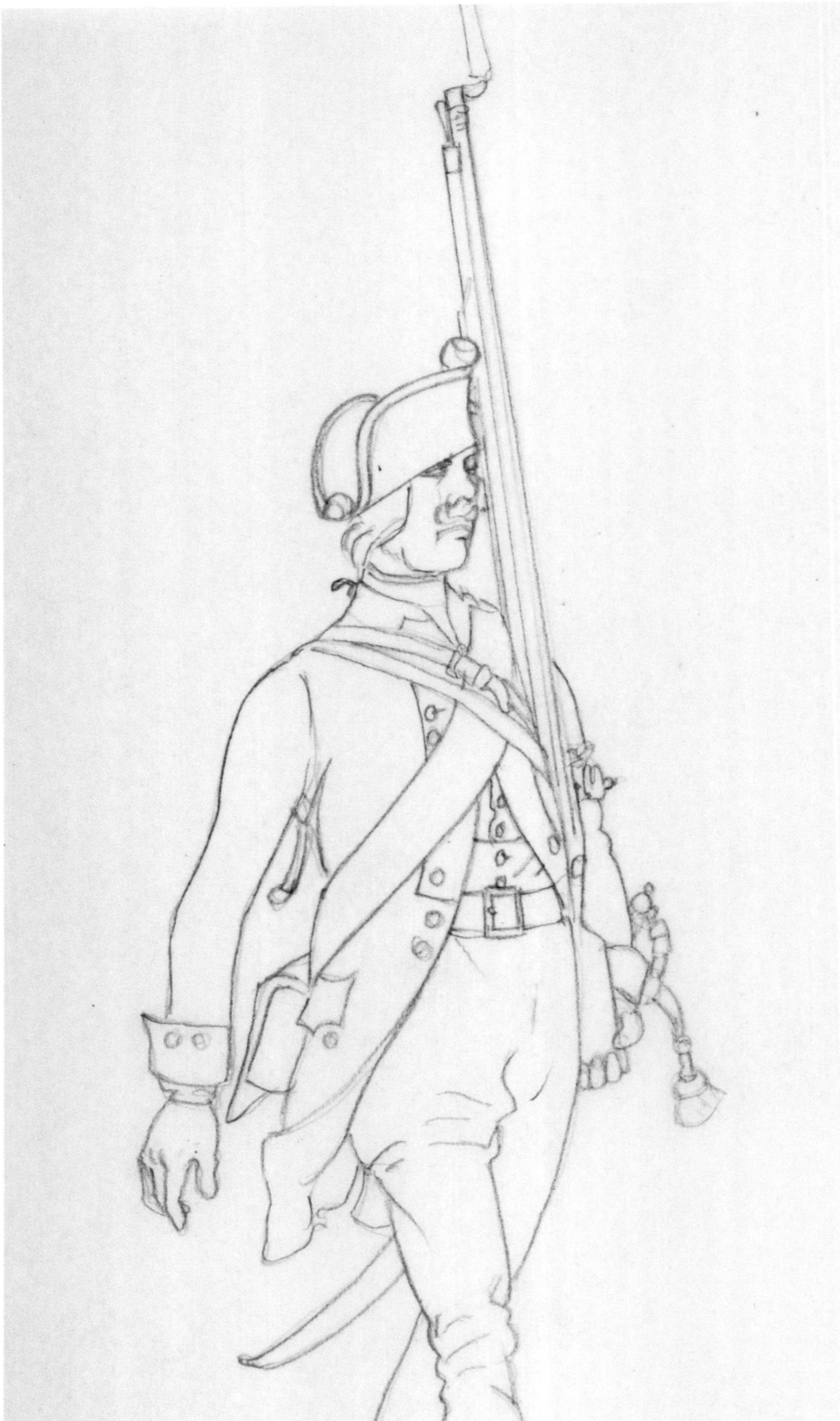

Musketeer sketch, von Specht Infantry Regiment, Brunswick troops in Canada 1778.

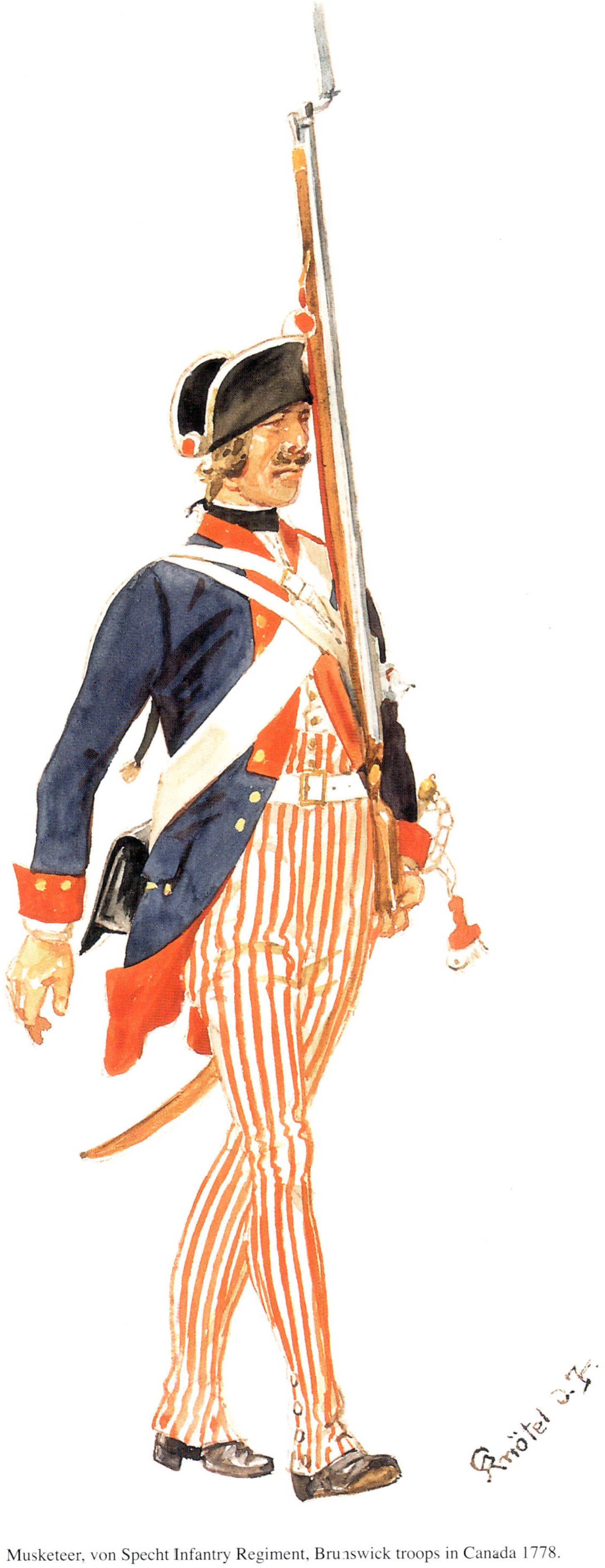

Musketeer, von Specht Infantry Regiment, Brunswick troops in Canada 1778.

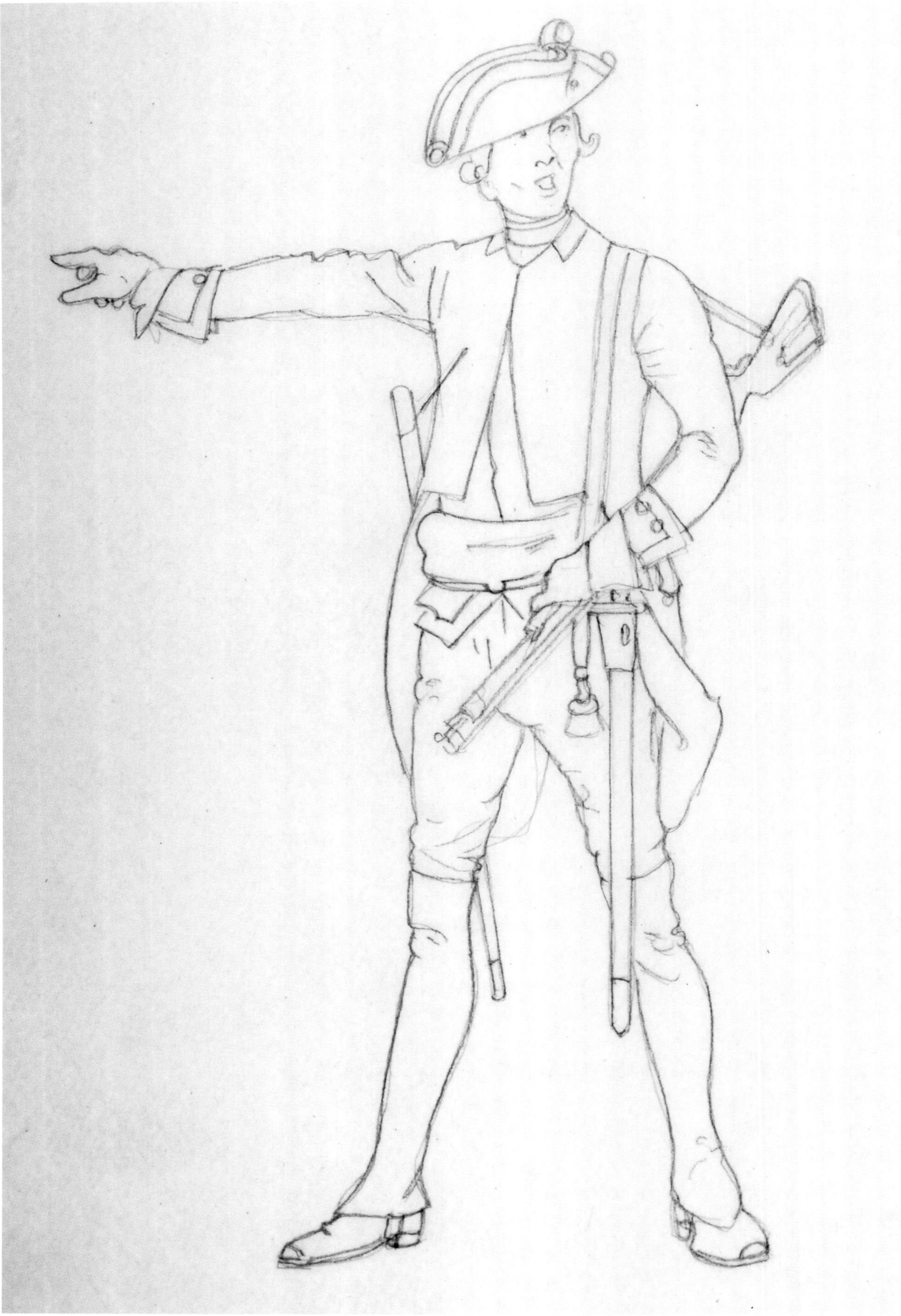

Noncommissioned Officer sketch, Barner Light Infantry Battalion, Brunswick troops in Canada 1776.

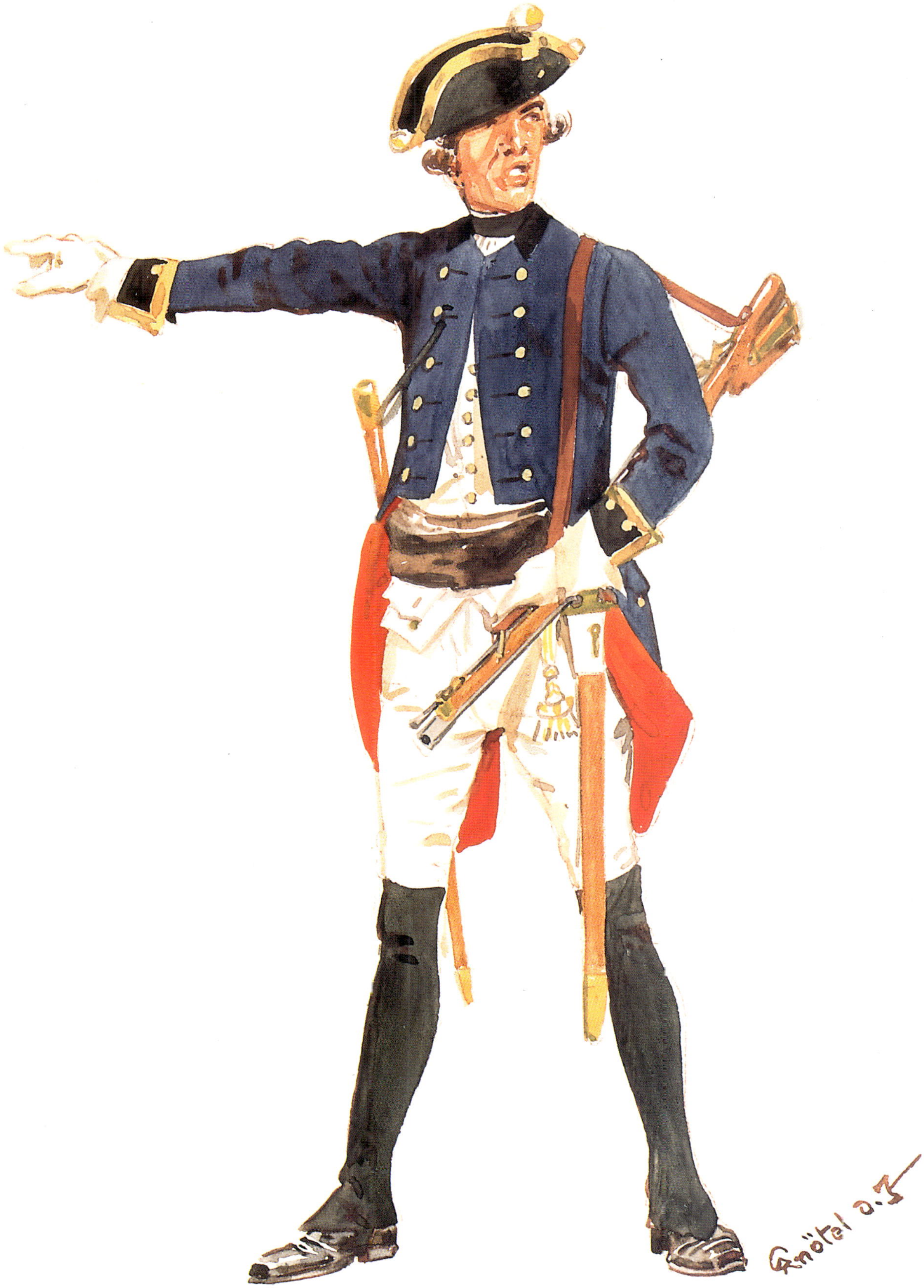

Noncommissioned Officer, Barner Light Infantry Battalion, Brunswick troops in Canada 1776. The Barner Light Battalion was especially formed for the campaign in America. This NCO carries a rifle and a hunter's sword.

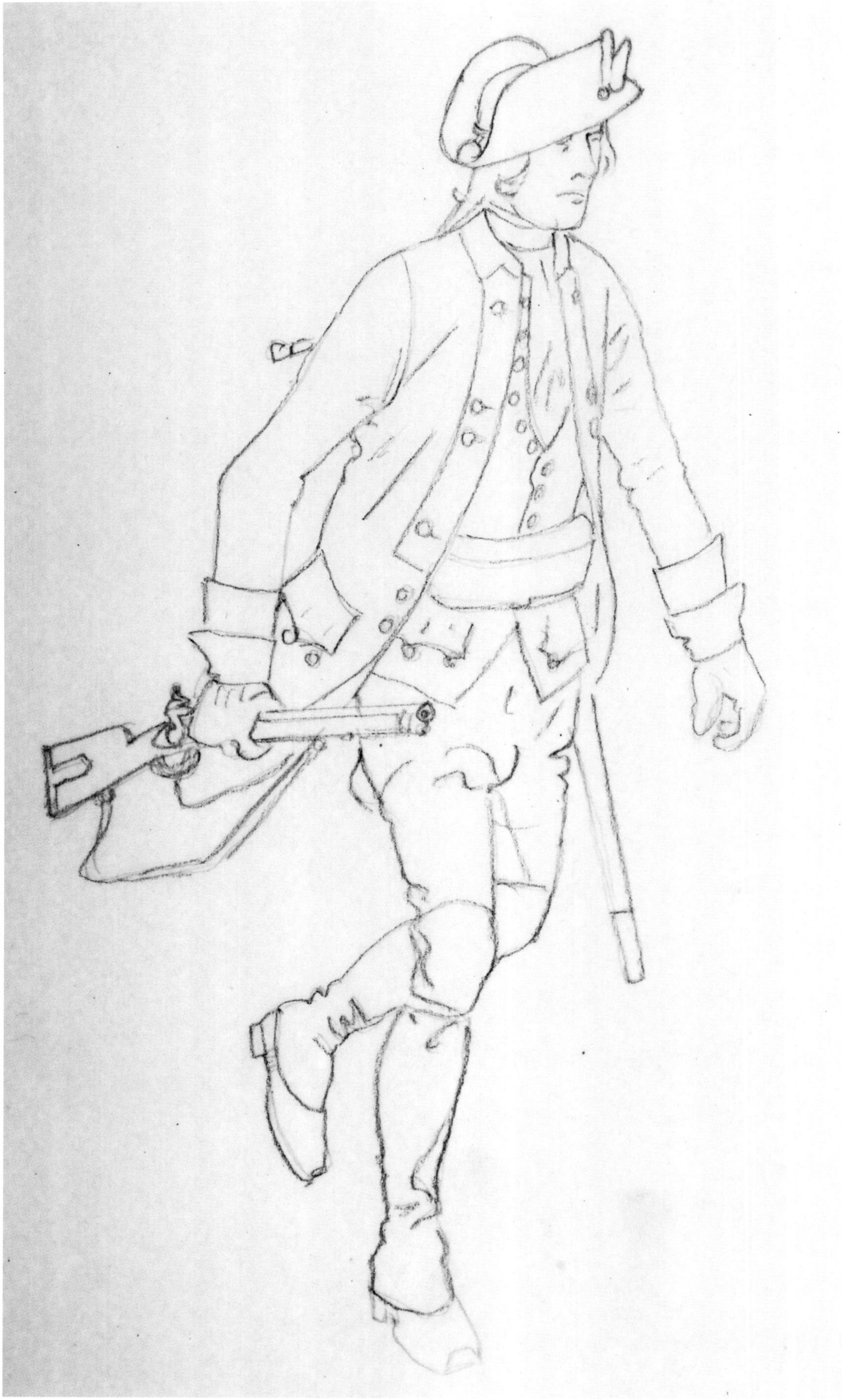

Jäger sketch, Barner Light Infantry Battalion, Brunswick troops in Canada 1776.

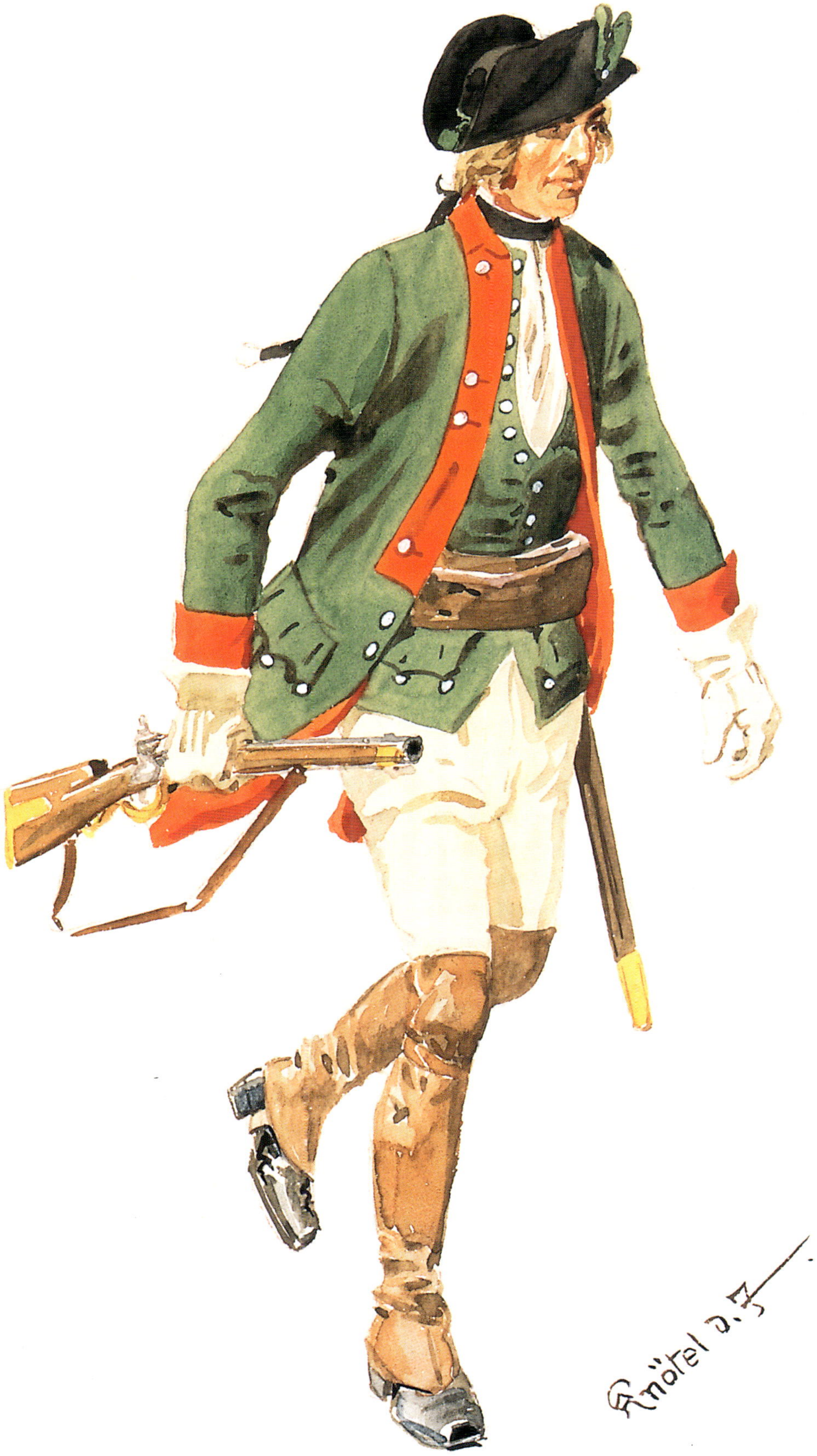

Jäger, Barner Light Infantry Battalion, Brunswick troops in Canada 1776. This is the well know uniform of the Jägers, here shown with brown leather gaiters. Jägers were trained marksmen.

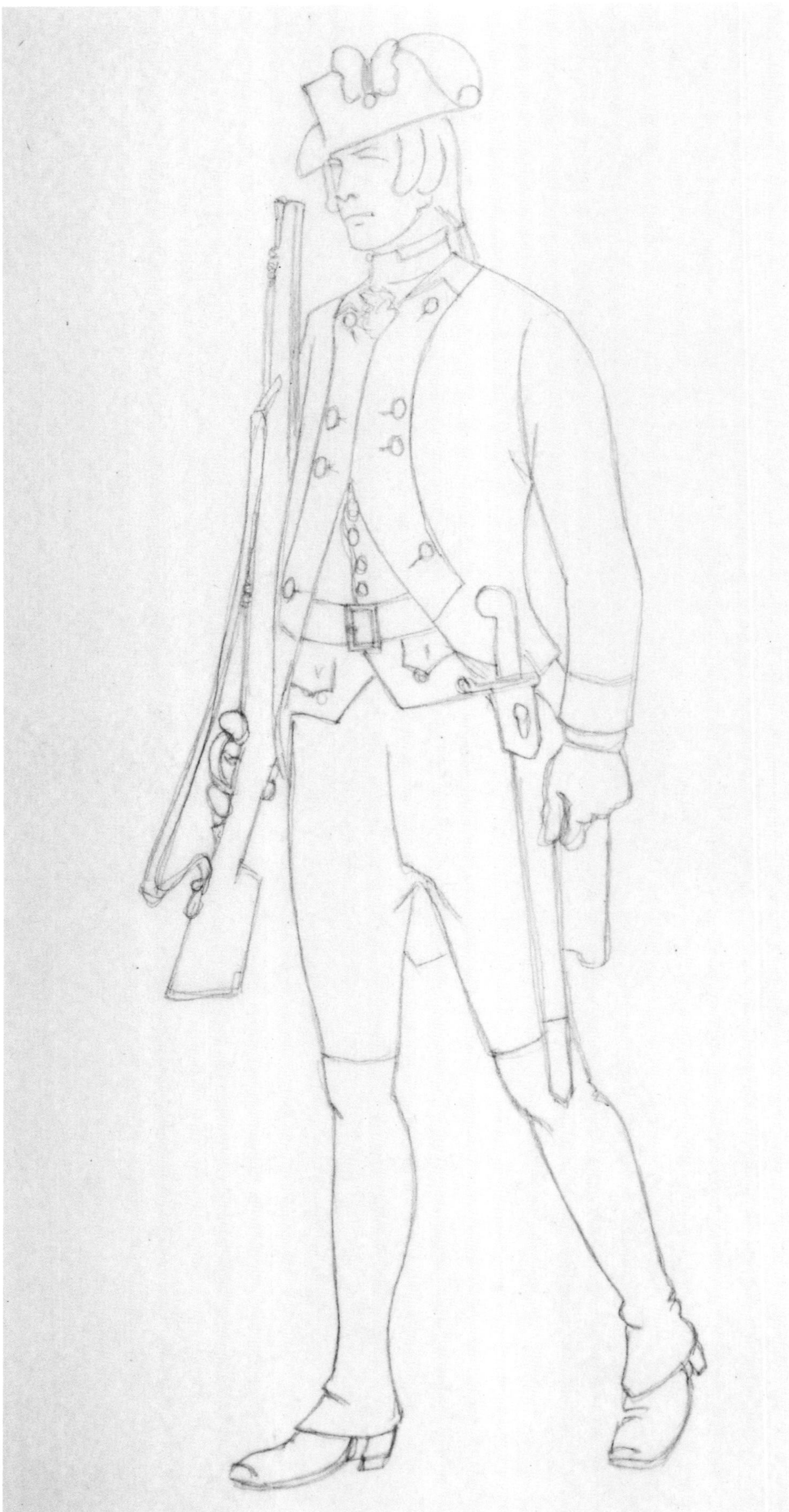

Jäger sketch, Barner Light Infantry Battalion, Brunswick troops in Canada 1776.

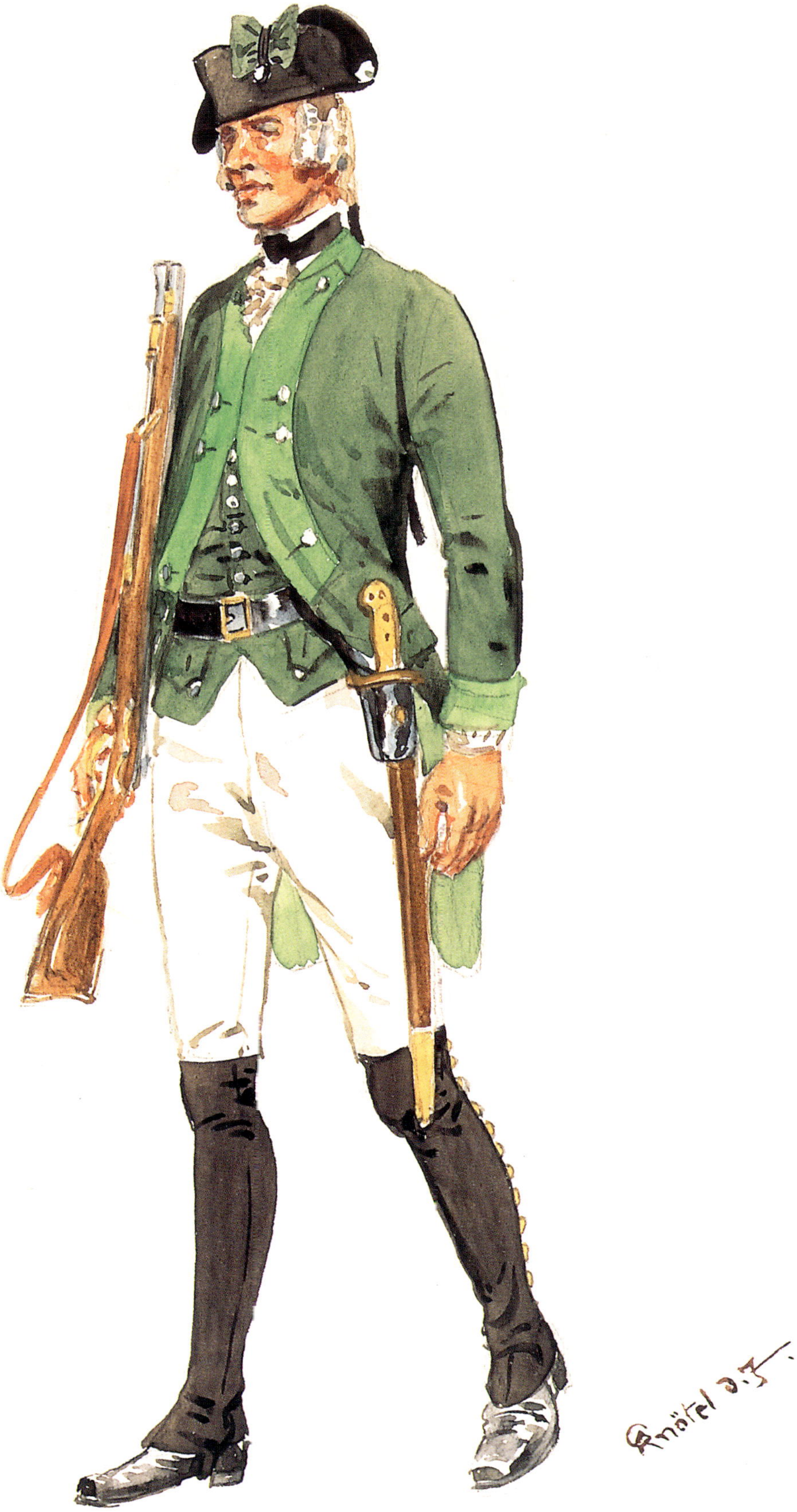

Jäger, Barner Light Infantry Battalion, Brunswick troops in Canada 1776. This version of the Jäger with light green facings is a bit controversial and not confirmed by official sources.

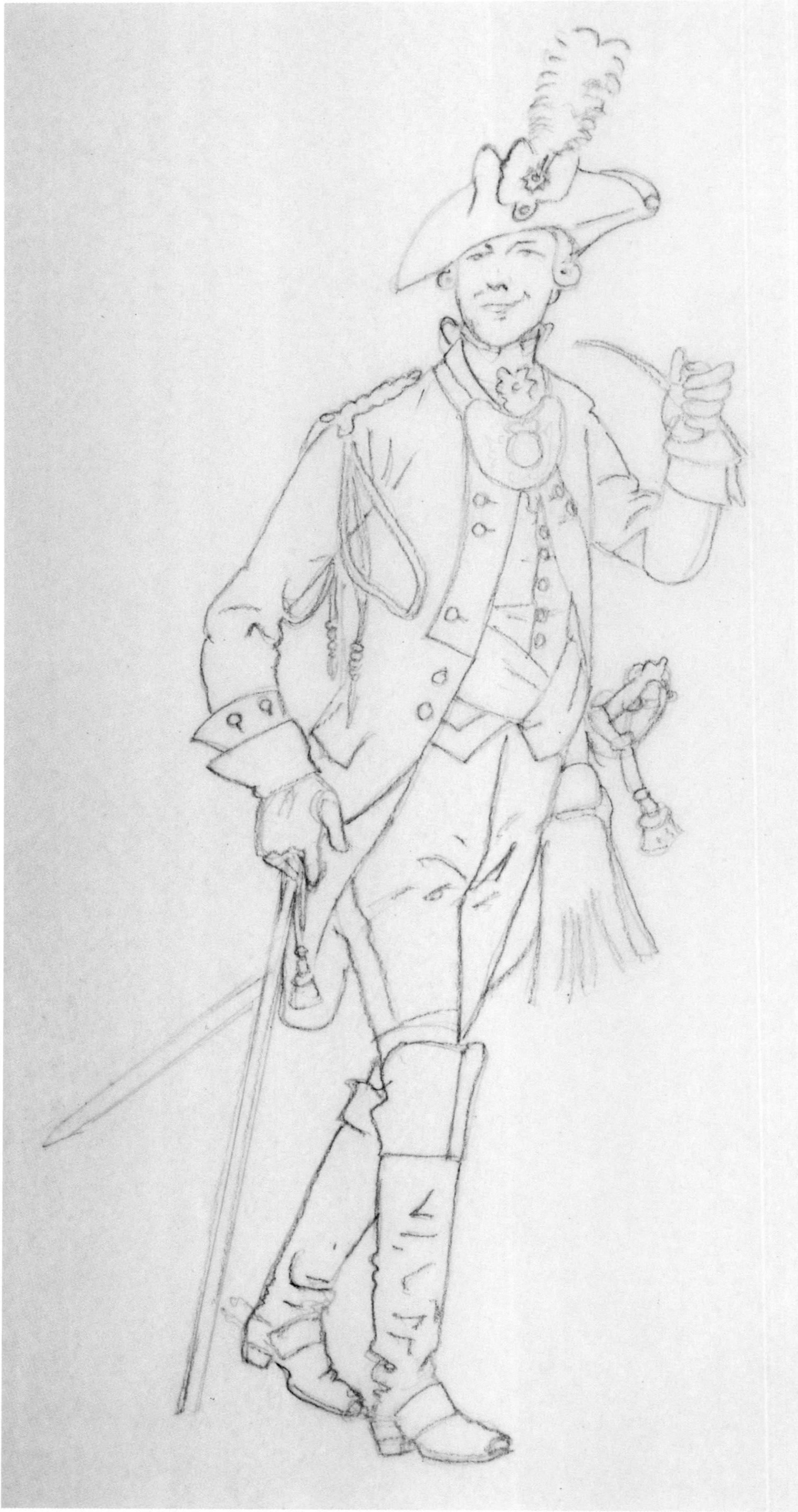

Officer sketch, Dragoon Regiment, Brunswick troops in Canada 1776.

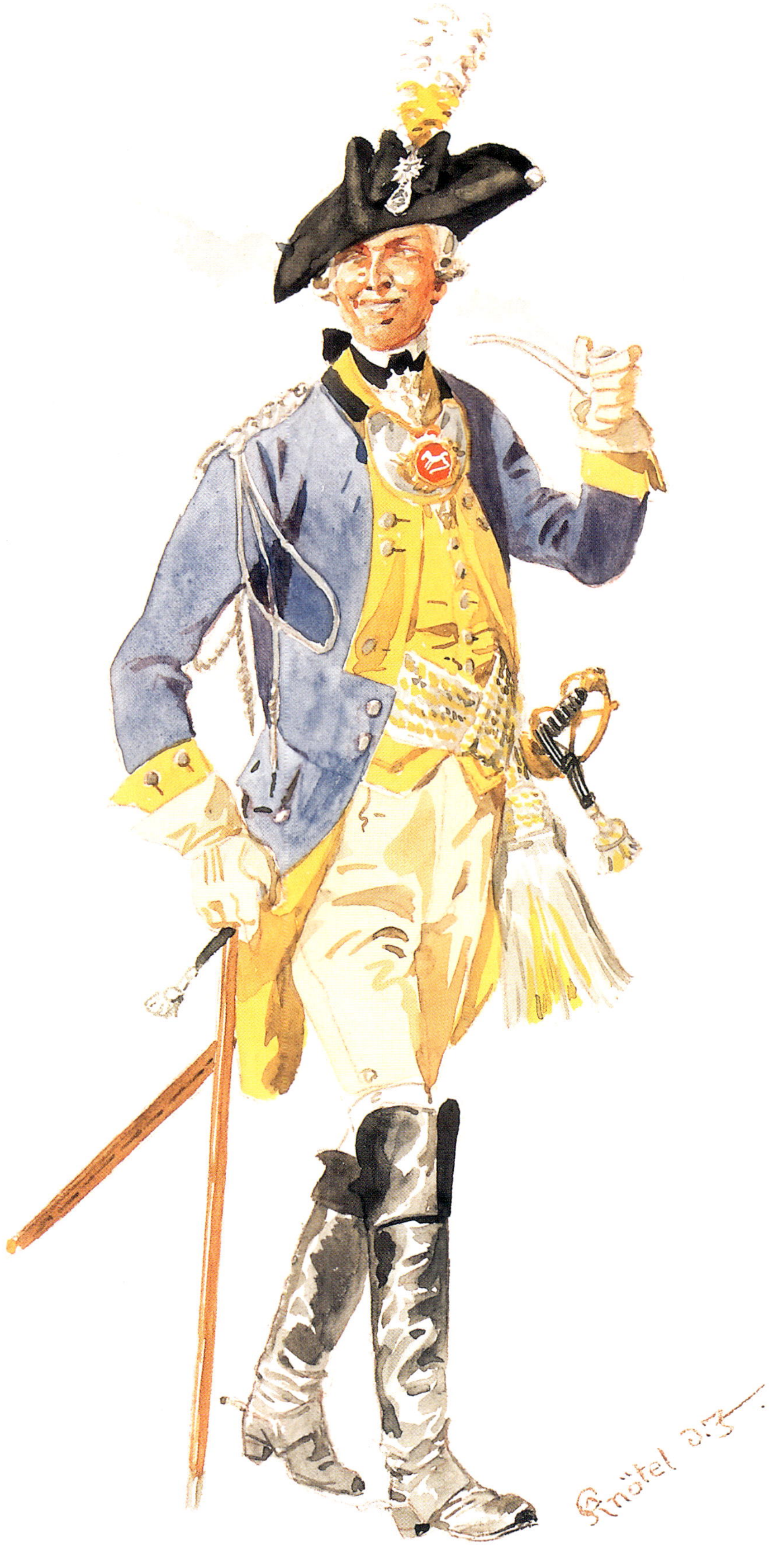

Officer, Dragoon Regiment, Brunswick troops in Canada 1776. The gorget is not a distinction usually worn by cavalry. While the unit served as infantry, its use was tolerated.

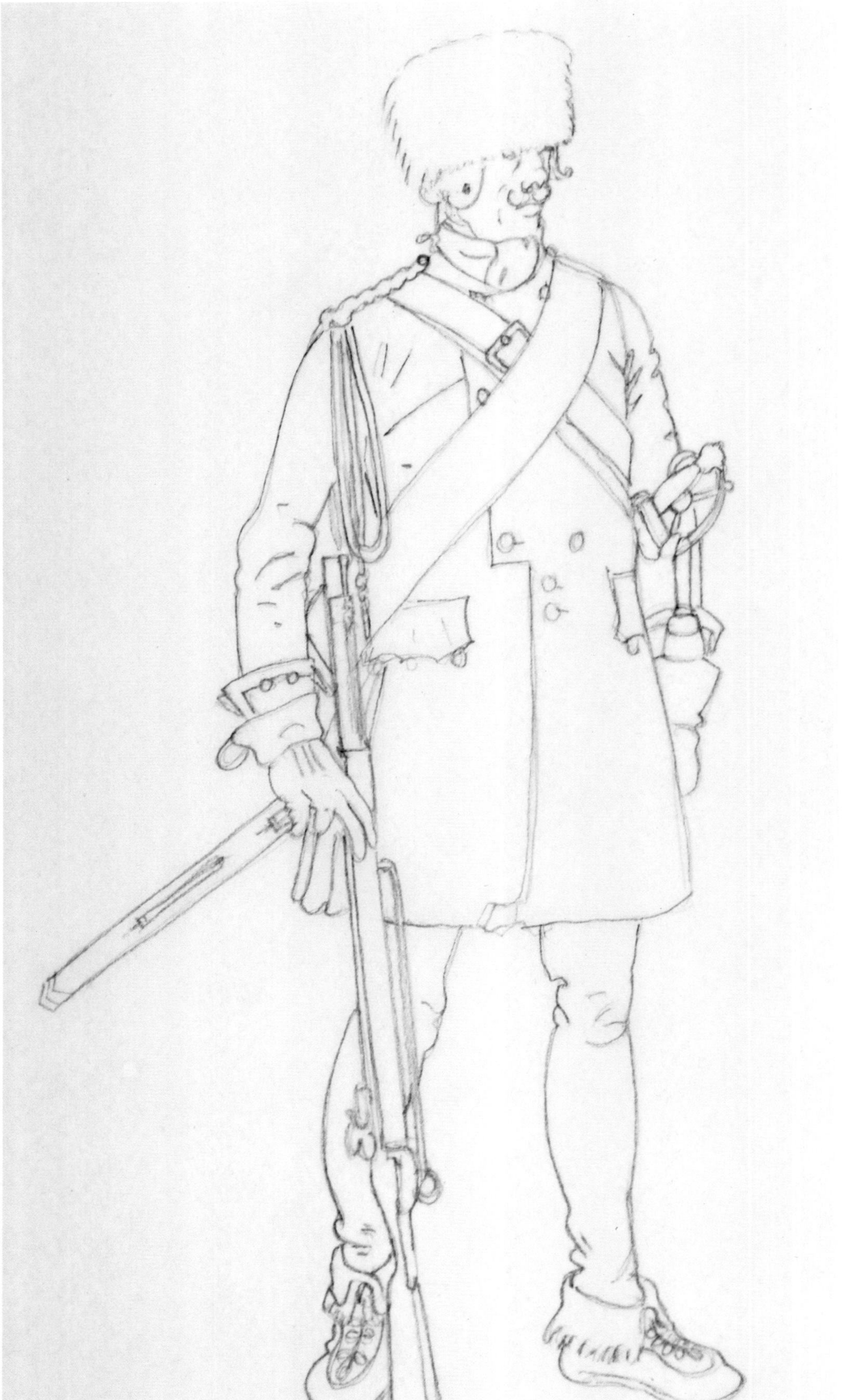

Noncommissioned Officer sketch, Dragoon Regiment, Brunswick troops in Canada 1782.

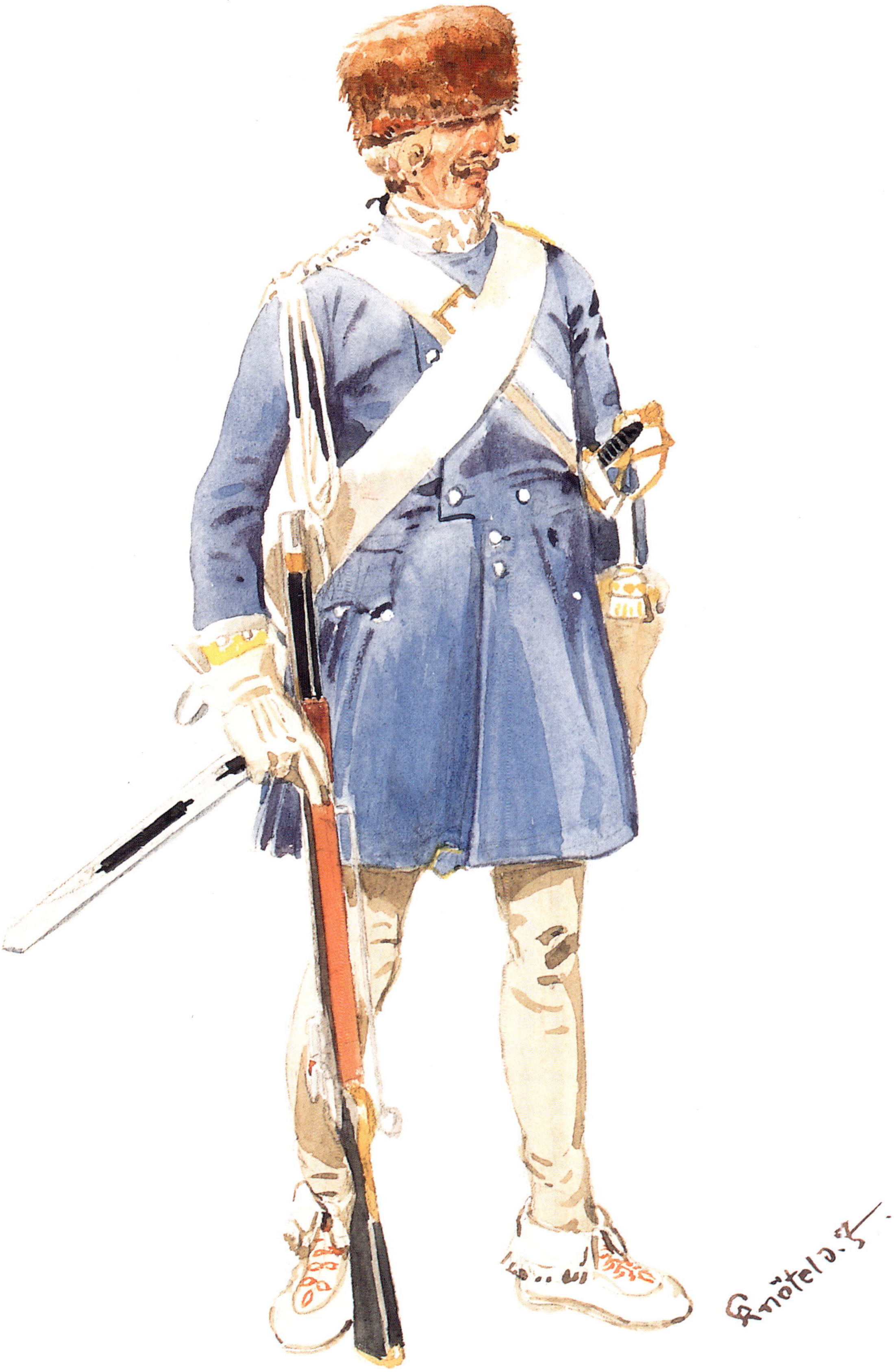

Noncommissioned Officer, Dragoon Regiment, Brunswick troops in Canada. Toward the end of 1782 noncommissioned officers and enlisted men received moccasins. In winter the fur cap replaced the hat and the coat was worn buttoned over for warmth and protection.

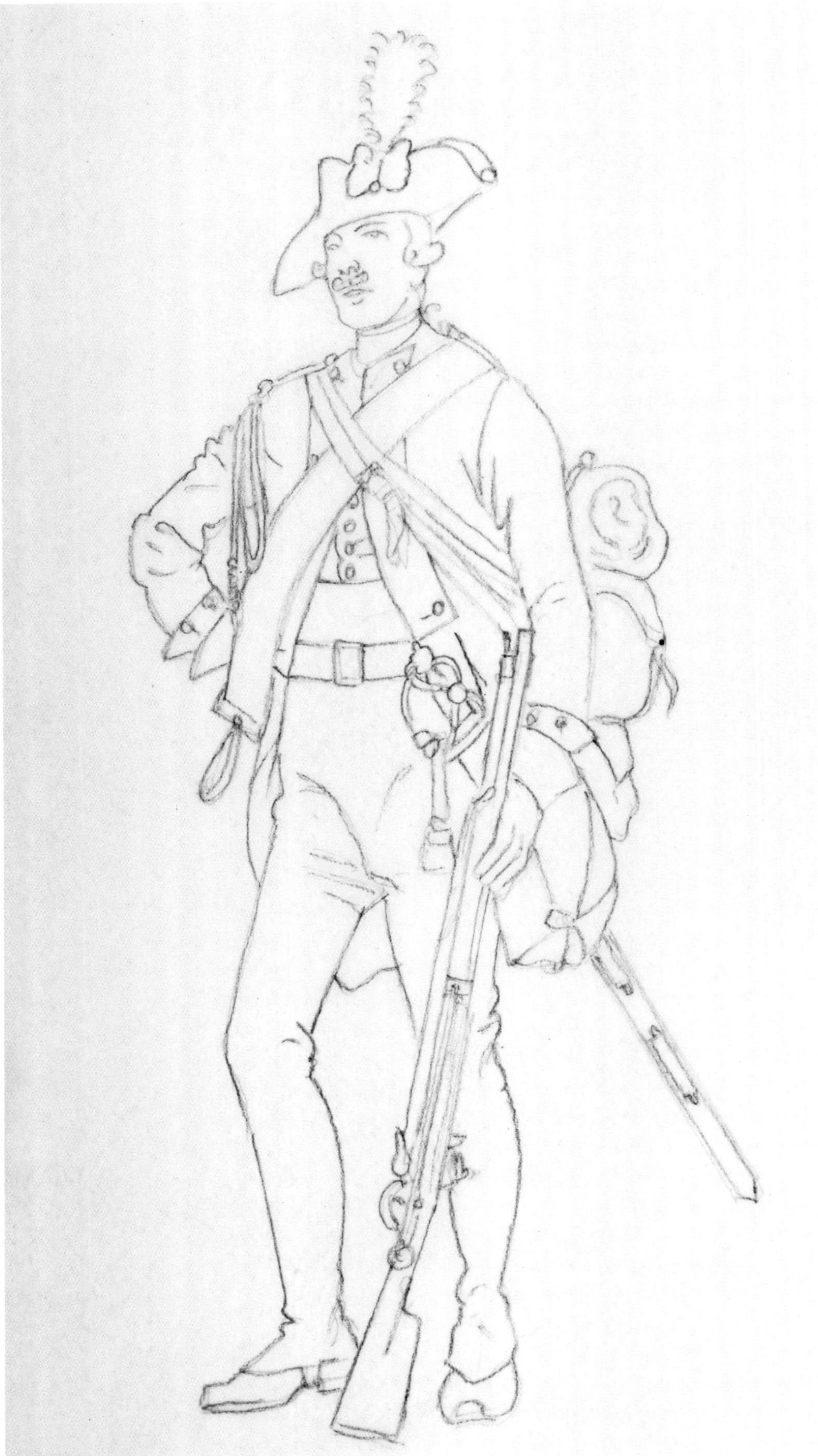

Dragoon sketch, Dragoon Regiment, Brunswick troops in Canada 1777.

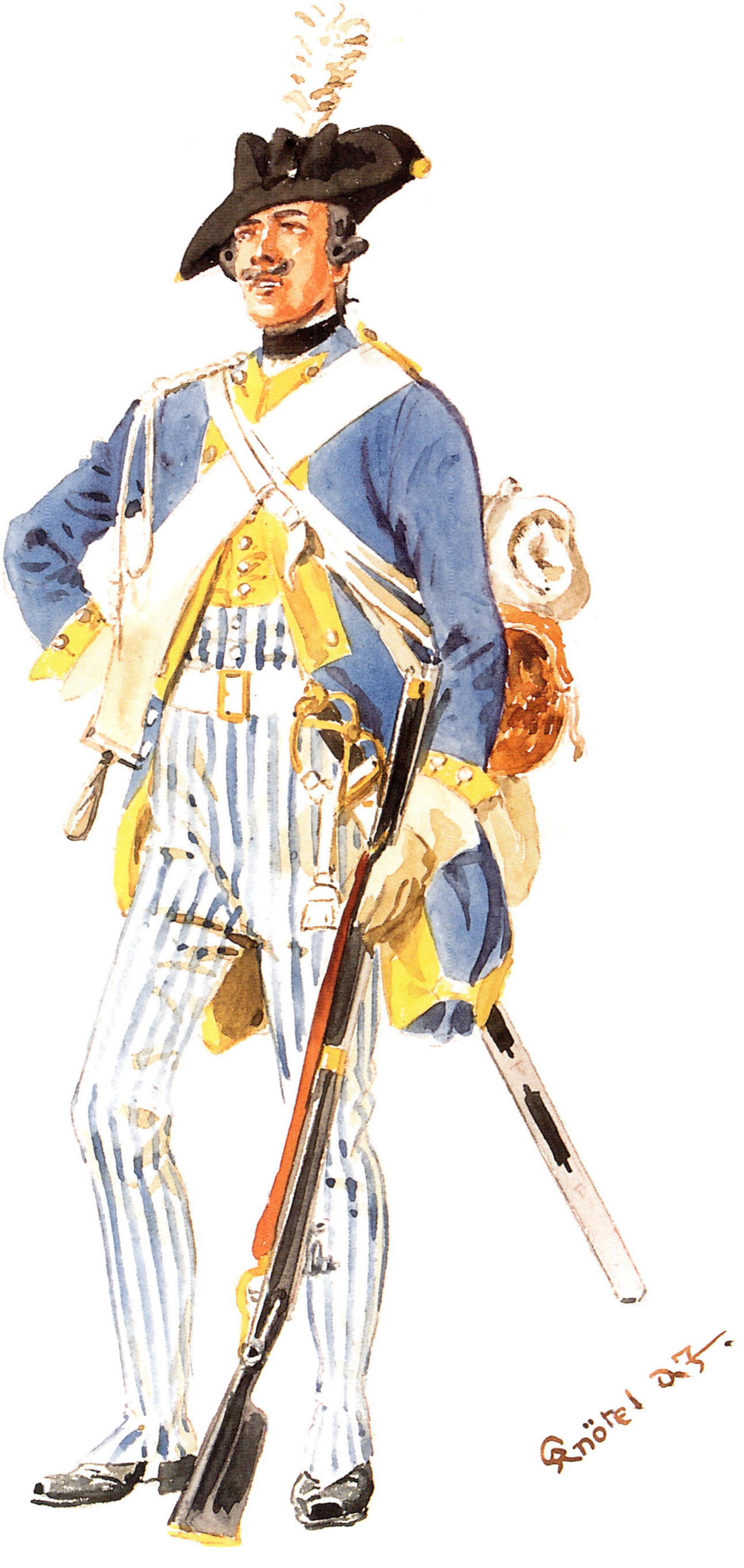

Dragoon, Dragoon Regiment, Brunswick troops in Canada 1777. This dragoon is already equipped and dressed for foot-service. He discarded his heavy boots and carries a haversack and blanket.

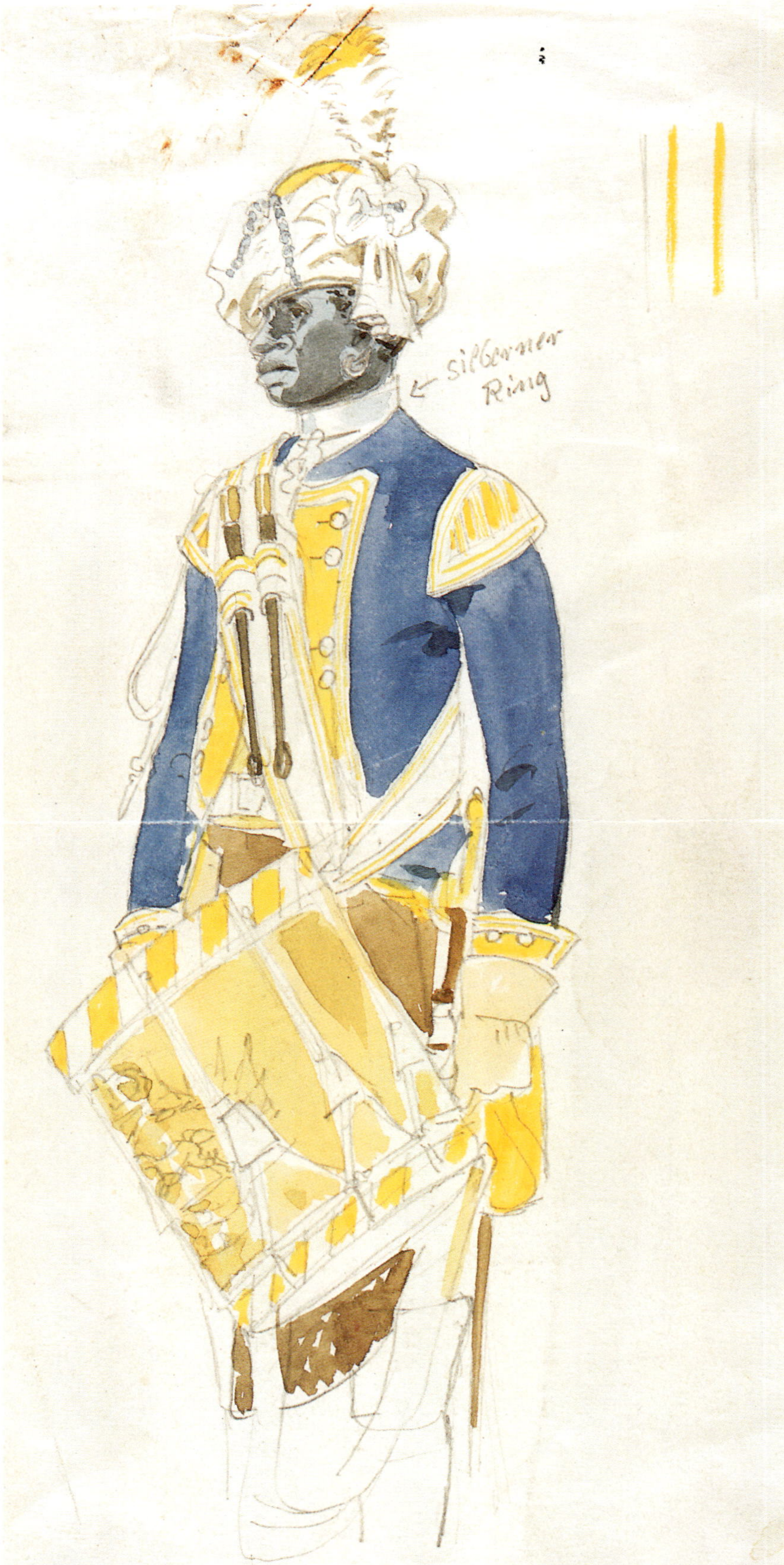

Drummer, Brunswick Dragoons, 1776-1783. Black musicians were highly fashionable in 18th century German armies. The dragoon regiment, reorganized after the destruction of the original corps in the battle of Bennington, recruited some African-Americans and dressed them in this curious mixture of German uniform and oriental headgear. Regimental records note that these musicians returned with the troops to Germany after the American War of Independence. Note the distinct silver neck ring and earring. Painted by Knötel in 1959. Description courtesy of Alfred Umhey.

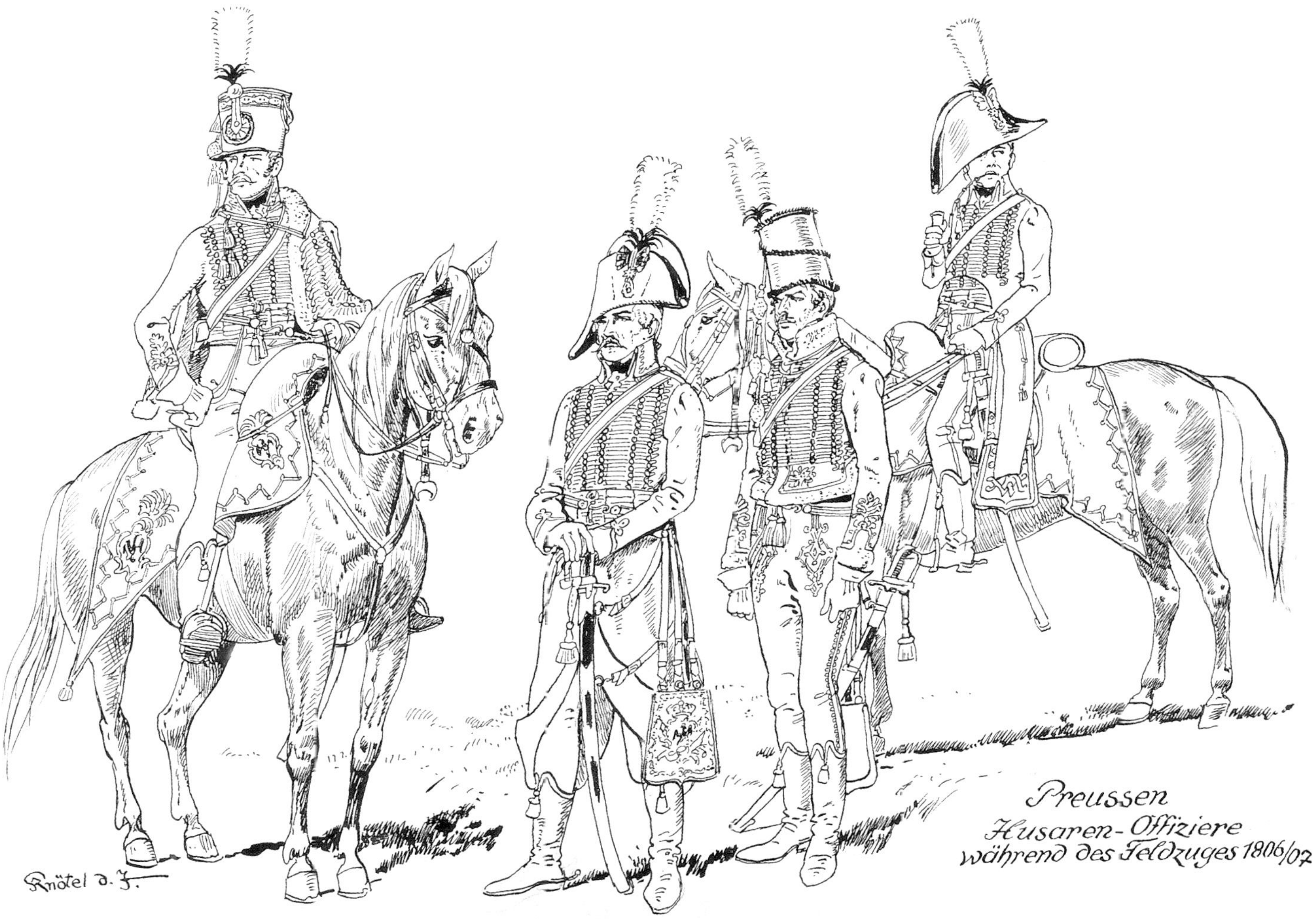

Hussar Officers sketch, Kingdom of Prussia 1806-1807.

Pages 84-85
French Dragoons charging a square of Prussian grenadiers at the final phase of the battle of Jena, October 14, 1806. These dramatic horse charges were frequently beaten by defensive infantry squares that delivered deadly musketry volleys. The kneeling infantry have deployed an impenetrable bayonet wall.

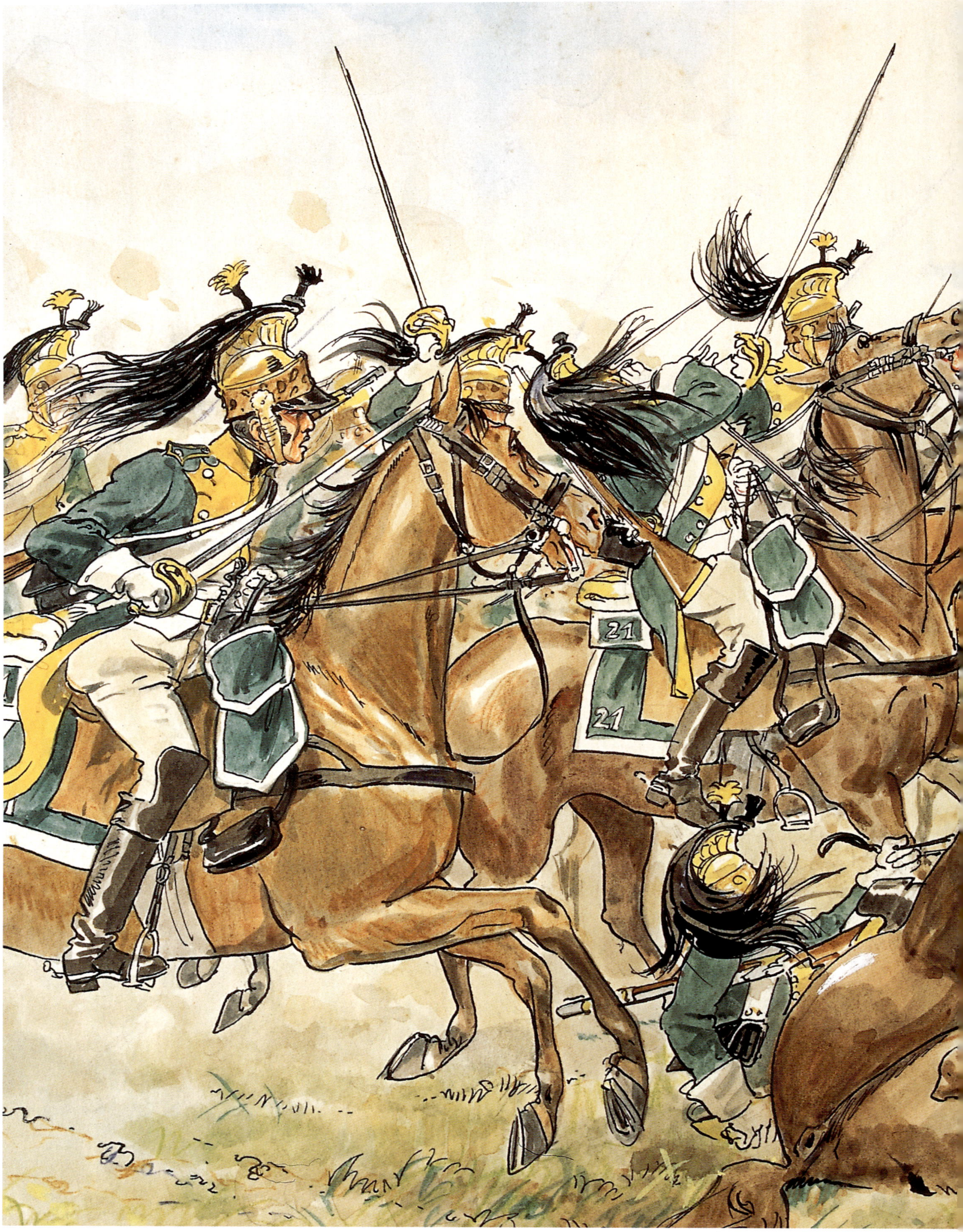

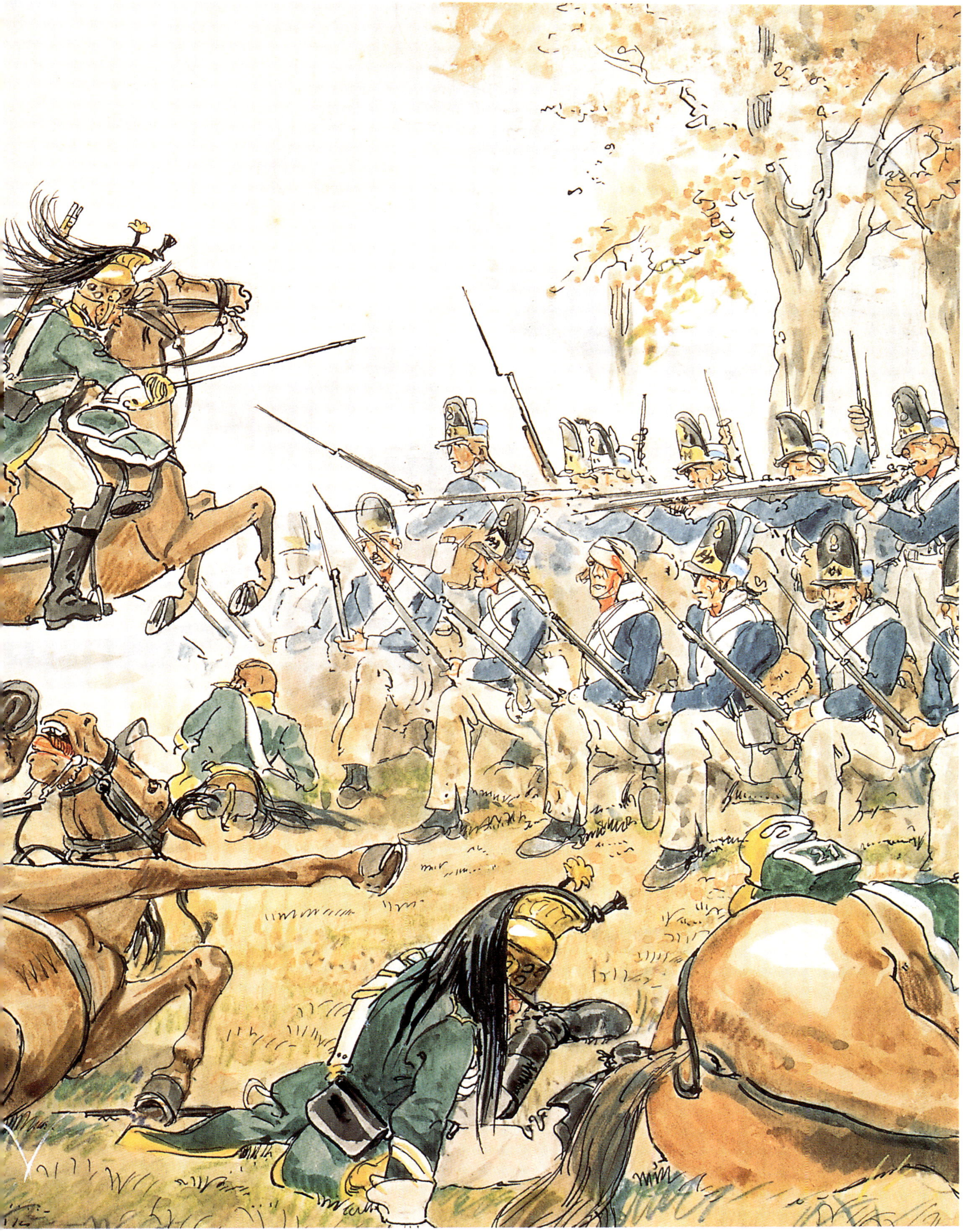

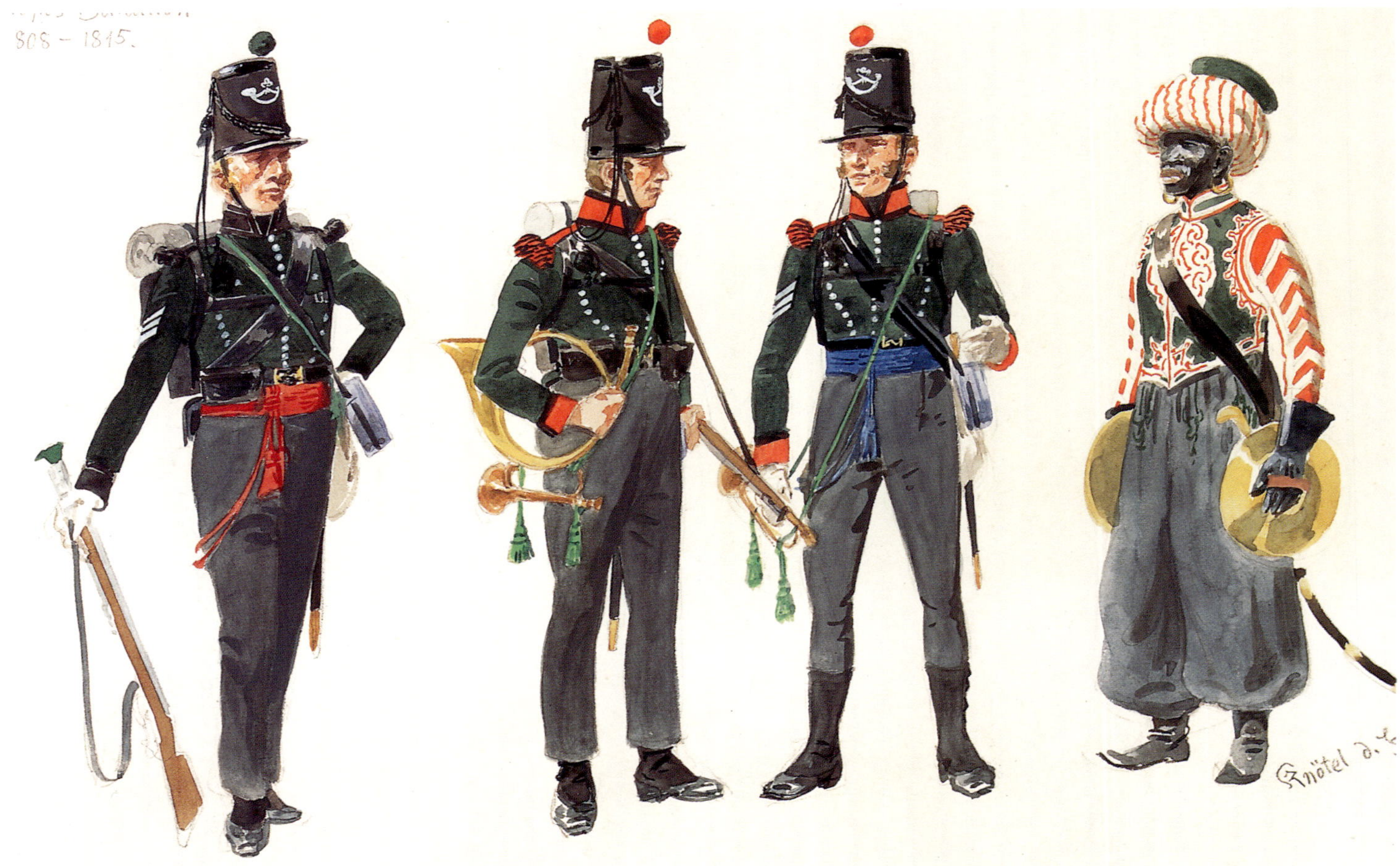

Sergeant, Bugler, Staff Bugler and Janissary, King's German Legion, 2nd Light Battalion, United Kingdom 1808-1815. These are the famous defenders of the farm La Haye Sainte in the battle of Waterloo. The buglers wore red facings instead of the men's black ones. The Black musician is dressed in oriental style. This was common for so-called "turkish instruments". Description courtesy of Alfred Umhey.

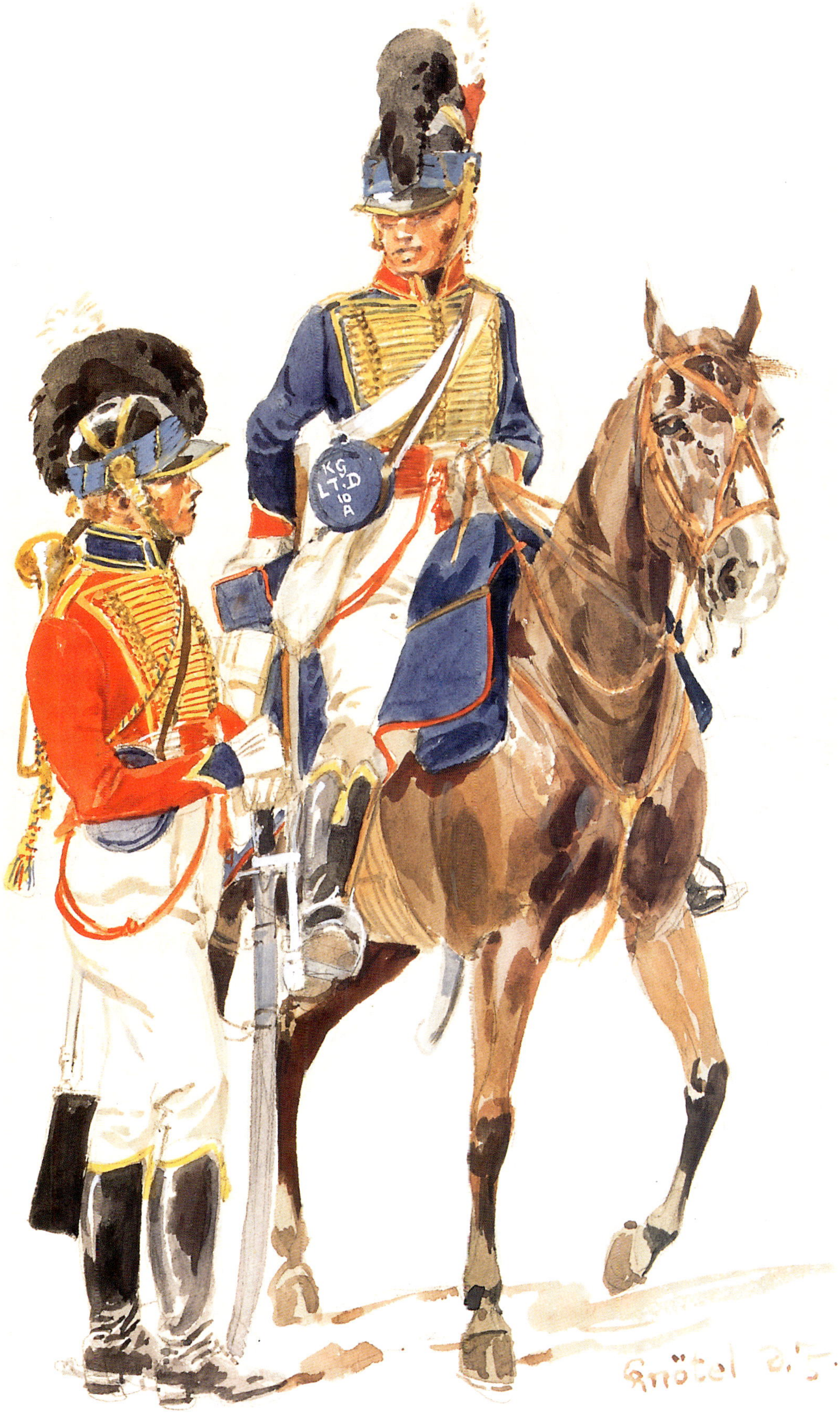

Mounted Dragoon and Trumpeter, King's German Legion, 1st Light Dragoon Regiment, United Kingdom 1807. Later 1st Hussars. This is the typical British light cavalry uniform with the fur crested "Tarleton" helmet. The trumpeter wore reversed color, i.e. the coat in the regimental facing color. Description courtesy of Alfred Umhey.

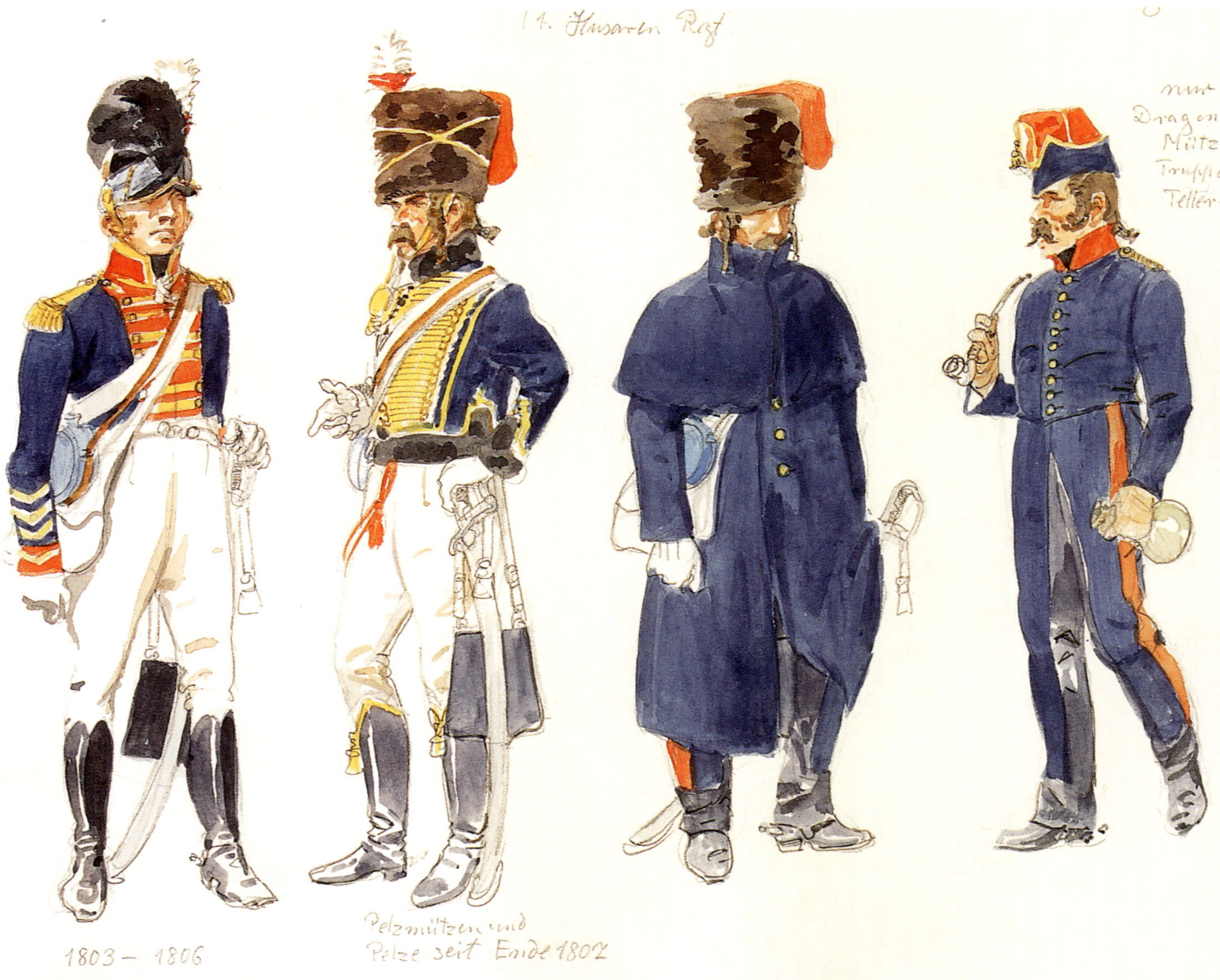

1st Light Dragoon Regiment, King's German Legion, United Kingdom 1803-1807. 1st Hussar Regiment. Fur caps and pelisses since 1807. Only the light dragoons wore these caps. All other troop formations wore flat-topped caps.

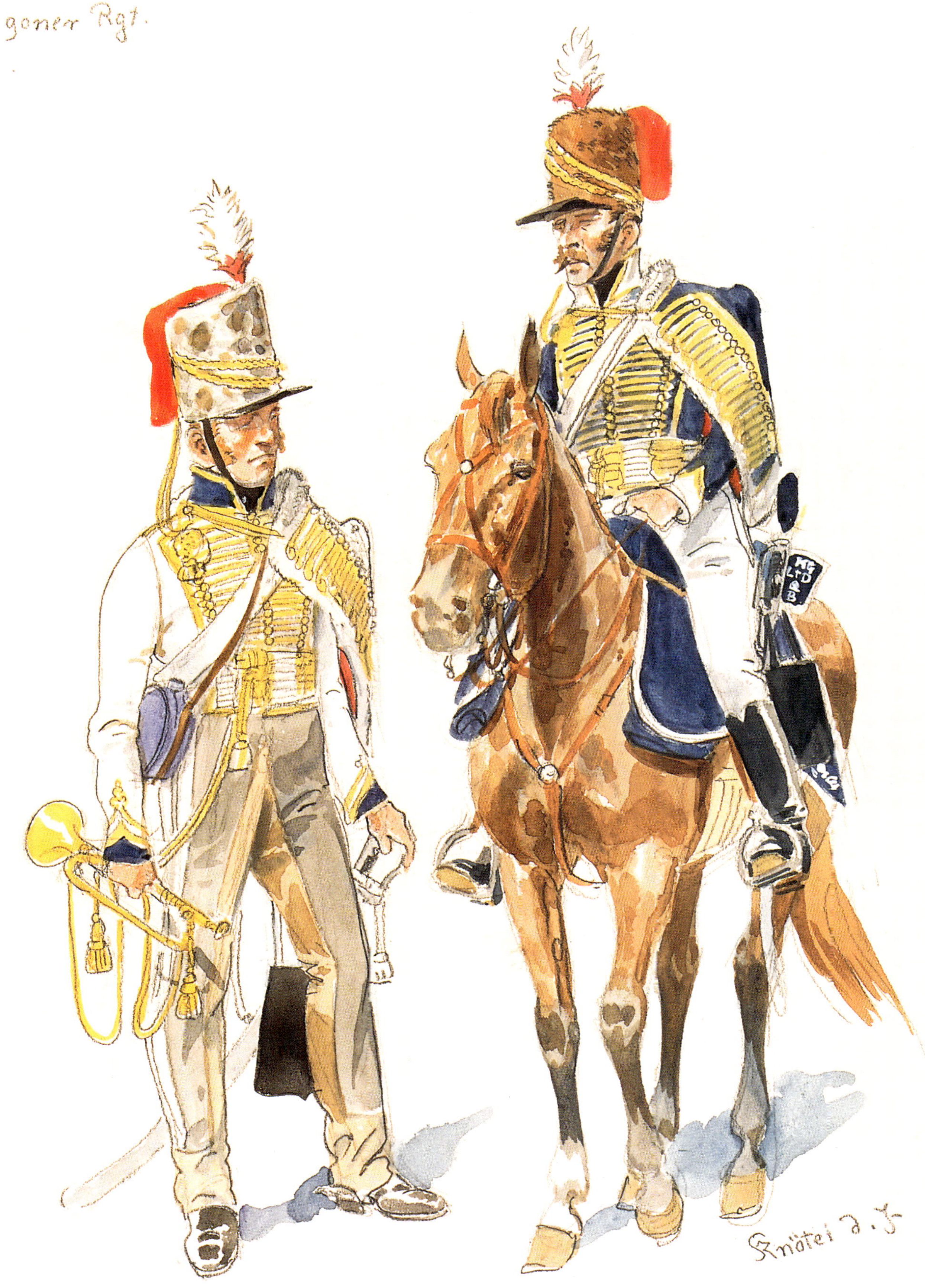

Mounted Dragoon and Trumpeter, King's German Legion, 2nd Light Dragoon Regiment, Hussars, United Kingdom 1809-1810. Here the change of dress has already been completed. Both wore the traditional hussar uniform, the trumpeter again in reversed colors.

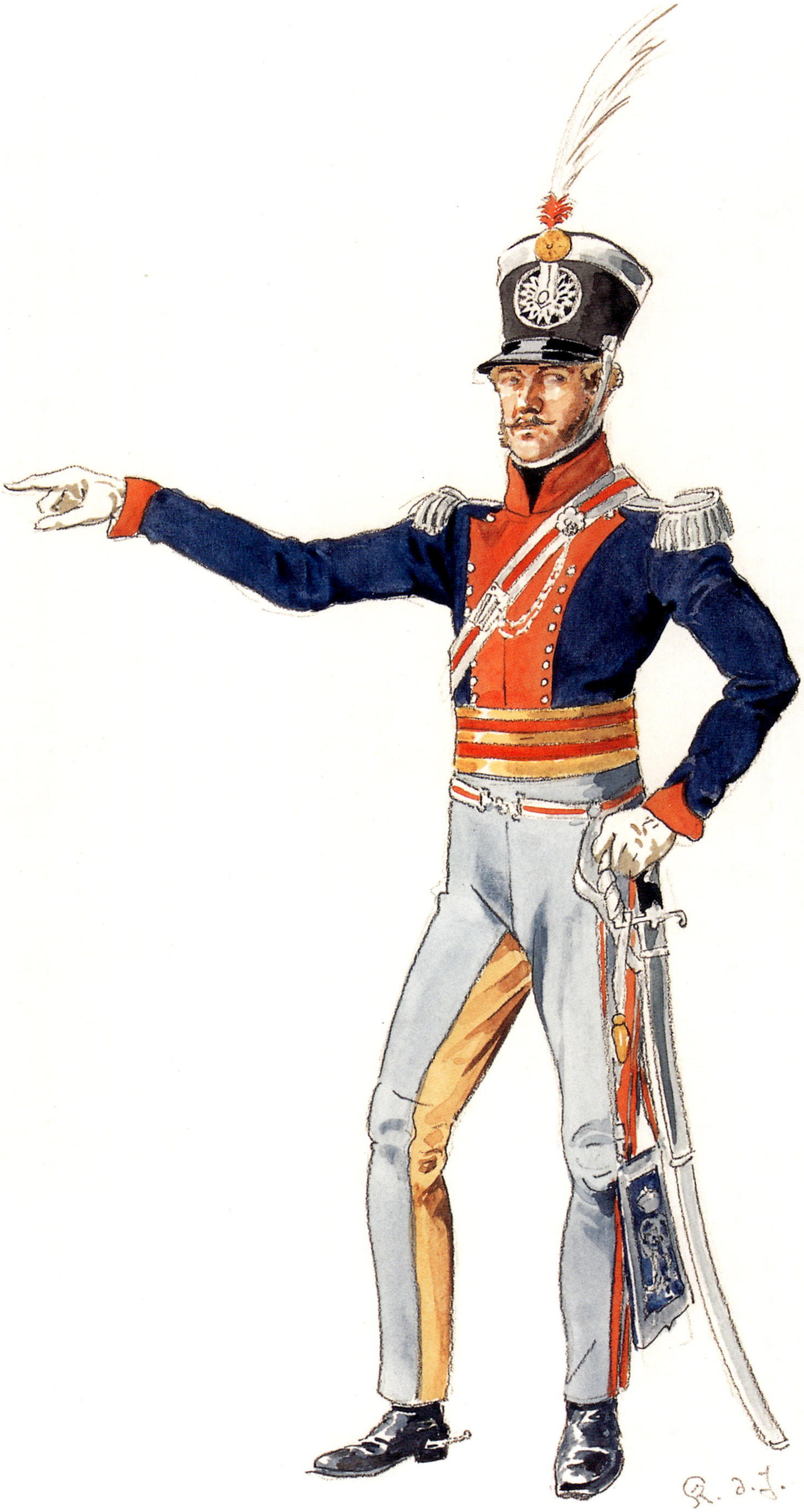

Officer, King's German Legion, 2nd Light Dragoon Regiment, United Kingdom 1815. After an oil painting in the Musée Royale de l'Armée in Brussels.

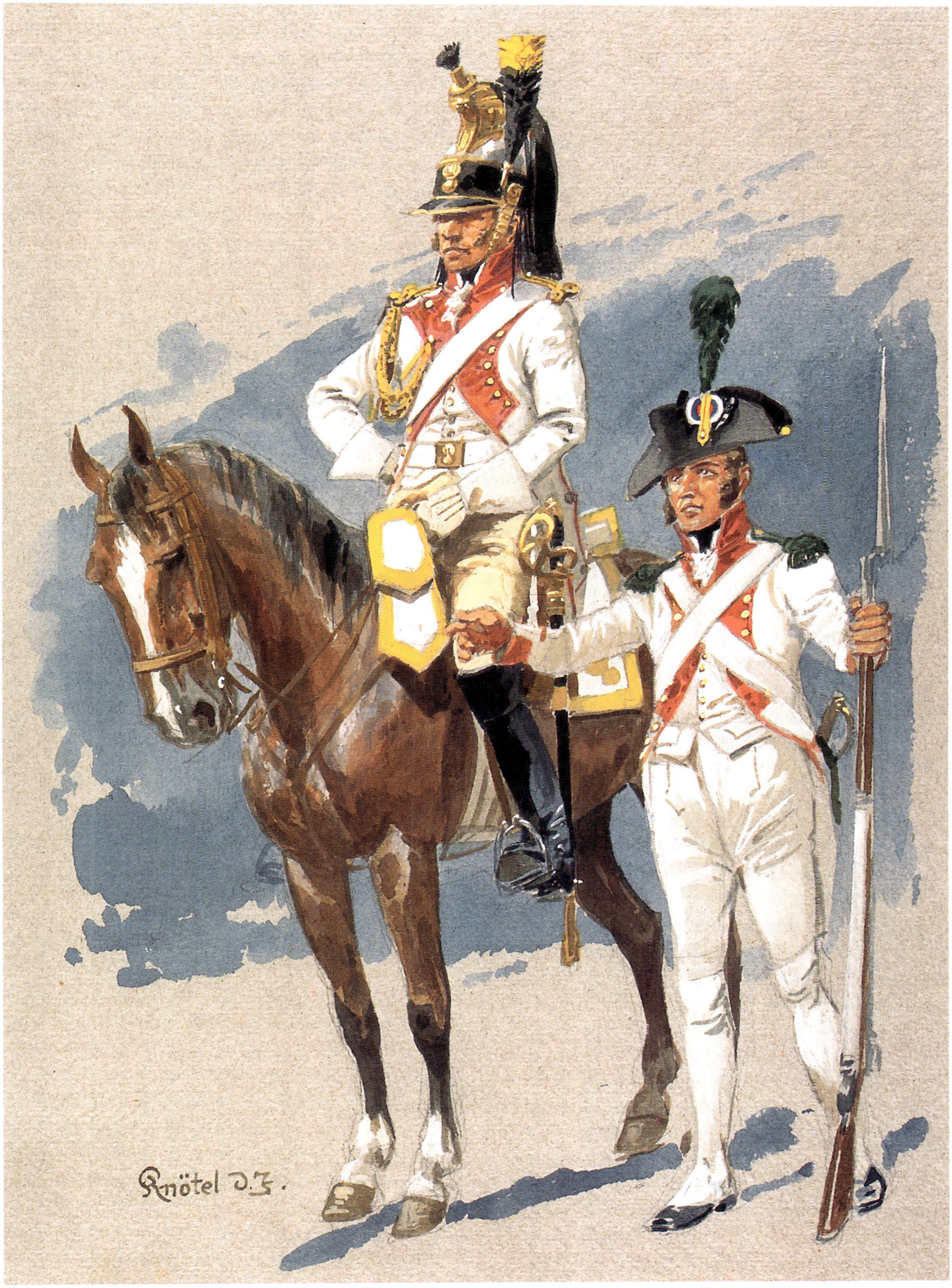

Cavalryman and Foot Chasseur, Münster National Guard. Raised in 1807, originally in the Grand Duchy of Cleves-Berg and existed from then to 1813. In 1808 Münster came under French control. The uniform did not change.

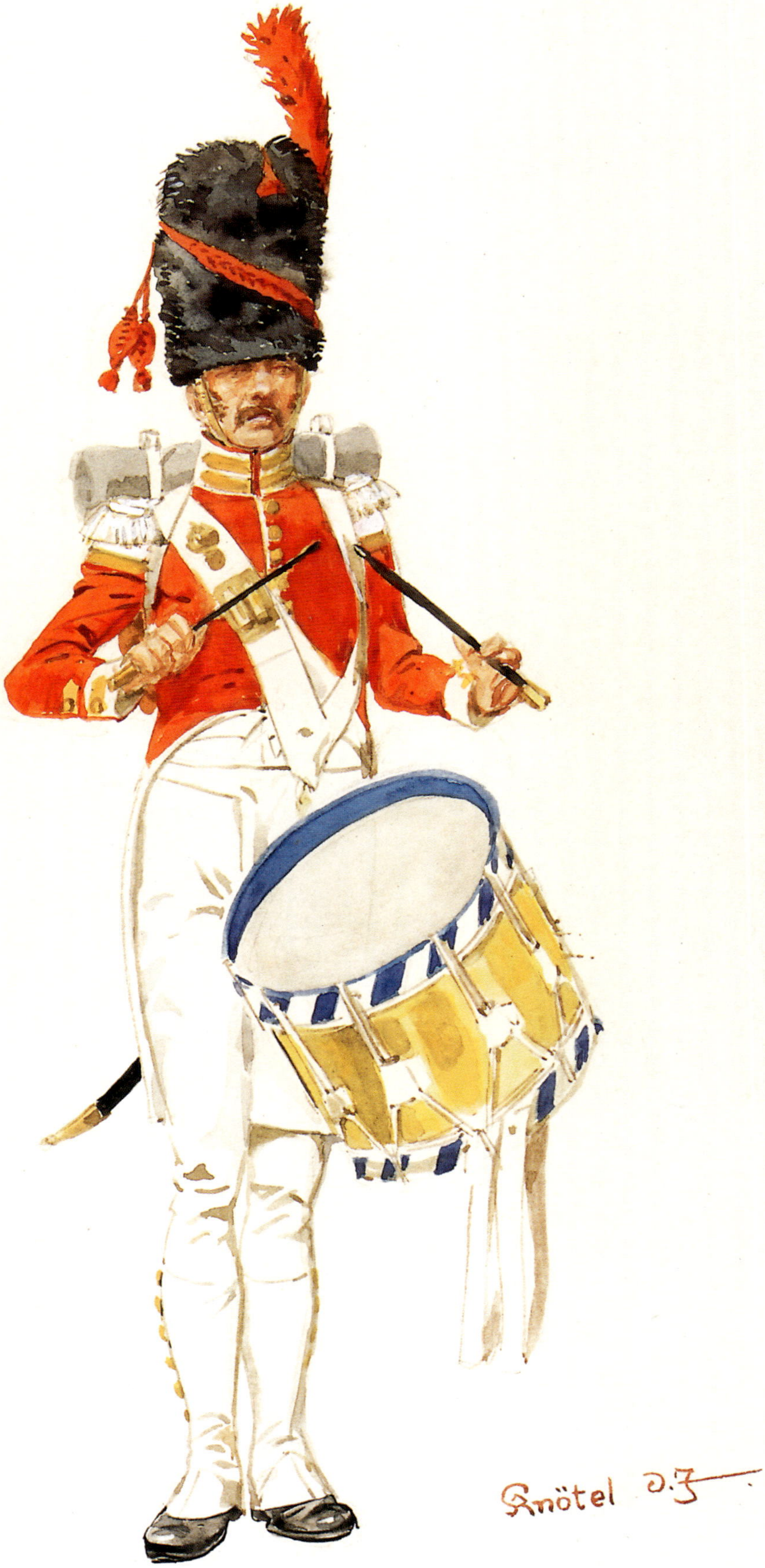

Drummer, Guard Grenadiers, Kingdom of Westphalia 1812. Following the pattern of the French Imperial Guard, the Westphalian Grenadiers still retained traditional white uniforms. The drummer is in a typical coat of facing color.

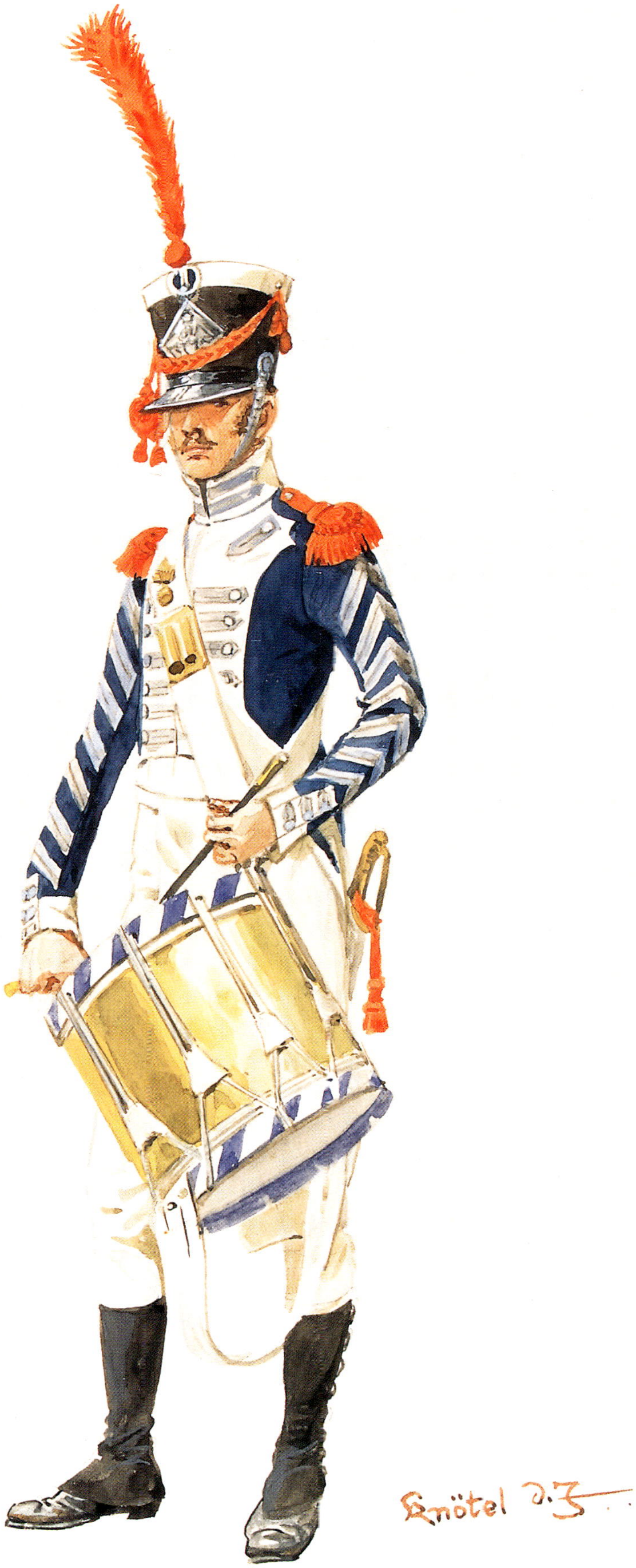

Drummer, Queens Regiment, Kingdom of Westphalia 1812.

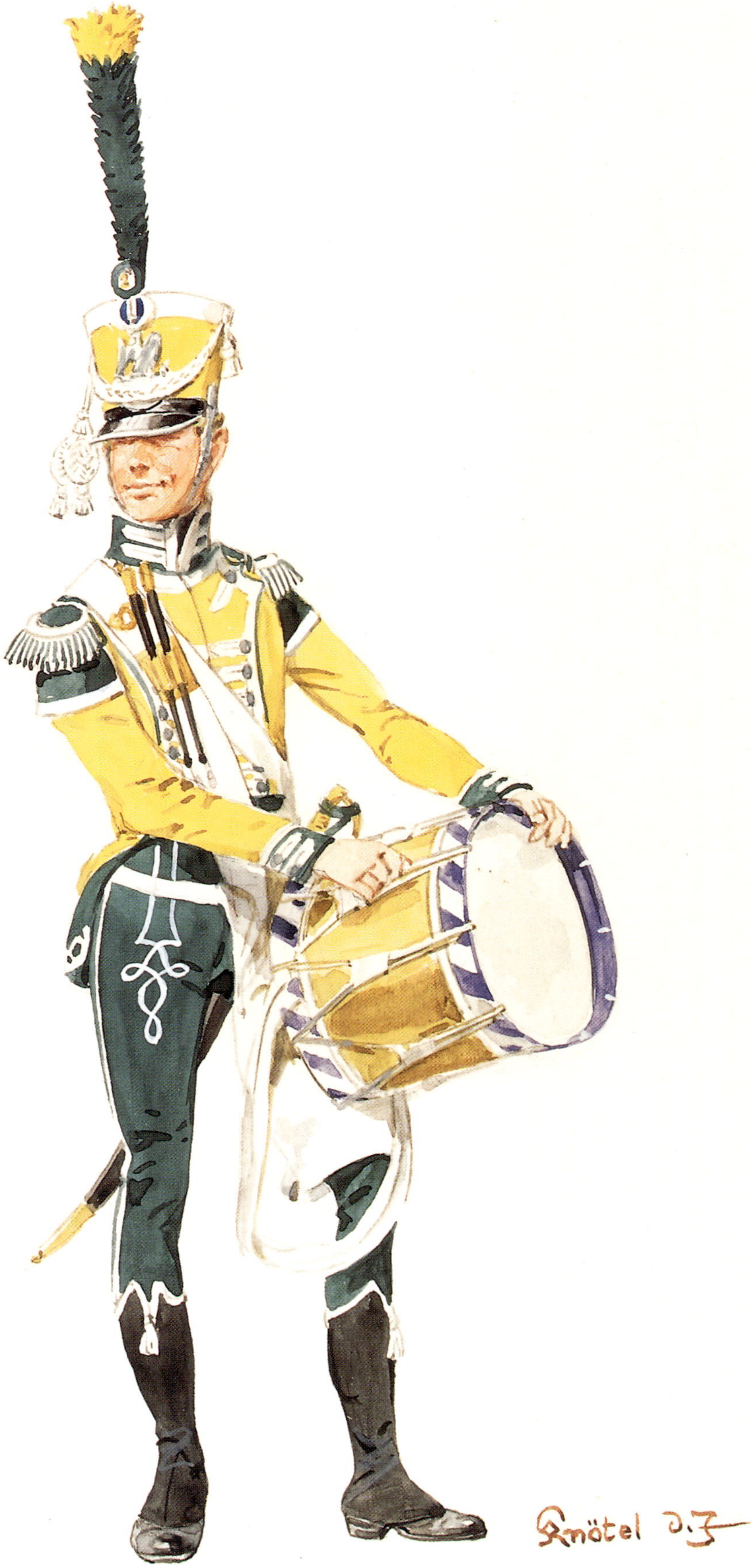

Drummer, Jäger Guard, in full dress uniform, Kingdom of Westphalia 1812. Although named Jäger, this regiment carried ordinary muskets. The drummer's bright yellow coat reflects the facing color.

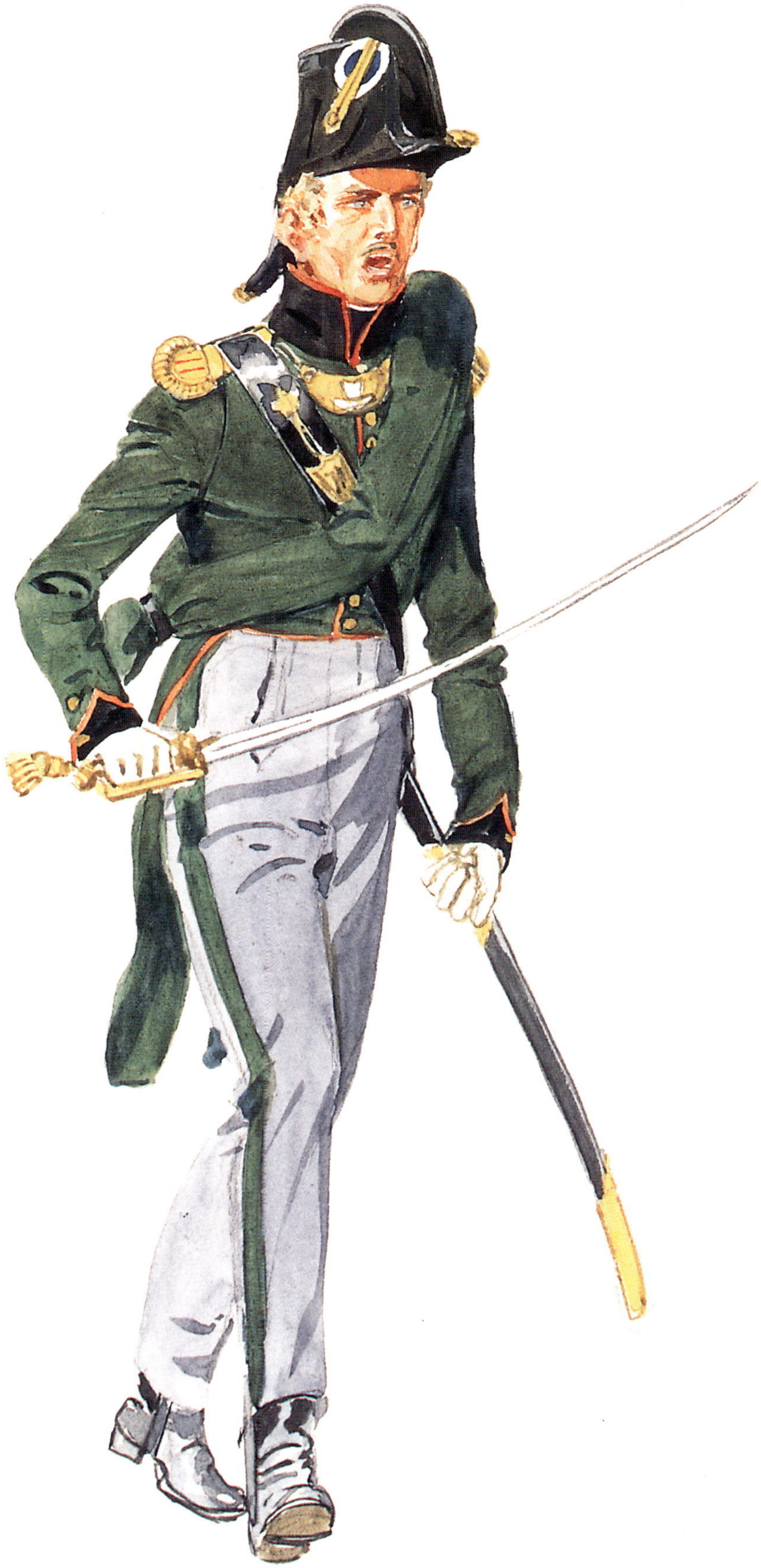

Officer, Jäger Carabiniers, in field uniform, Kingdom of Westphalia 1812. The field uniform was simple and frequently the bicorne replaced the full dress shako for officers.

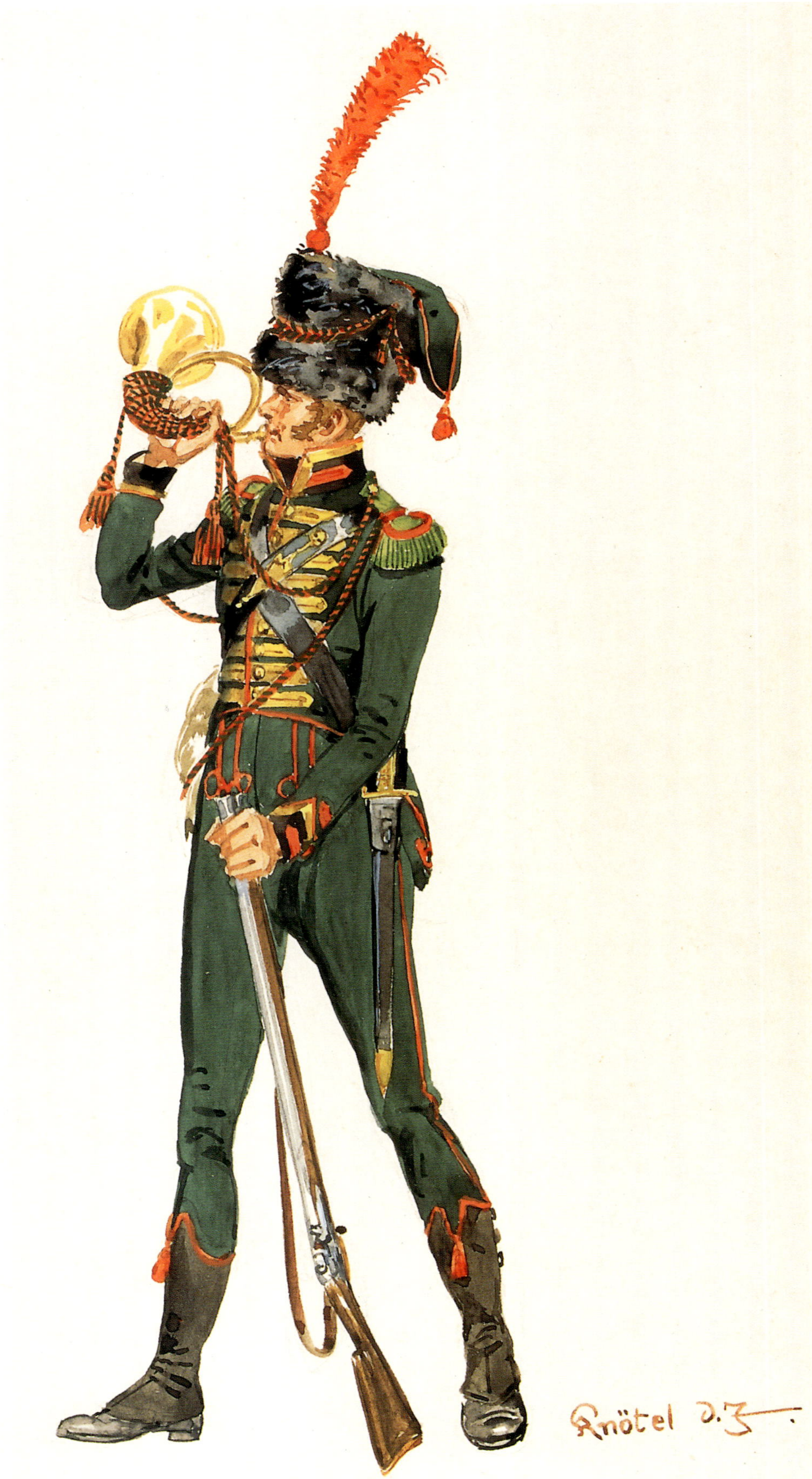

Bugler, Elite Jäger Carabiniers, Kingdom of Westphalia 1812. While the privates wore shakos, this bugler is distinguished by his fur cap. The unit's coats were of the traditional Jäger green. They were armed with rifles and recruited from foresters.

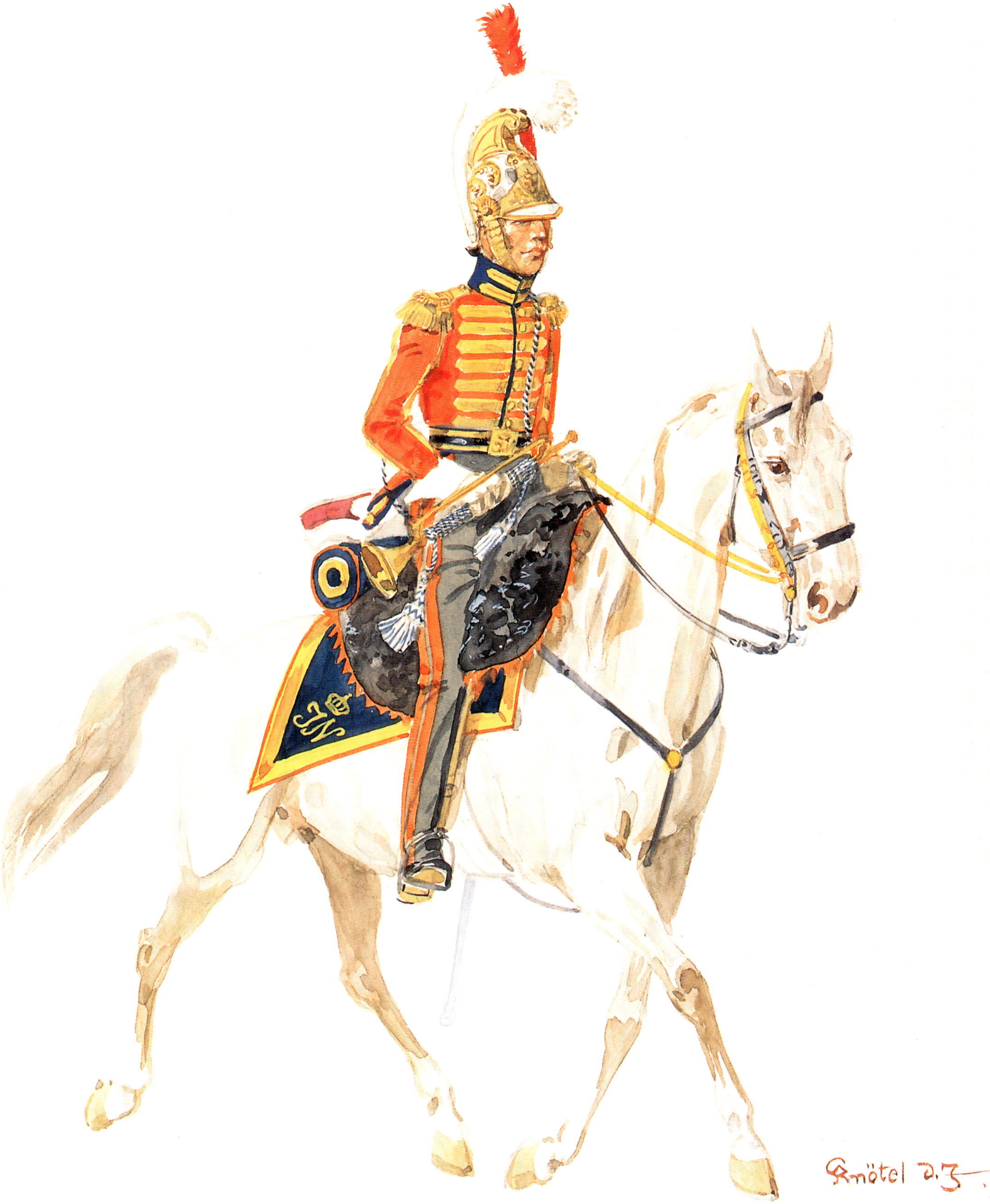

Trumpeter, Lifeguards, in field uniform, Kingdom of Westphalia 1813. As the King's personal bodyguard, this unit accompanied him into the Russian campaign and escorted him, after the downfall of his kingdom up to Cologne, to France. Description courtesy of Alfred Umhey.

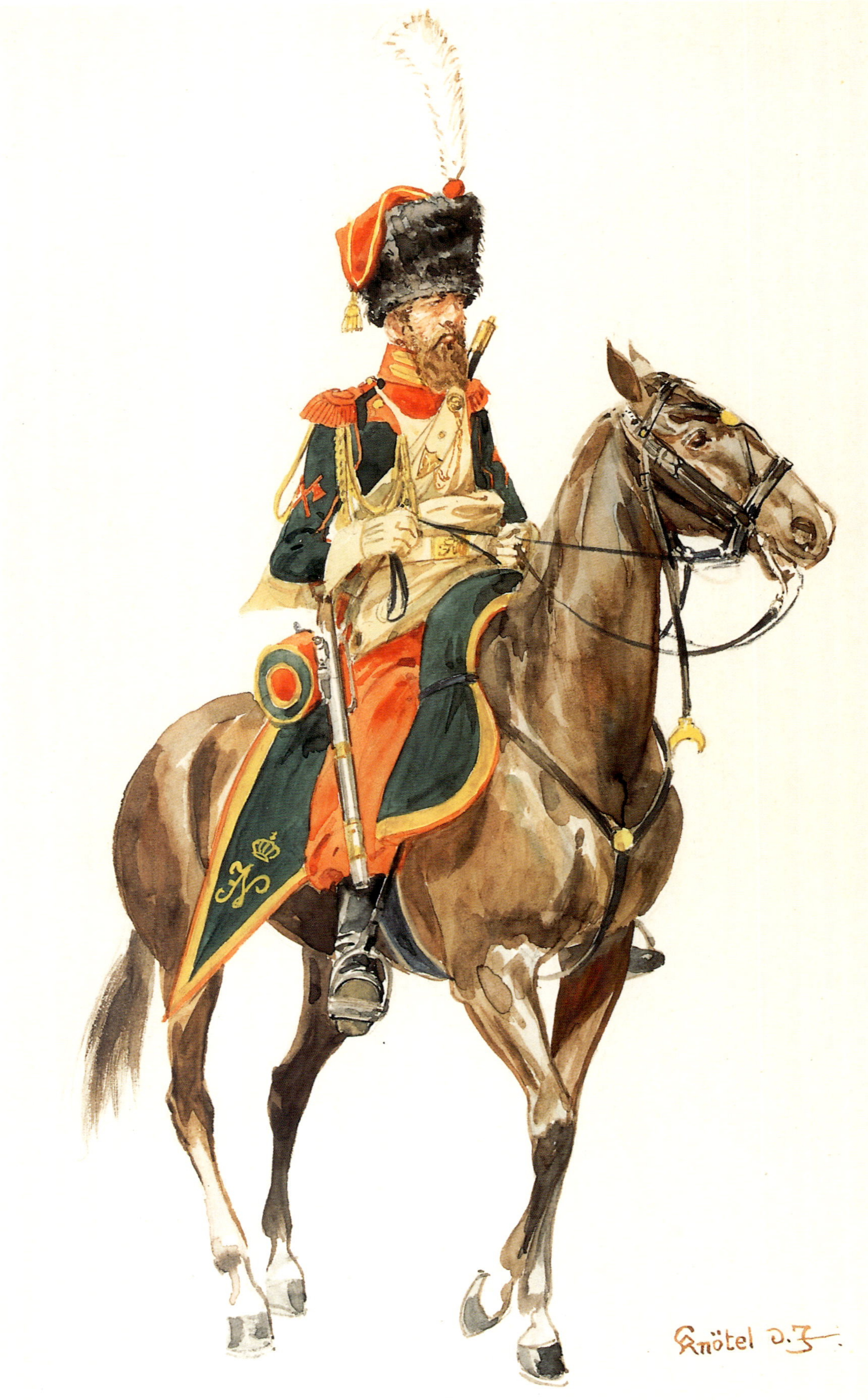

Sapper (Carpenter), Guard Chevau-Légers (Light Horse), Kingdom of Westphalia 1813. Some of the cavalry regiments were also allowed to have sappers. Sappers were the only men allowed to grow beards. The ax and apron are distinctions of his profession.

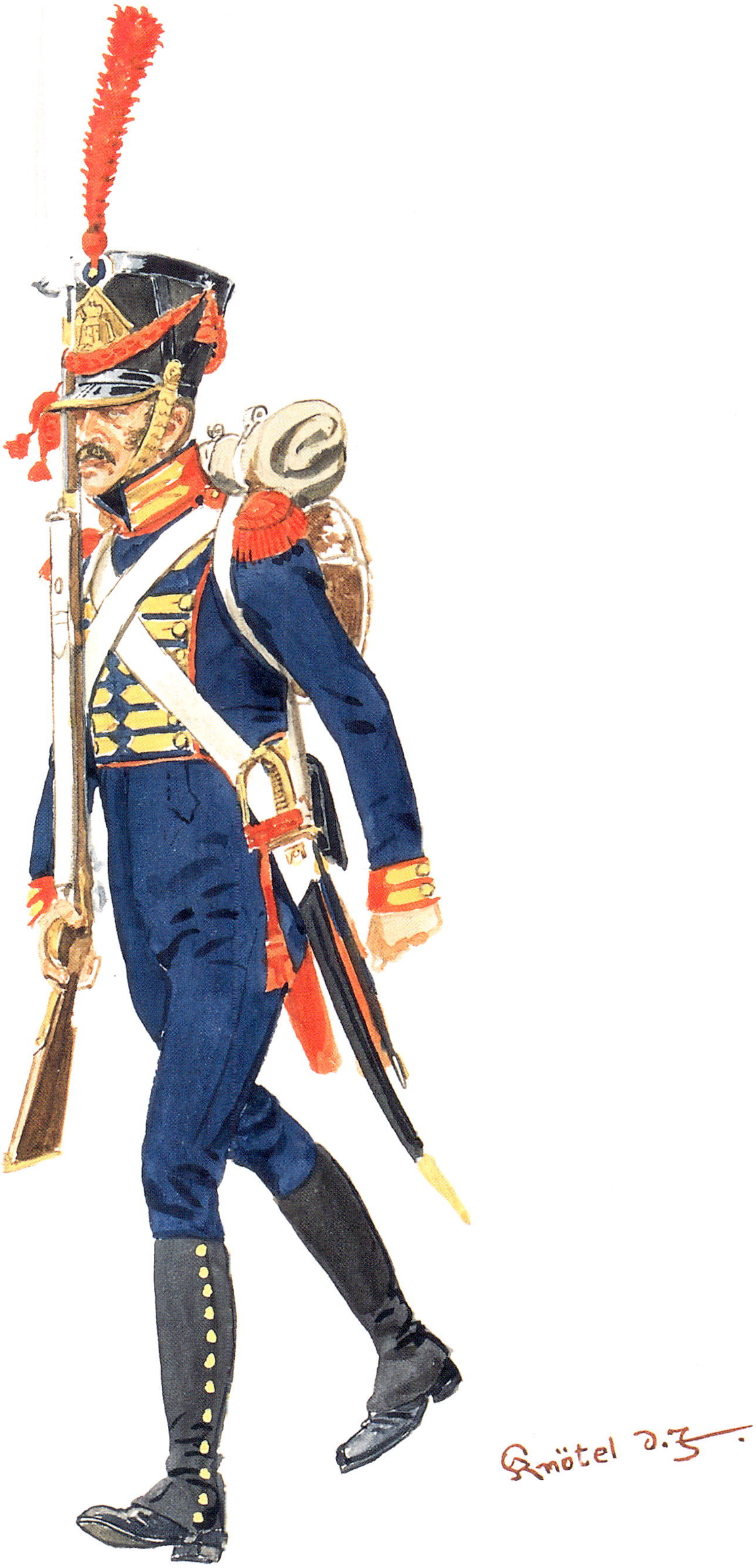

Gunner, Foot artillery of the Royal Guard, Kingdom of Westphalia 1813. The yellow lace on the uniform indicates that this gunner belongs to a guard unit.

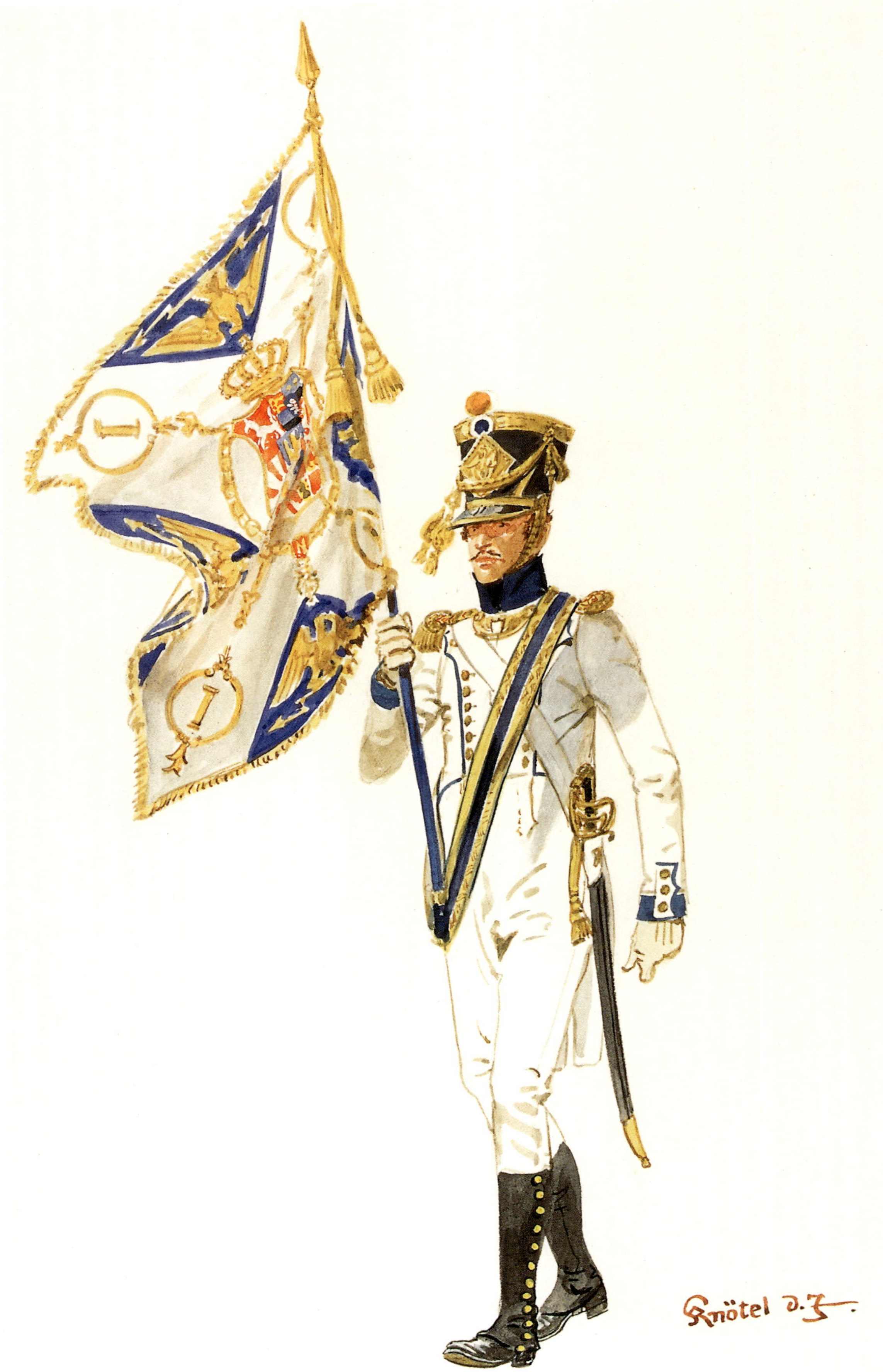

Standard bearer, I and II Battalions from the 1st Line Infantry Regiments, Kingdom of Westphalia 1808-1811.

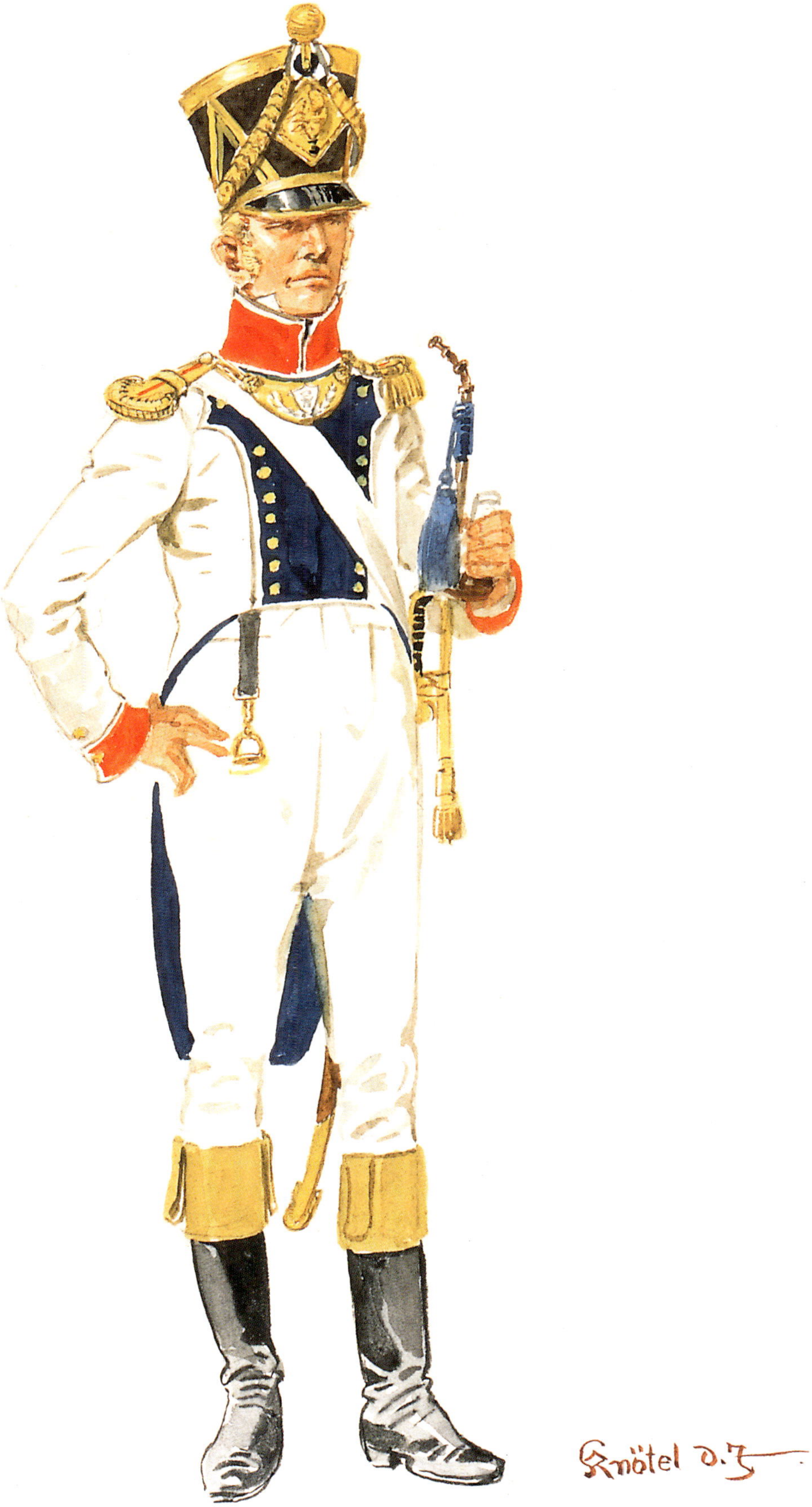

Officer from Regimental Artillery of the 3rd Line Infantry Regiment, Kingdom of Westphalia 1811-1812. Before the 1812 Russian campaign many regiments received regimental artillery with guns captured from Austria in 1809 to increase their firepower. The gunners wore regimental uniform with red collars and cuffs.

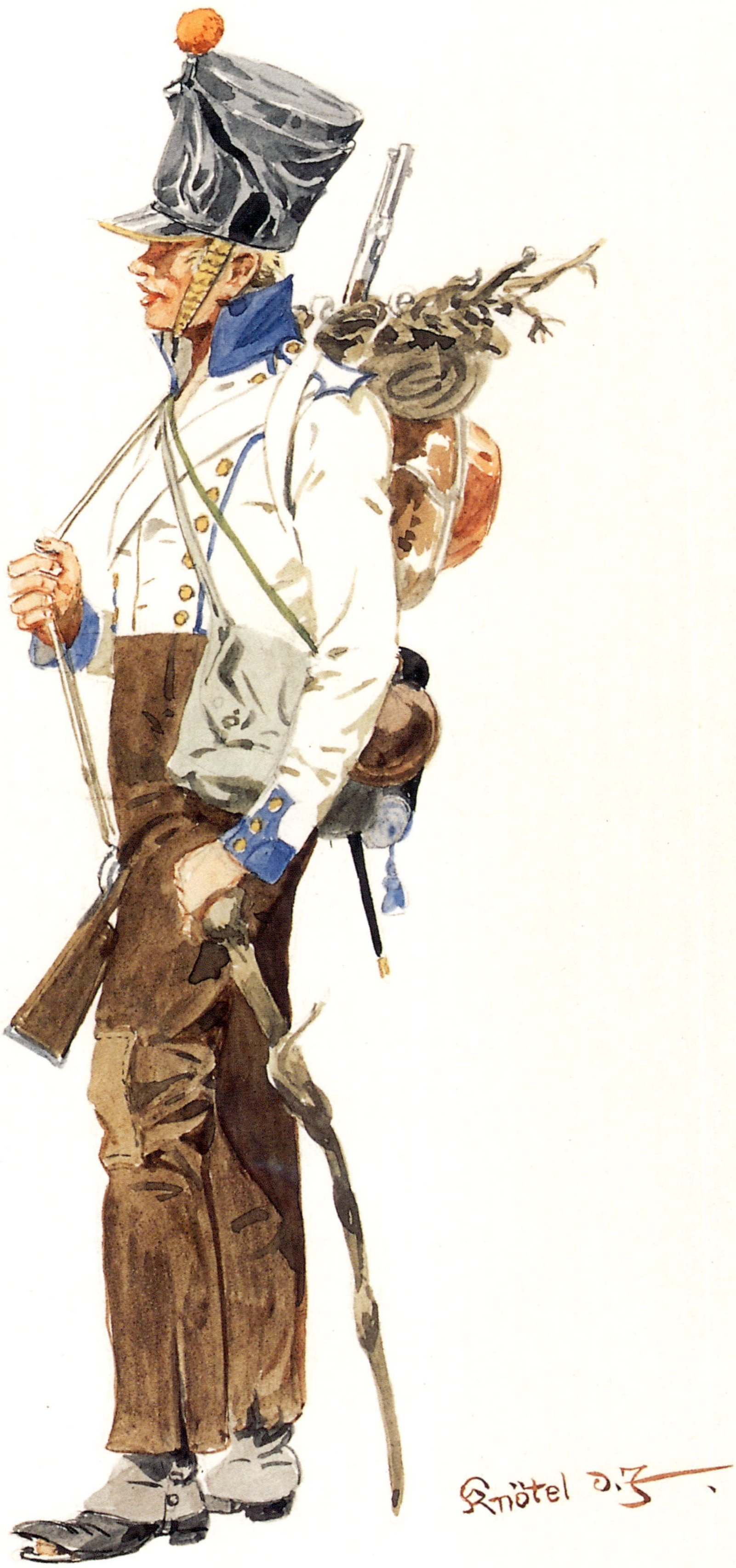

Fusilier, 4th Line Infantry Regiment, in Spain, Kingdom of Westphalia 1809. A typical feature in the Spanish campaign were the brown trousers made locally from the cloth confiscated in monasteries. Description courtesy of Alfred Umhey.

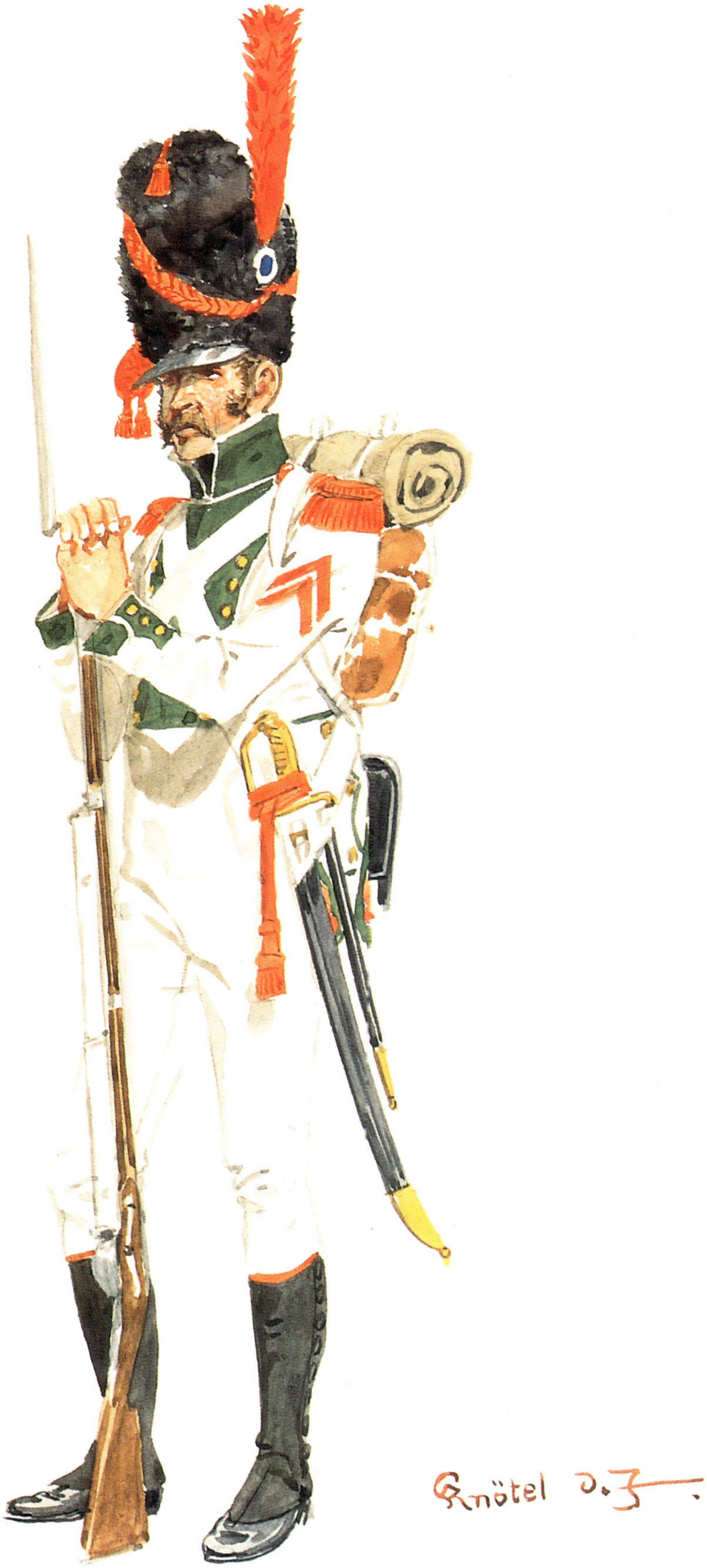

Grenadier, 5th Line Infantry Regiment, Kingdom of Westphalia 1808-1809. Westphalian fur caps were worn with a visor, otherwise uncommon in French and allied armies. The two red chevrons indicate fifteen years of service. Years served in other sovereigns' armies counted as part of total service. Description courtesy of Alfred Umhey

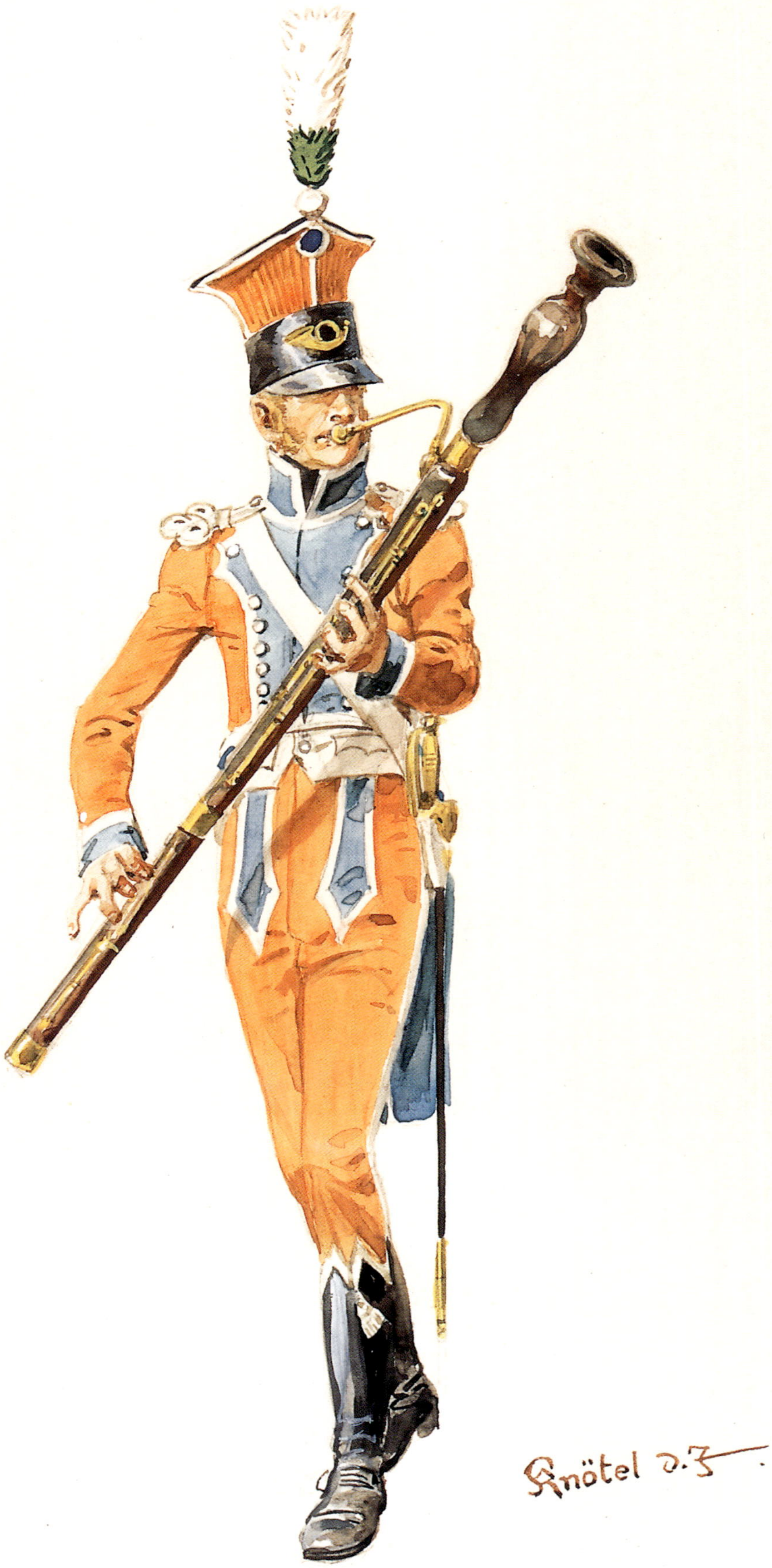

Musician, 2nd Light Infantry Battalion, Kingdom of Westphalia 1808. Musicians were often clad in bright colors. As a special feature, this musician wears a polish style schapska. The instrument is a bassoon.

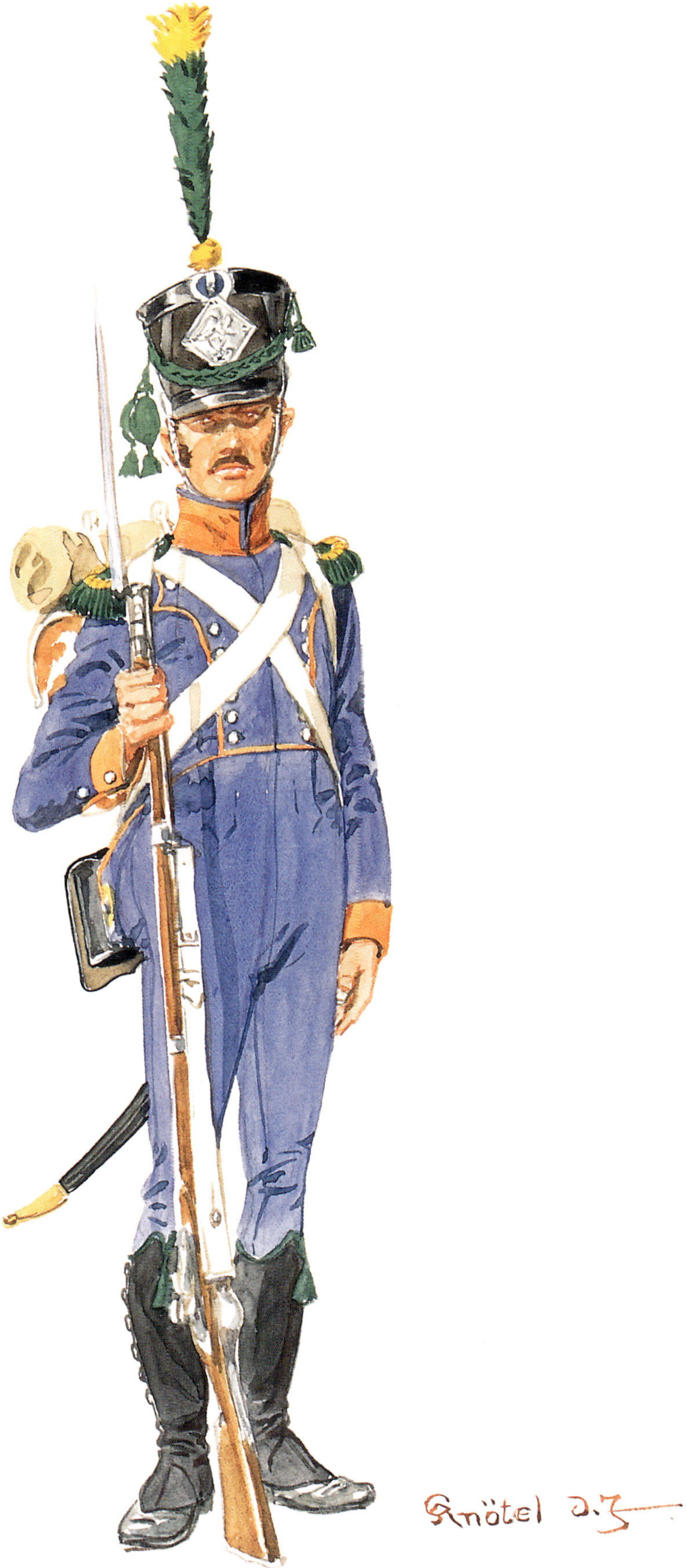

Voltigeur, 2nd Light Infantry Battalion, Kingdom of Westphalia 1809-1810. This is the first uniform of the light infantry, which later changed to green. Voltigeurs served as skirmishers in infantry units.

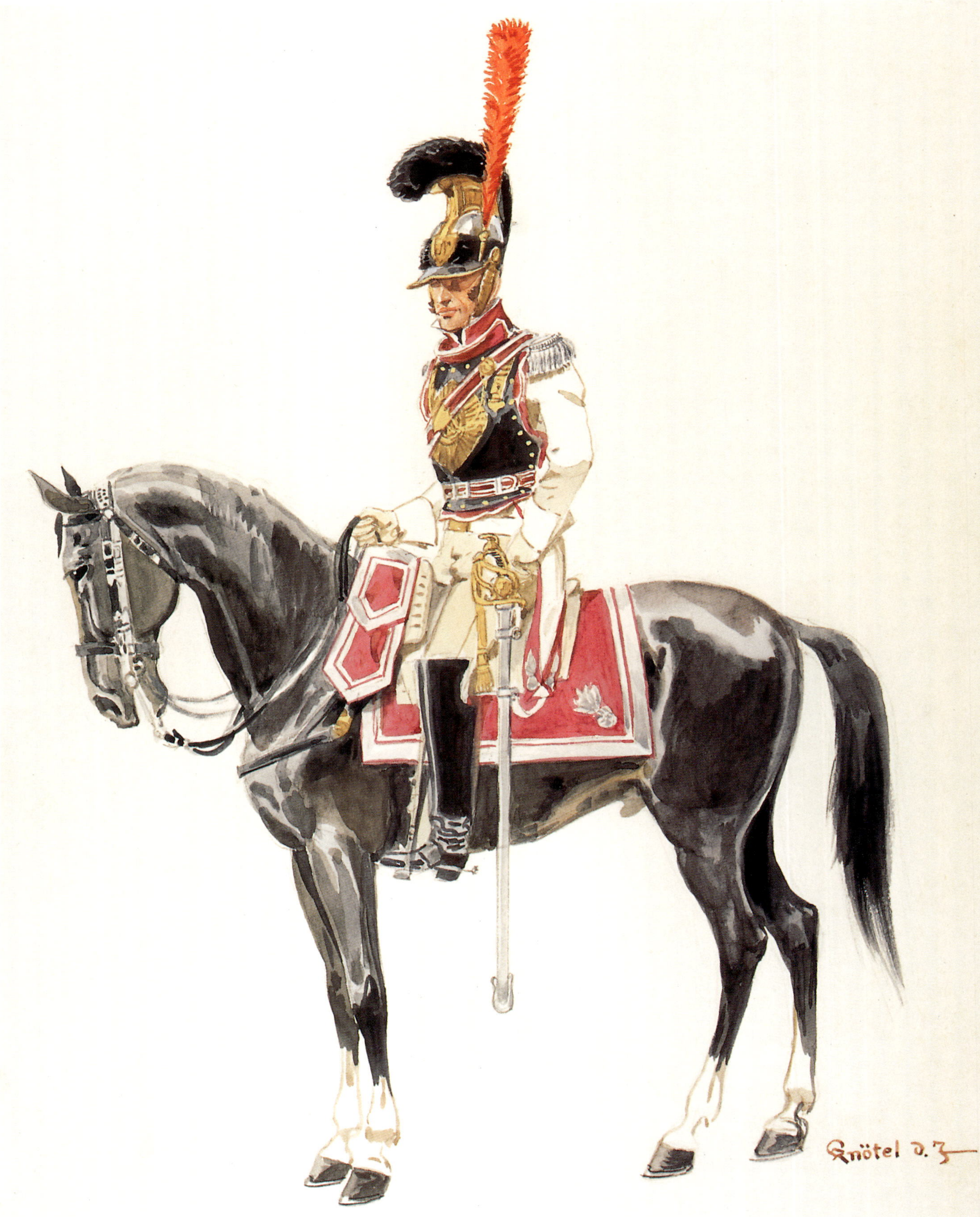

Officer, 1st Cuirassier Regiment, Kingdom of Westphalia 1808-1810. Clad in the traditional white coat of German heavy cavalry this officer wore only a breastplate instead of a full cuirass. Napoleon heavily opposed the creation of the Westphalian Cuirassiers because he only wanted his satellite armies to have light cavalry formations. Description courtesy of Alfred Umhey.

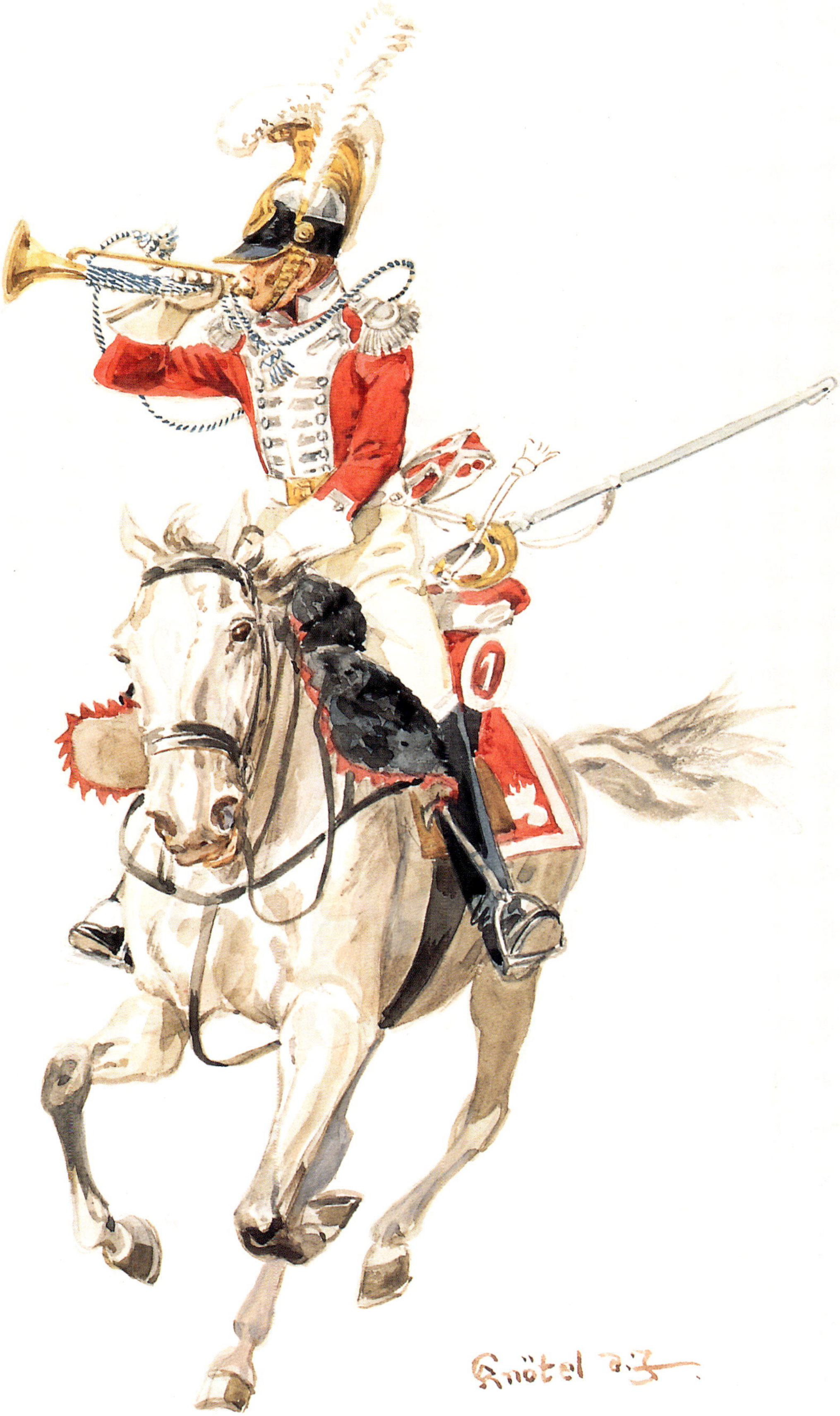

Trumpeter in full dress, 1st Cuirassier Regiment, Kingdom of Westphalia 1811. Troopers were armored, however, trumpeters were not hindered by the cumbersome cuirass in order to more easily draw breath to blow their instruments.

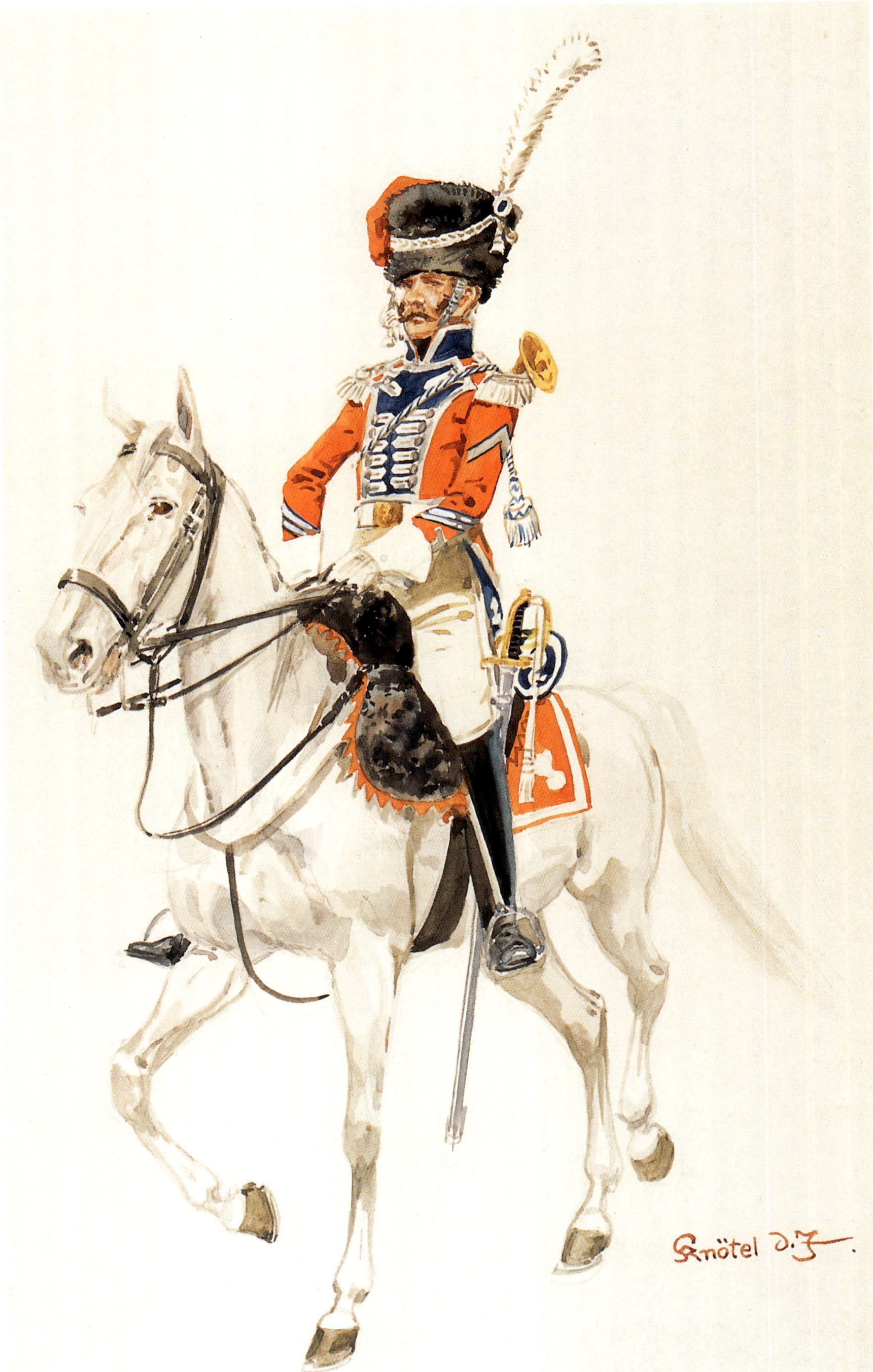

Trumpeter in full dress, 2nd Cuirassier Regiment, Kingdom of Westphalia 1812. The use of furcaps was not uncommon for trumpeters, even in the heavy cavalry. To contrast their white horses, they usually wore black sheepskin saddles.

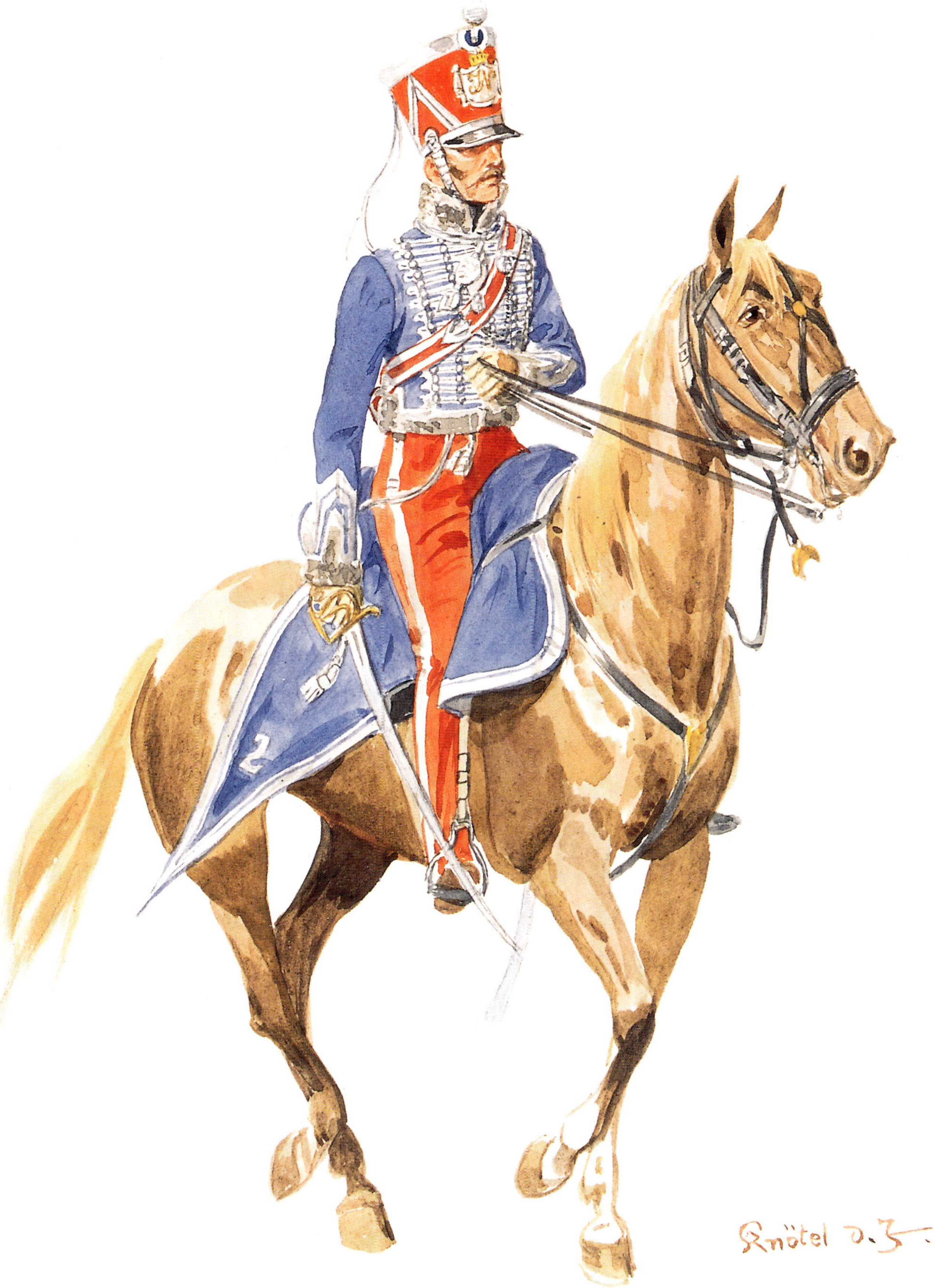

Officer, 2nd Hussar Regiment, Kingdom of Westphalia 1812-1813. The inverted V chevrons and the very elaborate shako late are particular on this figure.

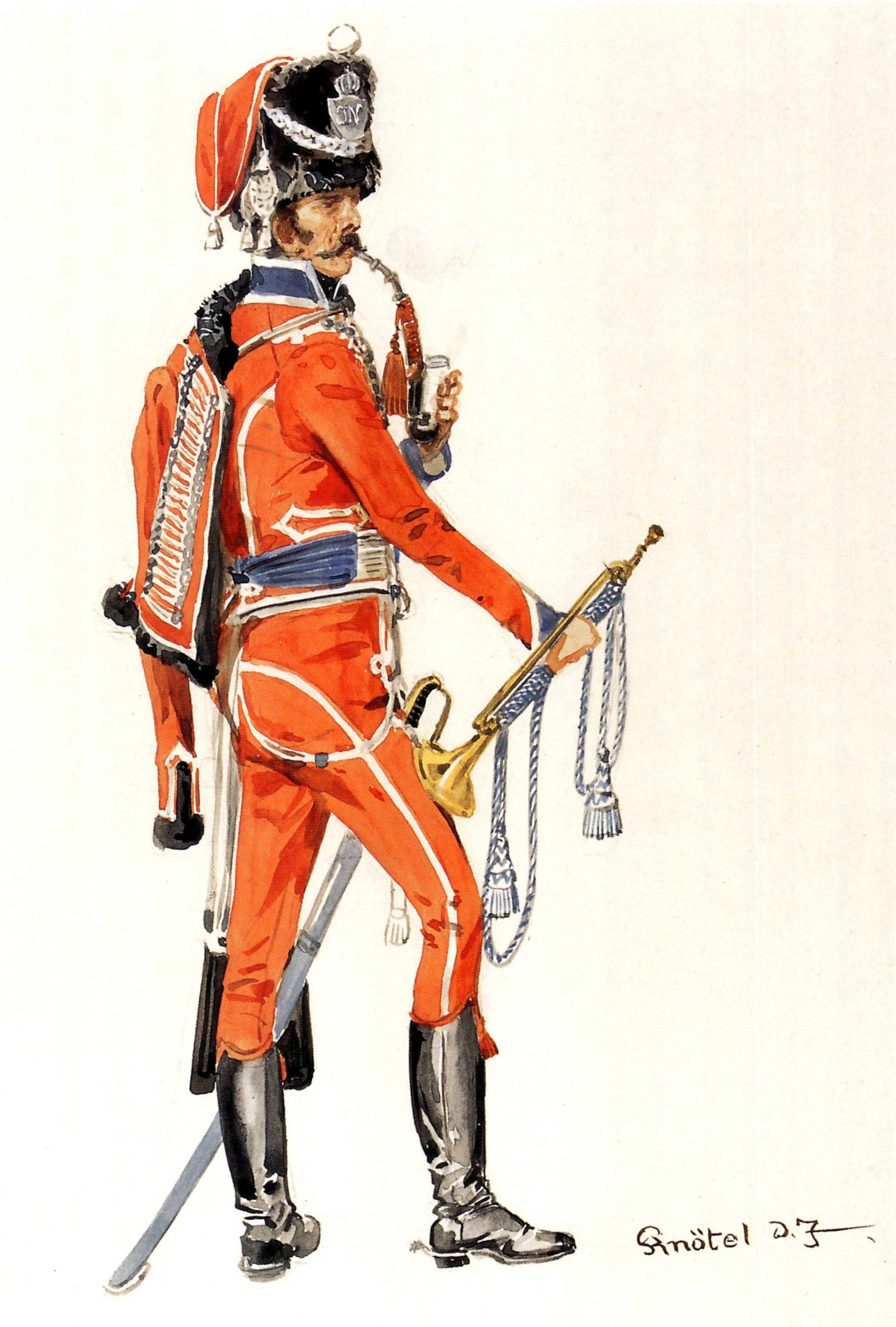

Trumpeter, 2nd Hussar Regiment, Kingdom of Westphalia 1812. This trumpeter is not just wearing reversed colors on the dolman, but is clad completely in the regiment's red facing color.

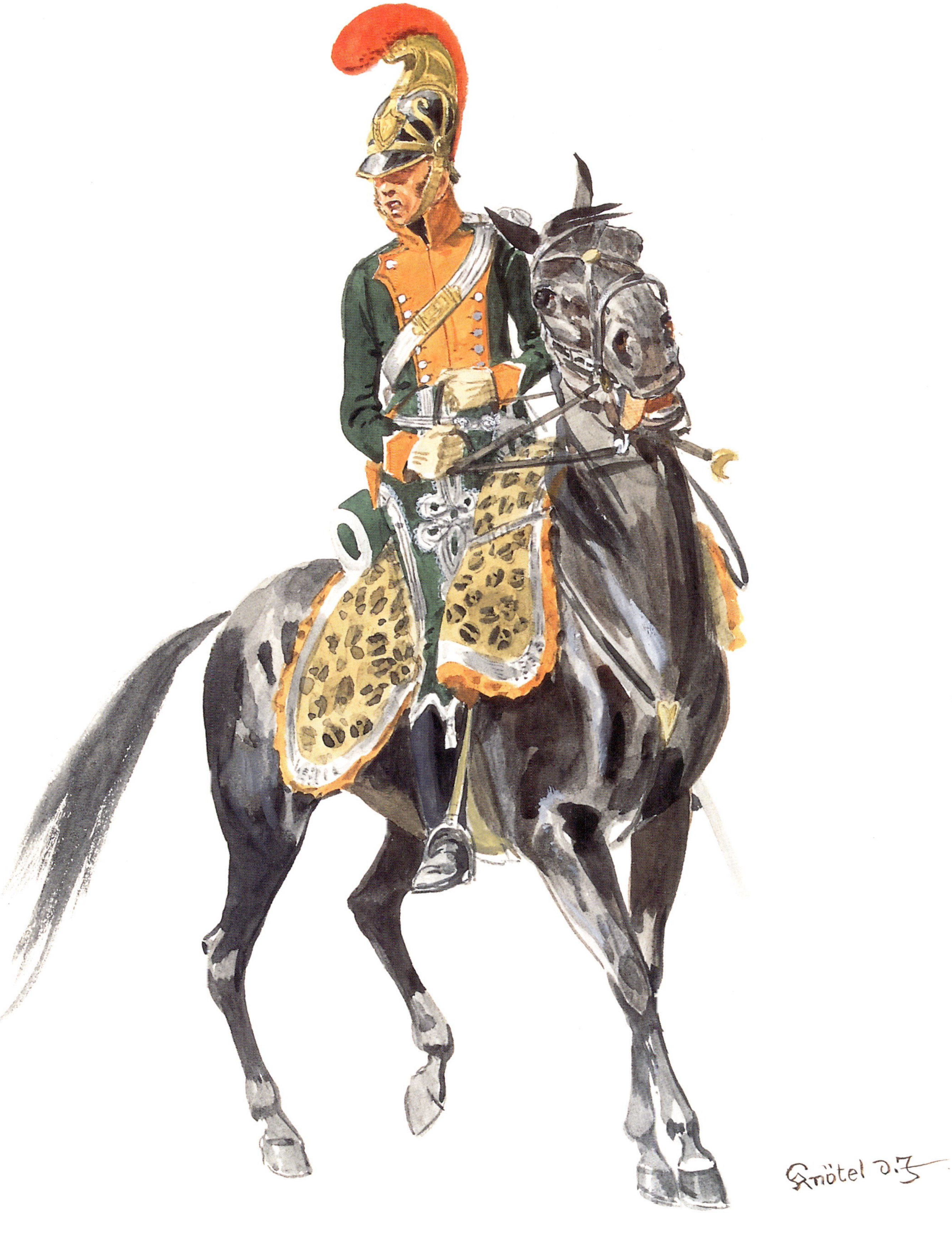

Officer in Parade uniform, Elite Company of 1st Chevau-Légers (Light Horse) Regiment, Kingdom of Westphalia 1812. The leopard skin shabraque was very popular with officers of light cavalry. The red crest is unusual it should be black for this unit. Description courtesy of Alfred Umhey.

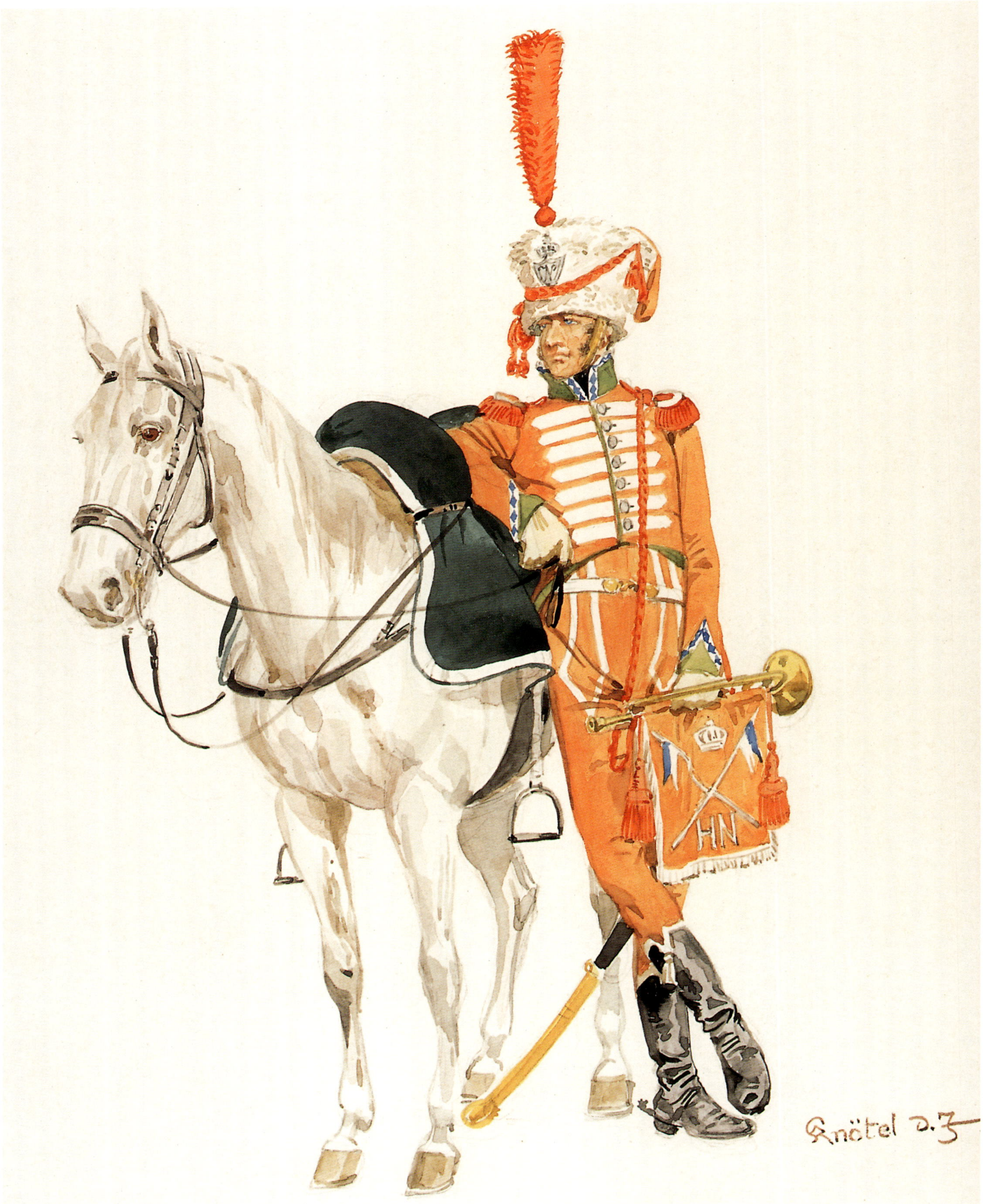

Trumpeter, Elite Company of 1st Chevau-Légers (Light Horse) Regiment, Kingdom of Westphalia 1811. This horseman displays every possible distinction of an Élite: white mount and colpak (fur cap) reversed colors for a trumpeter, red epaulettes plume and cords for a member of the first (elite) company of the regiment's first squadron.

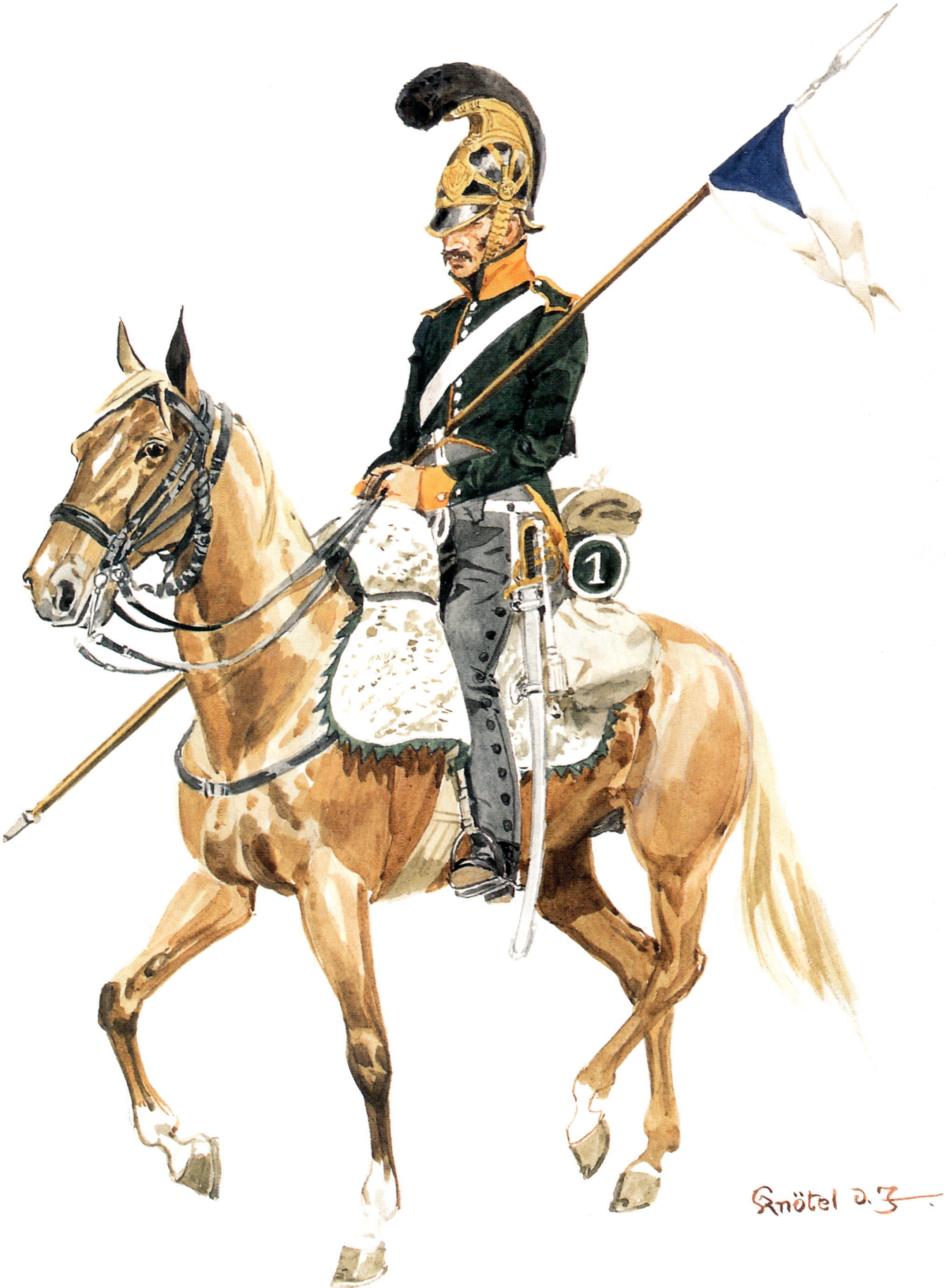

Lancer, in field uniform, 1st Chevau-Légers (Light Horse) Regiment, Kingdom of Westphalia 1812-1813. The uniform of the light horse lancers was very much inspired by their French counterparts.

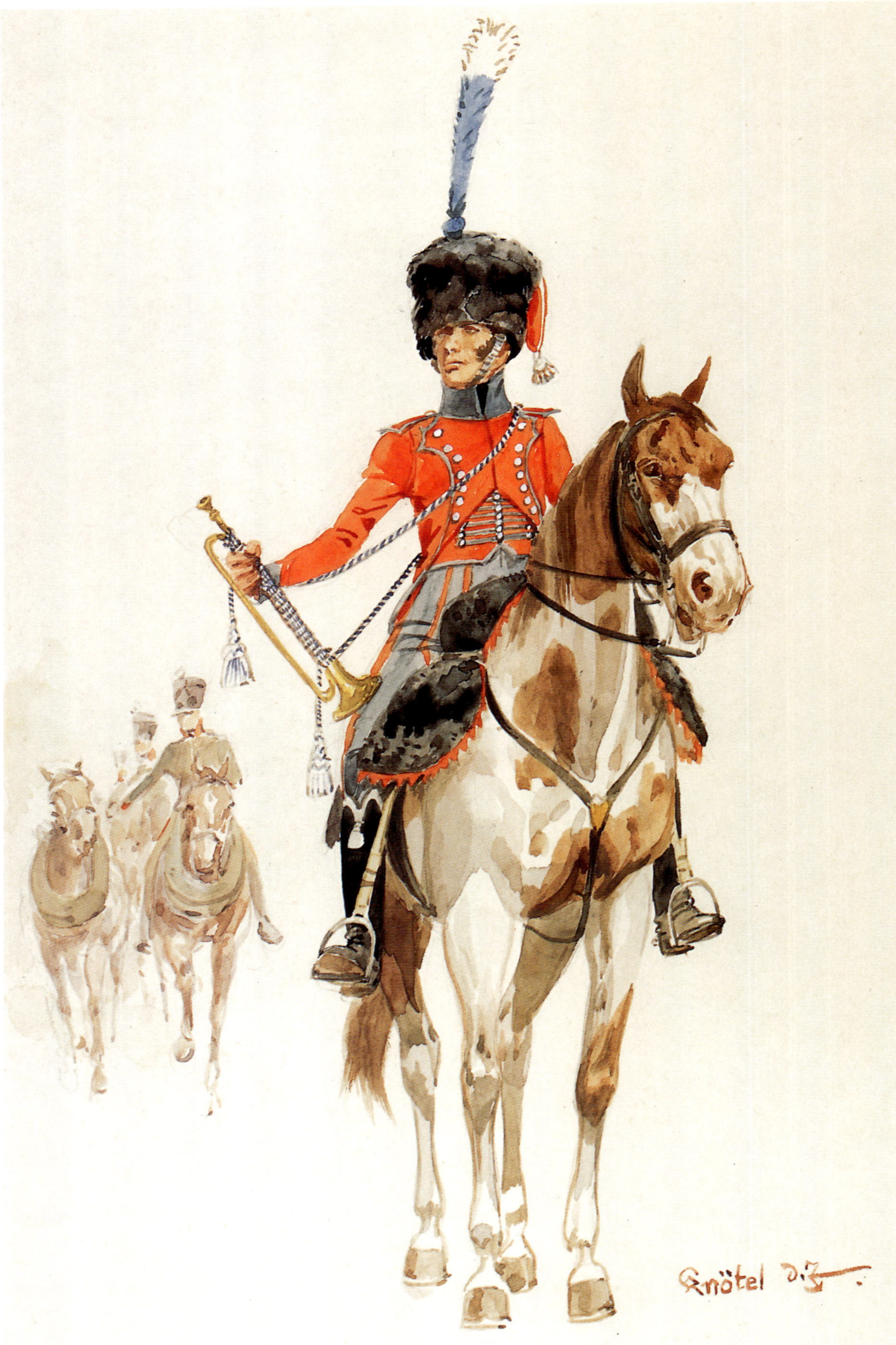

Trumpeter, Supply Train, Kingdom of Westphalia 1812. Even the musicians of the mundane baggage and supply train are colorfully attired.

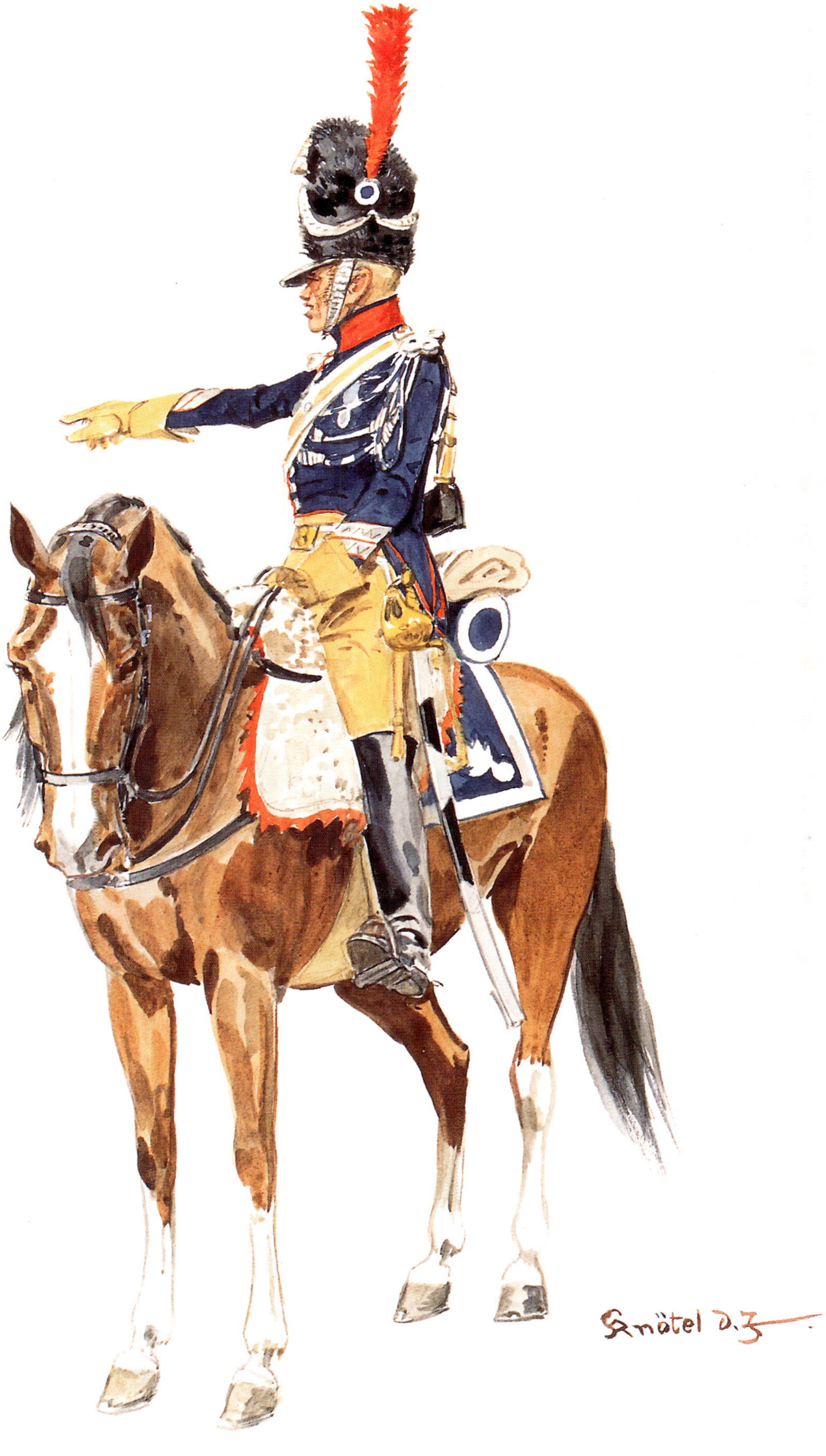

Gendarme, Kingdom of Westphalia 1812-1813. The Gendarmes were the military police, copied after the French.

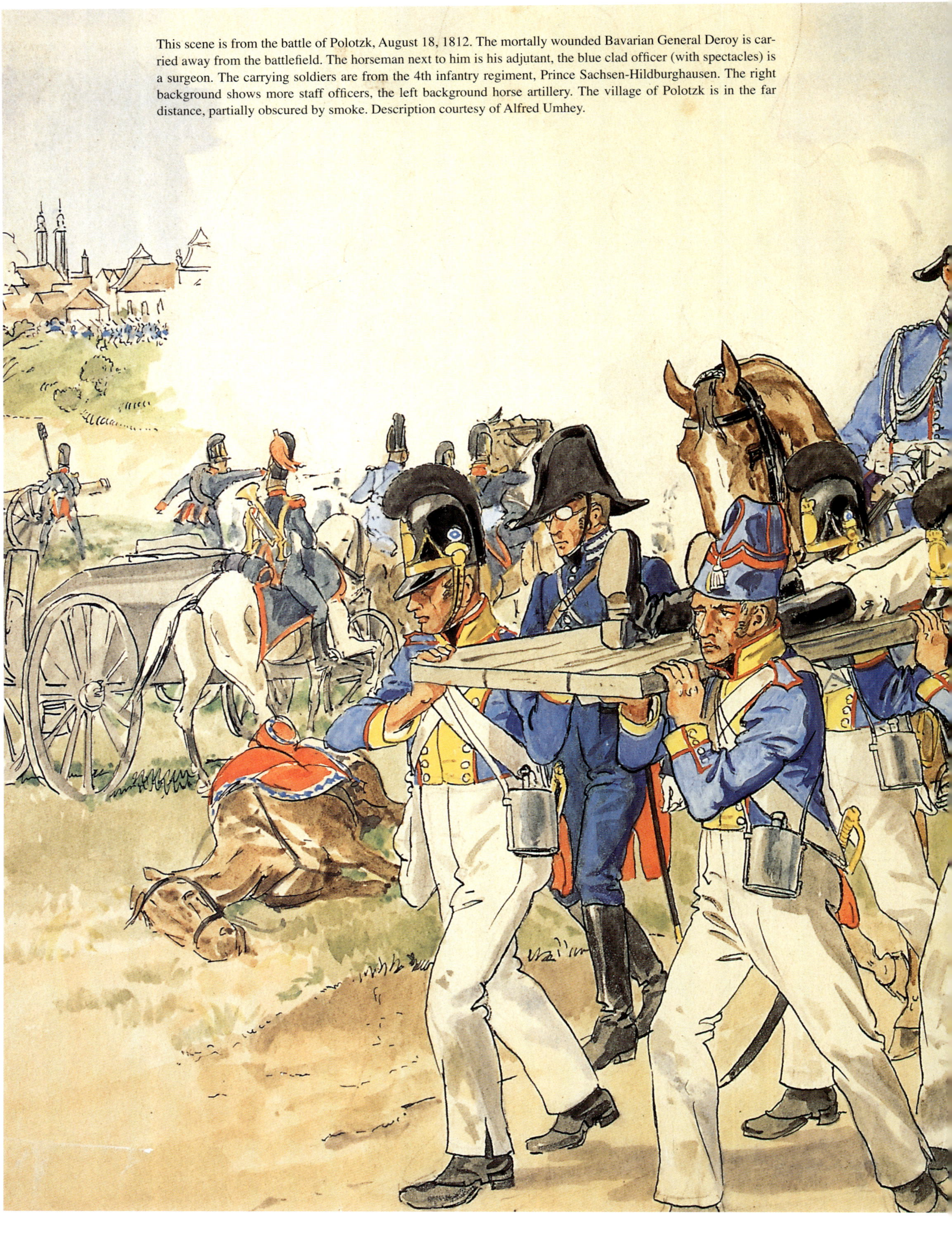

This scene is from the battle of Polotzk, August 18, 1812. The mortally wounded Bavarian General Deroy is carried away from the battlefield. The horseman next to him is his adjutant, the blue clad officer (with spectacles) is a surgeon. The carrying soldiers are from the 4th infantry regiment, Prince Sachsen-Hildburghausen. The right background shows more staff officers, the left background horse artillery. The village of Polotzk is in the far distance, partially obscured by smoke. Description courtesy of Alfred Umhey.

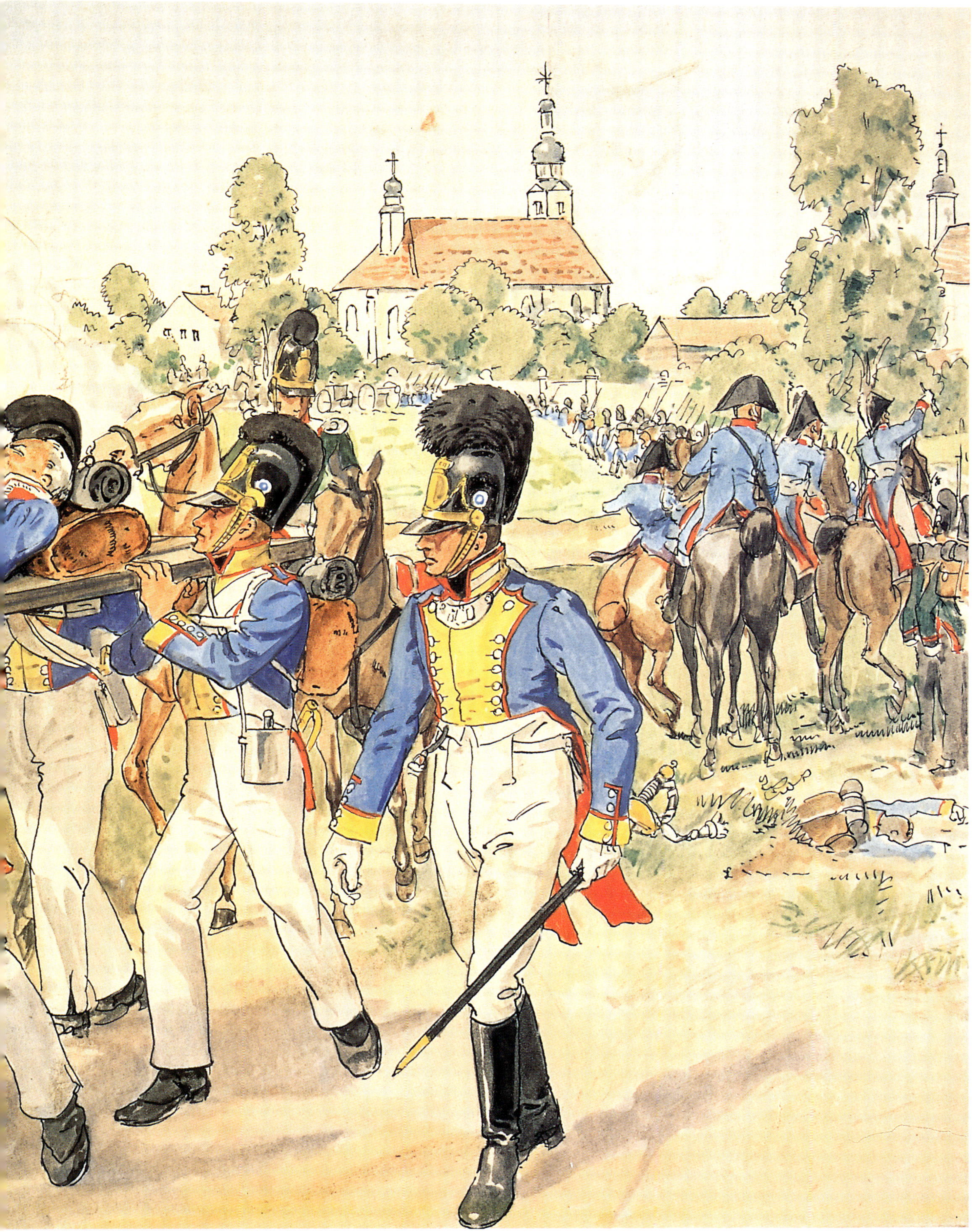

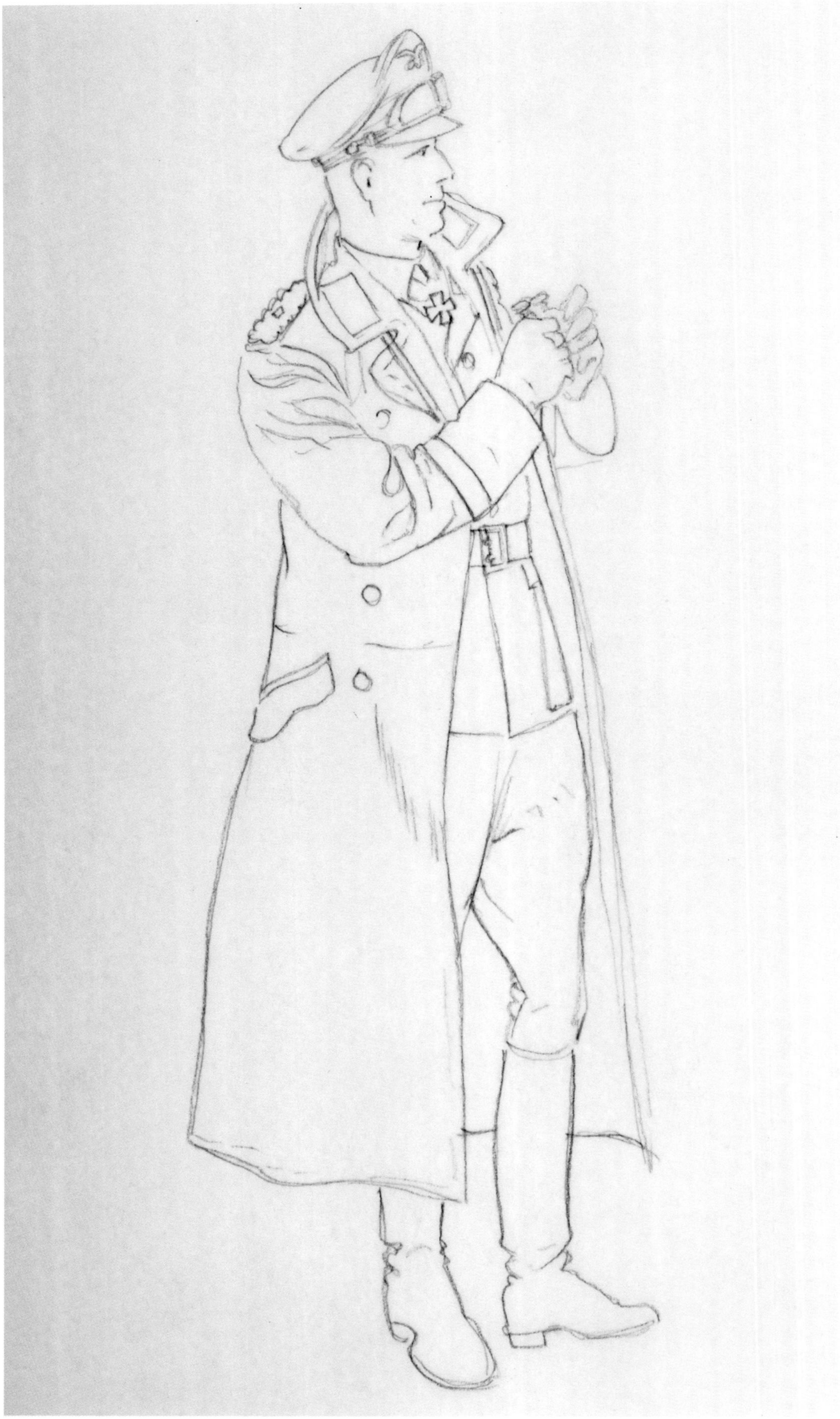

Staff Officer sketch, Hermann Göring Division, World War II.

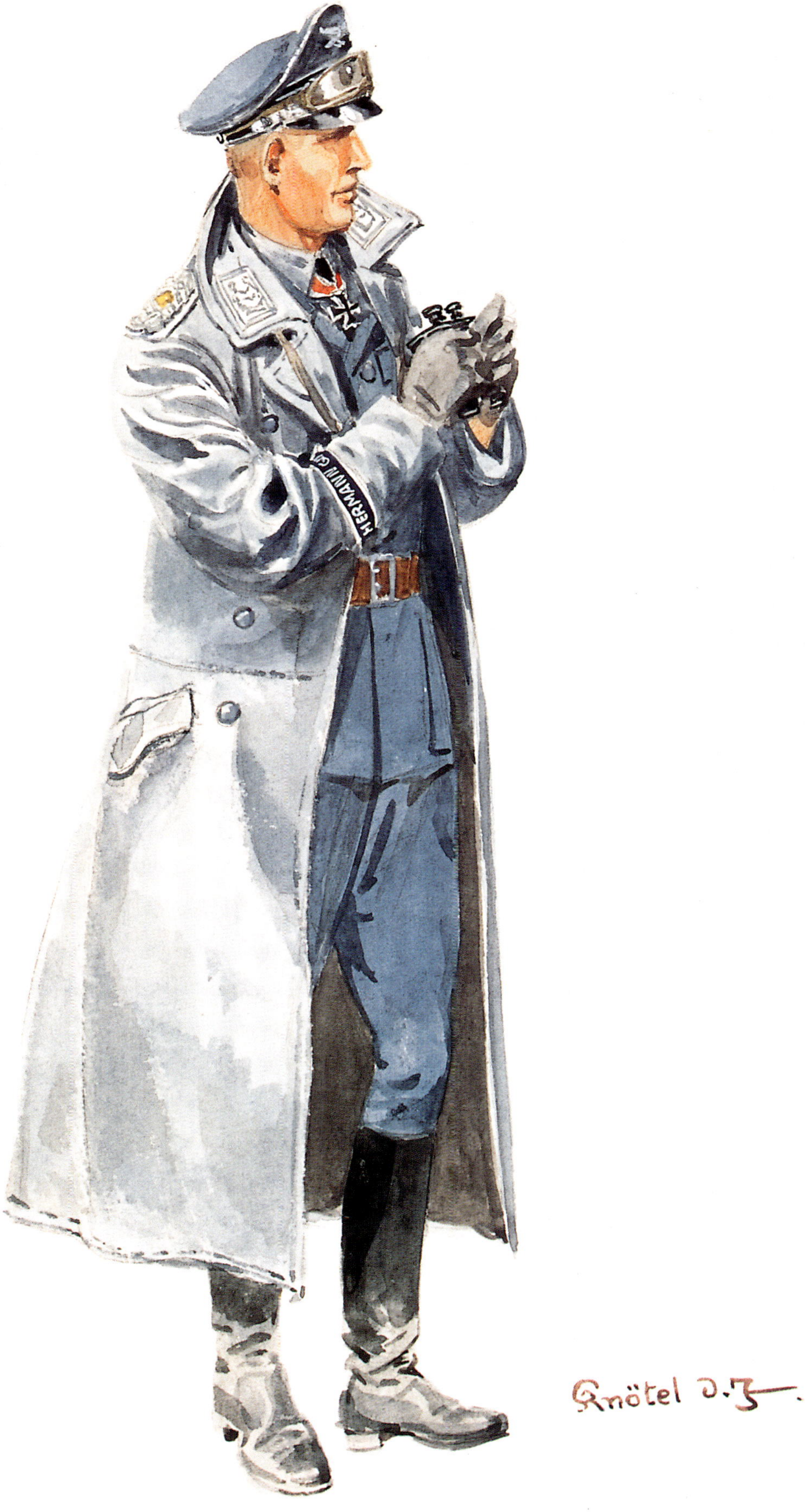

Staff Officer, Hermann Göring Division, World War II.

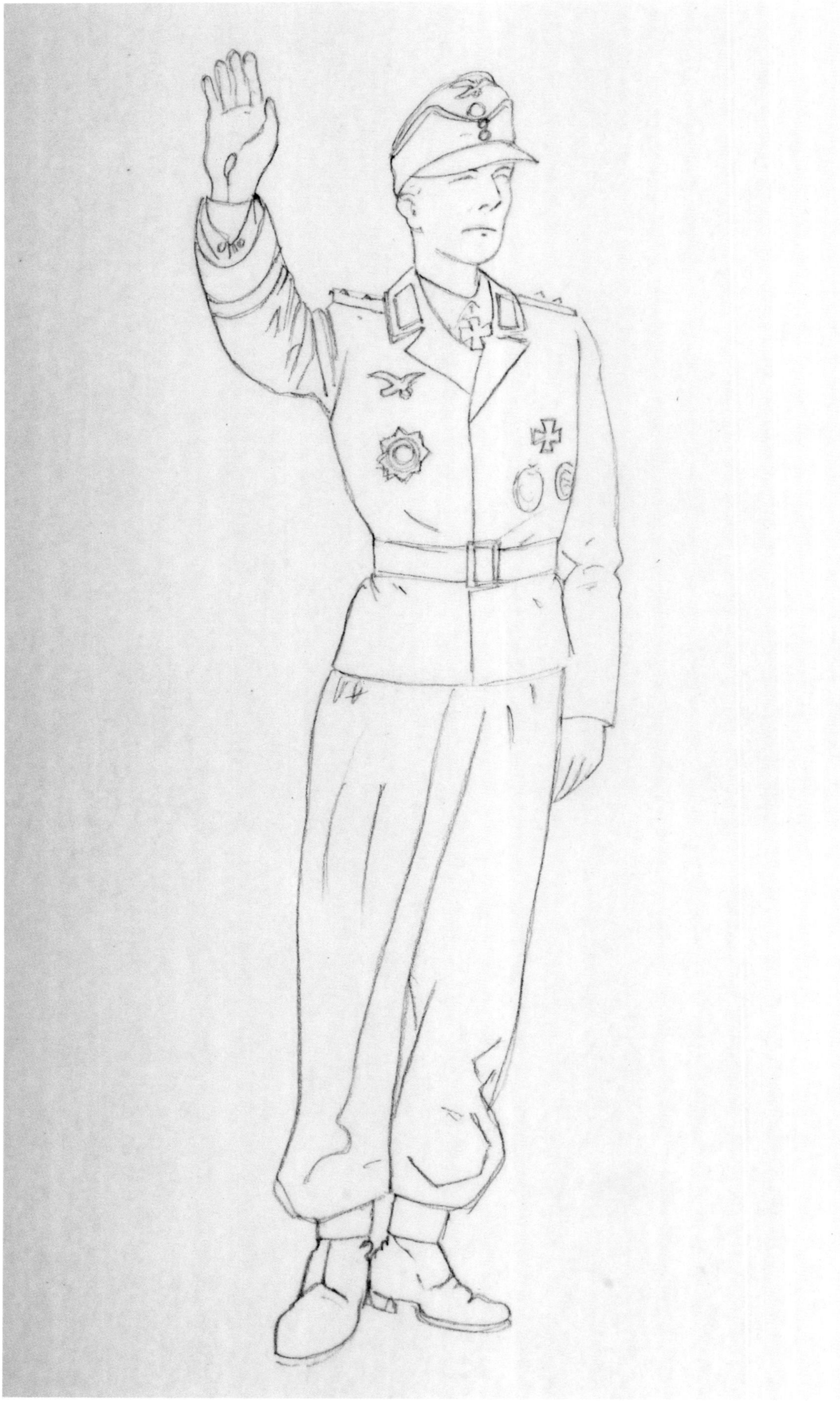

Captain sketch, Hermann Göring Division, World War II.

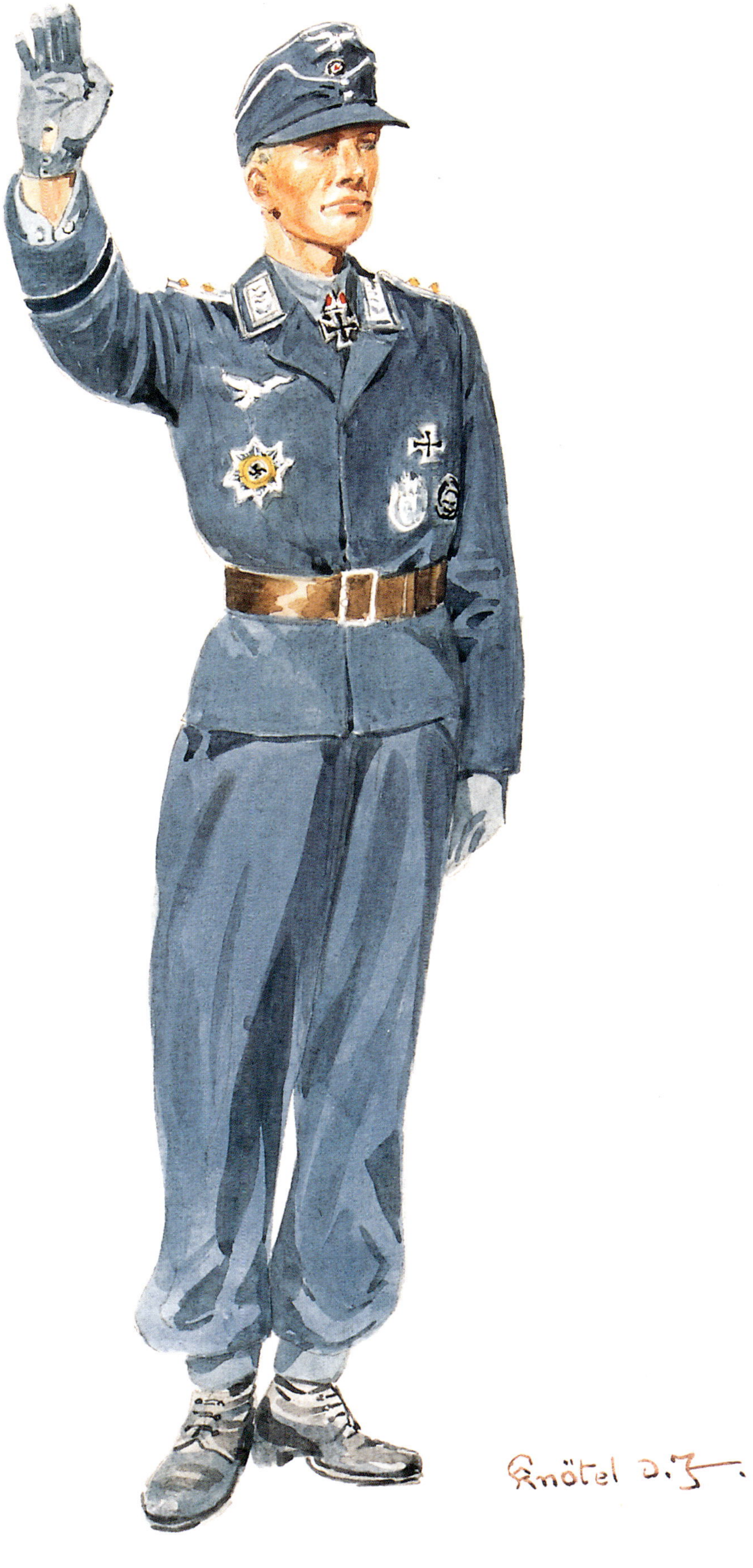

Captain Hermann Göring Division, World War II.

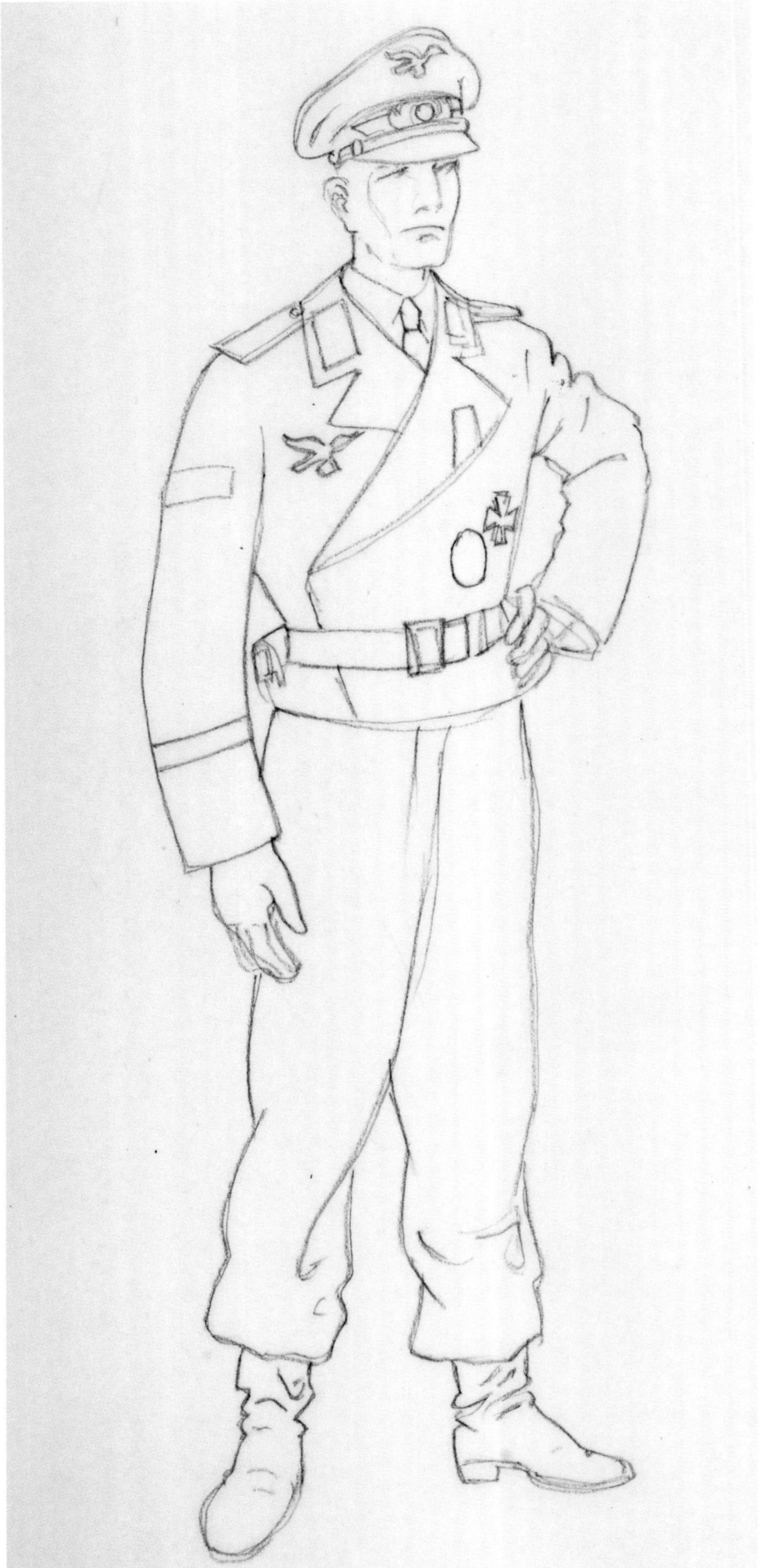

Lieutenant, Panzer tank gunner sketch, Hermann Göring Division, World War II.

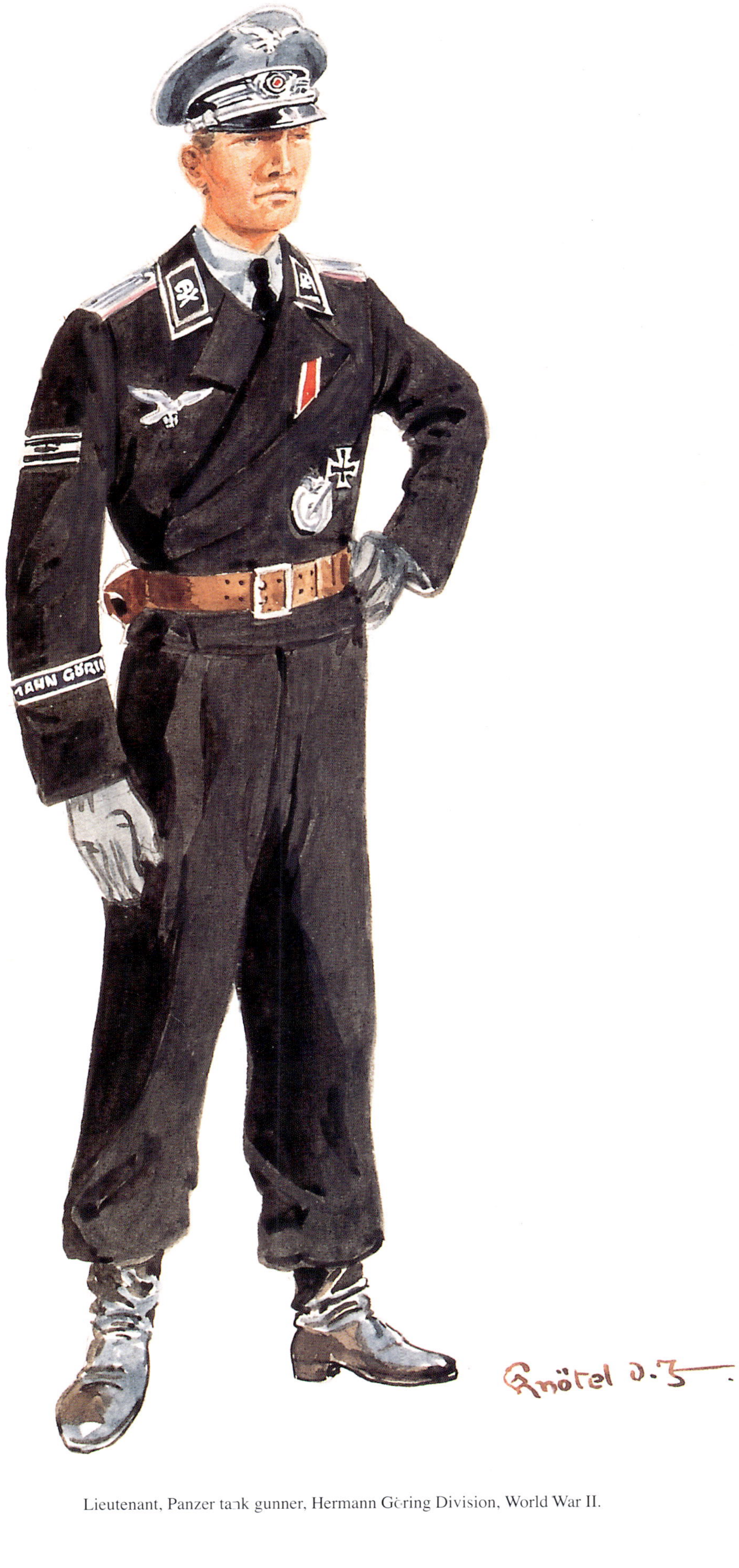

Lieutenant, Panzer tank gunner, Hermann Göring Division, World War II.

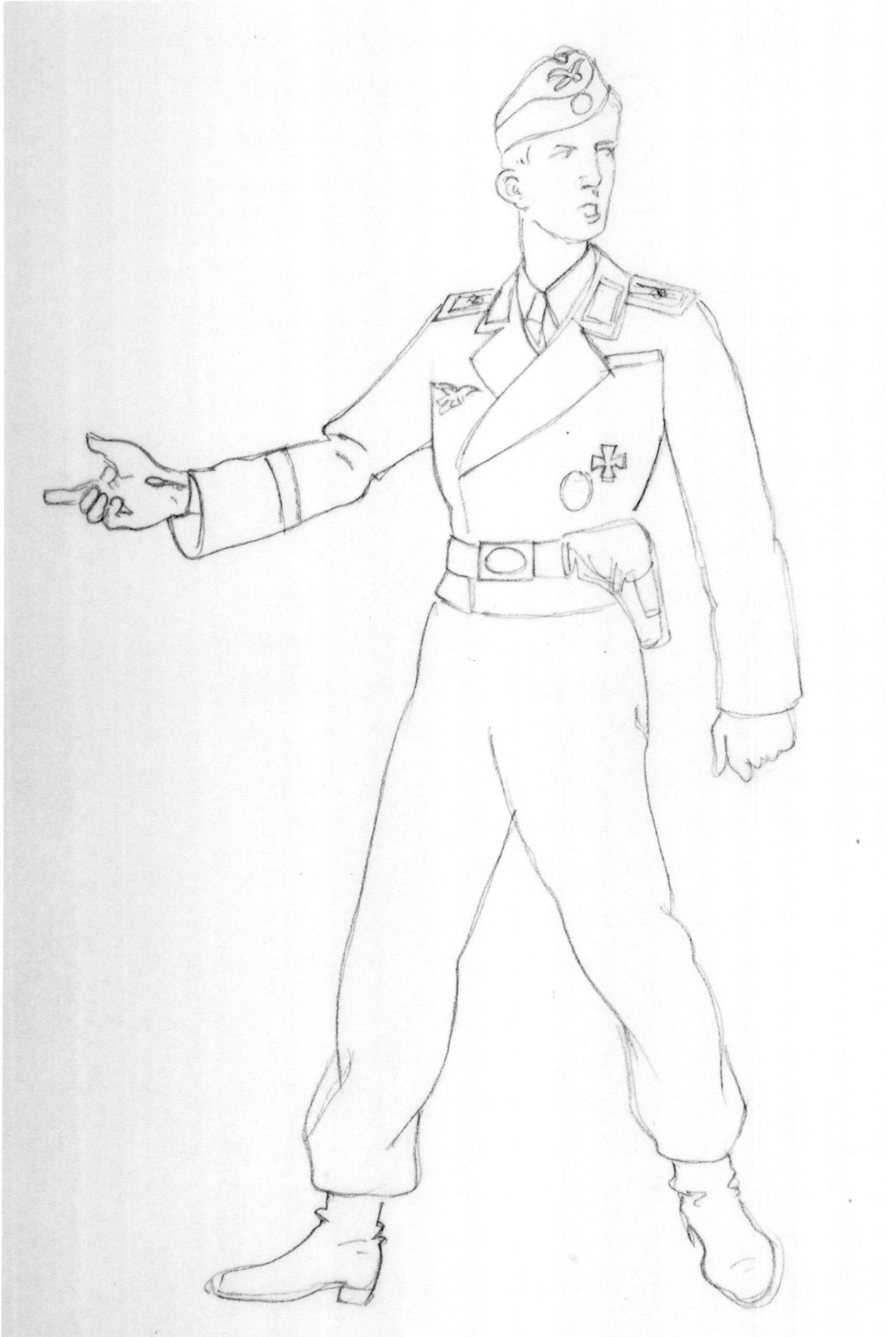

Sergeant, Armored Signal Corps sketch, Hermann Göring Division, World War II.

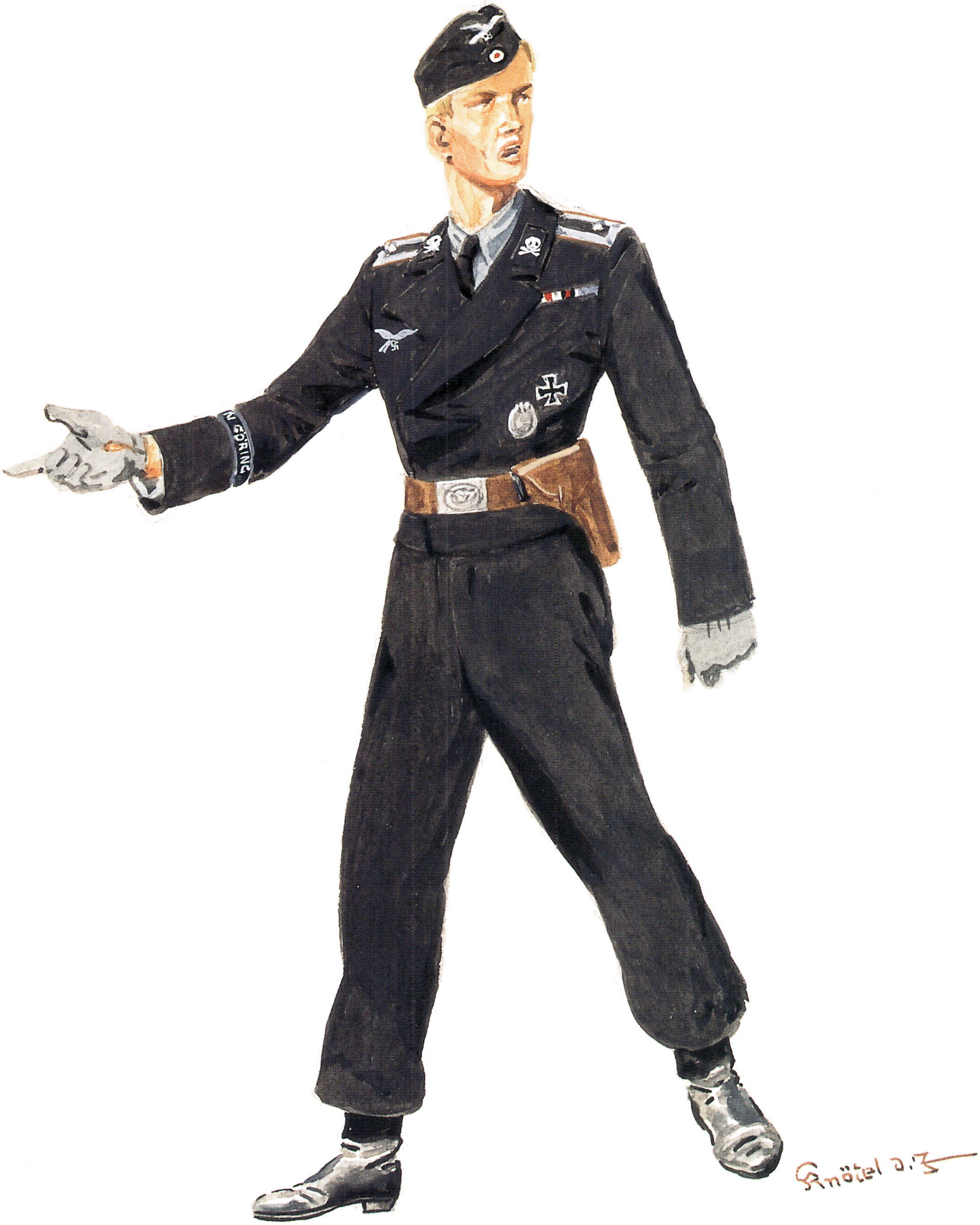

Sergeant, Armored Signal Corps, Hermann Göring Division, World War II.

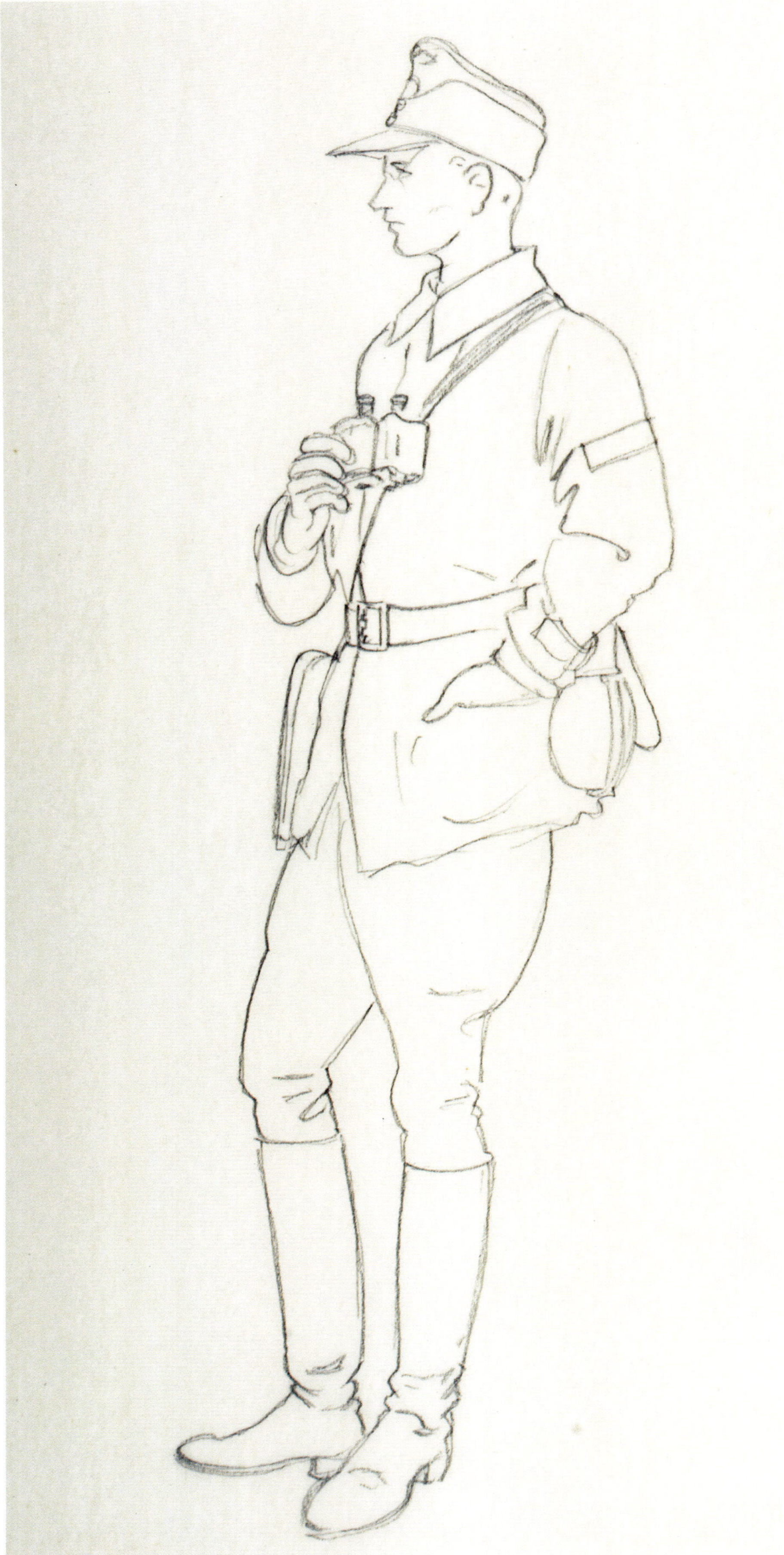

Lieutenant sketch, Hermann Göring Division, World War II.

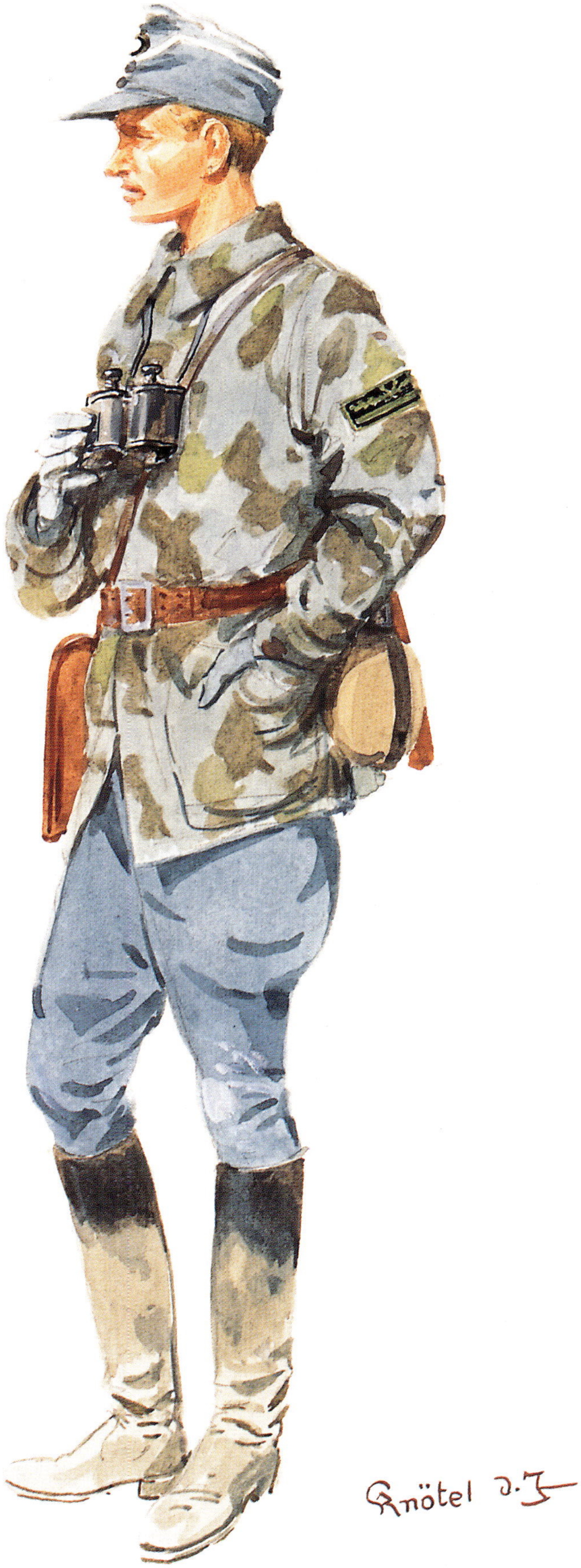

Lieutenant, Hermann Göring Division, World War II.

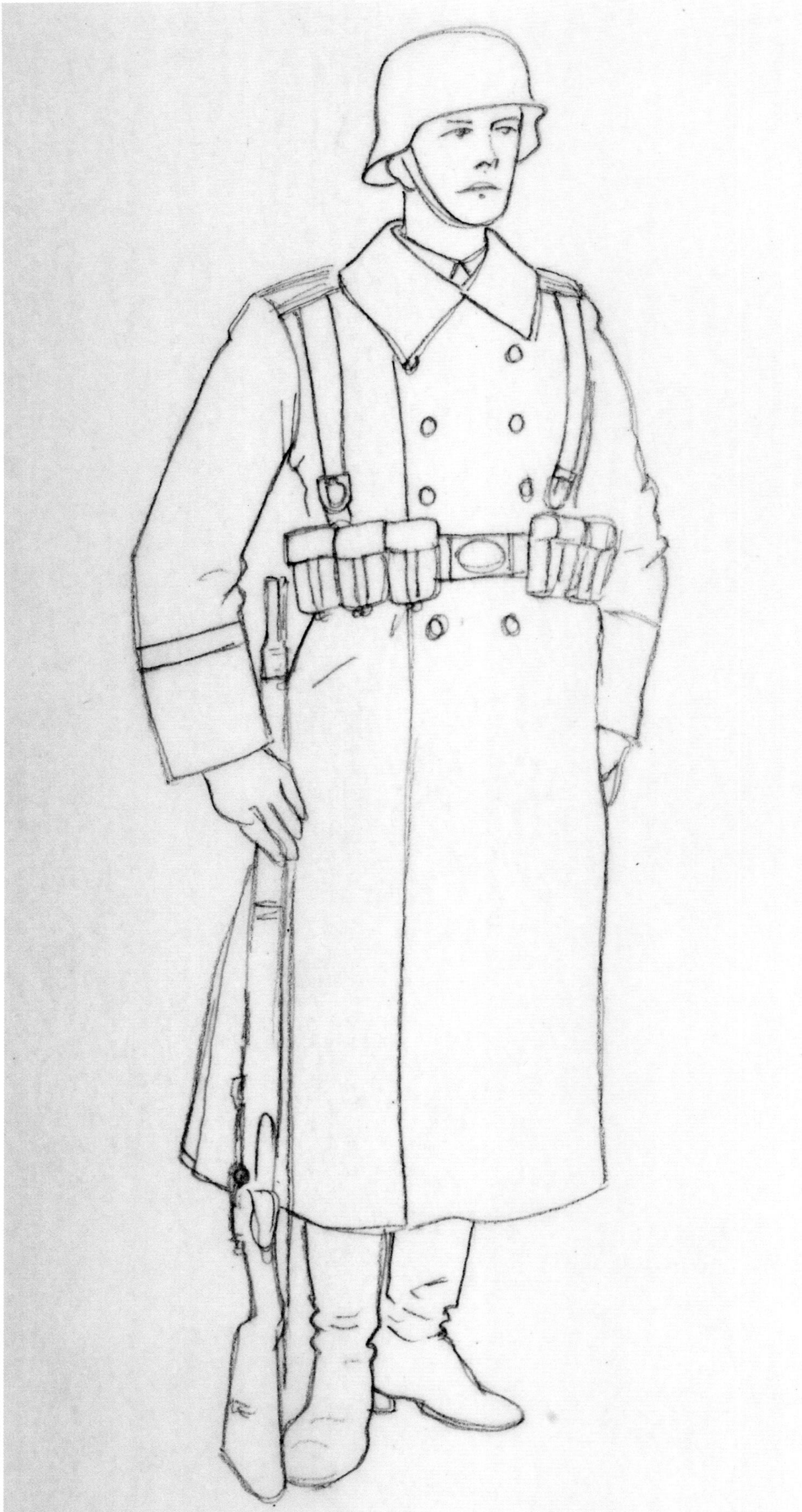

Panzer Grenadier in overcoat sketch, Hermann Göring Division, World War II.

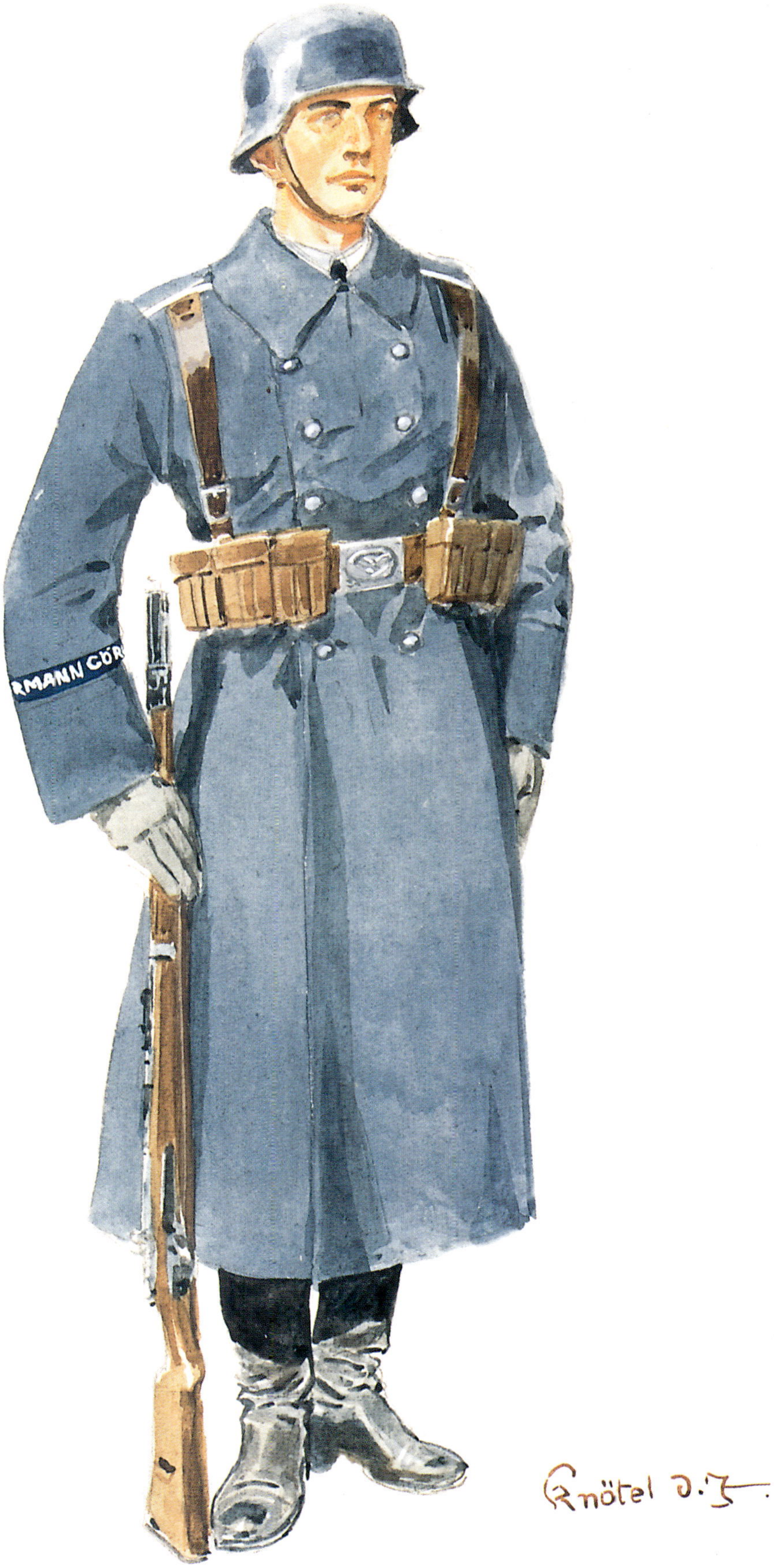

Panzer Grenadier in overcoat, Hermann Göring Division, World War II.

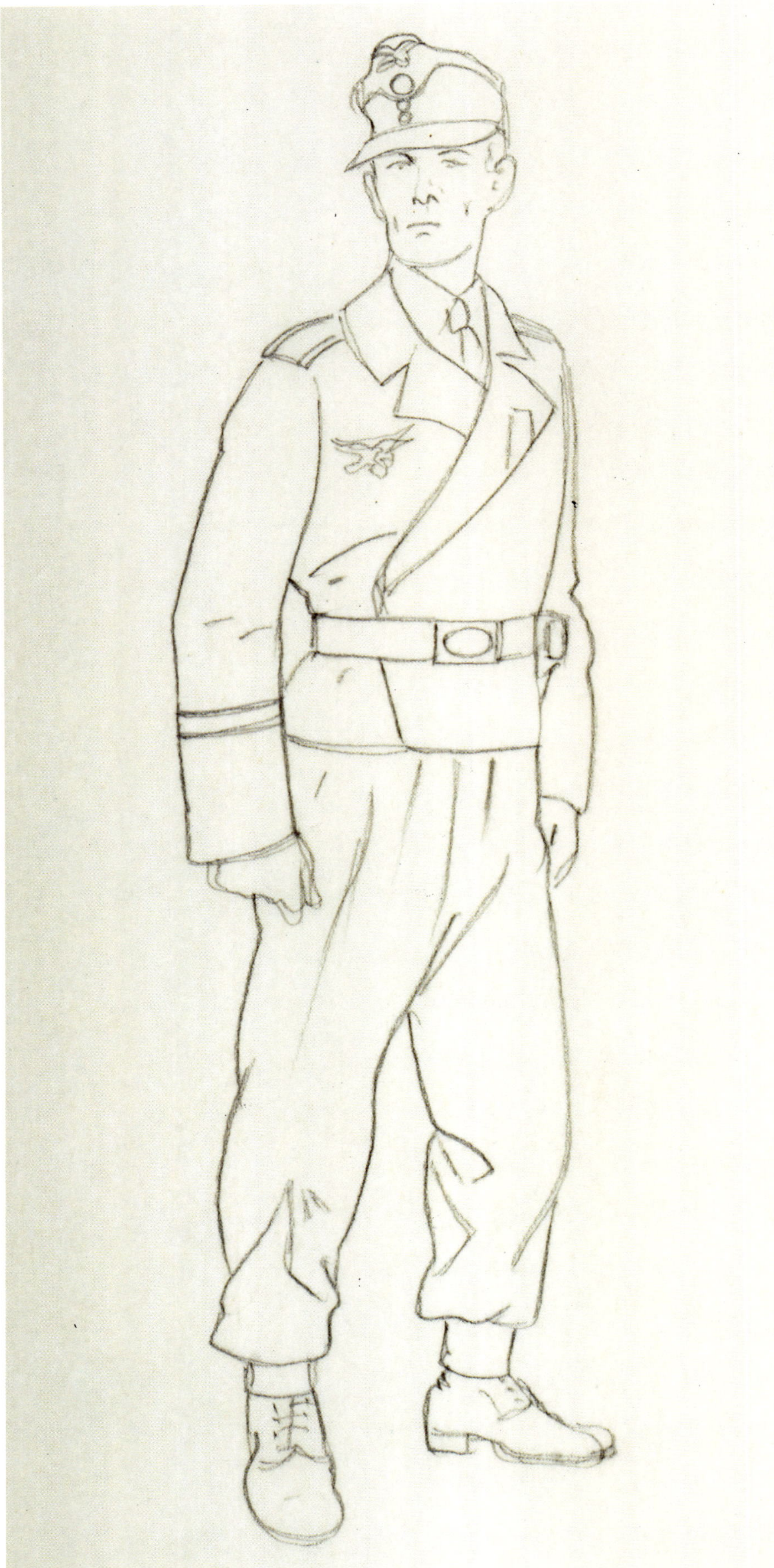

Tank gunner sketch, Hermann Göring Division, World War II.

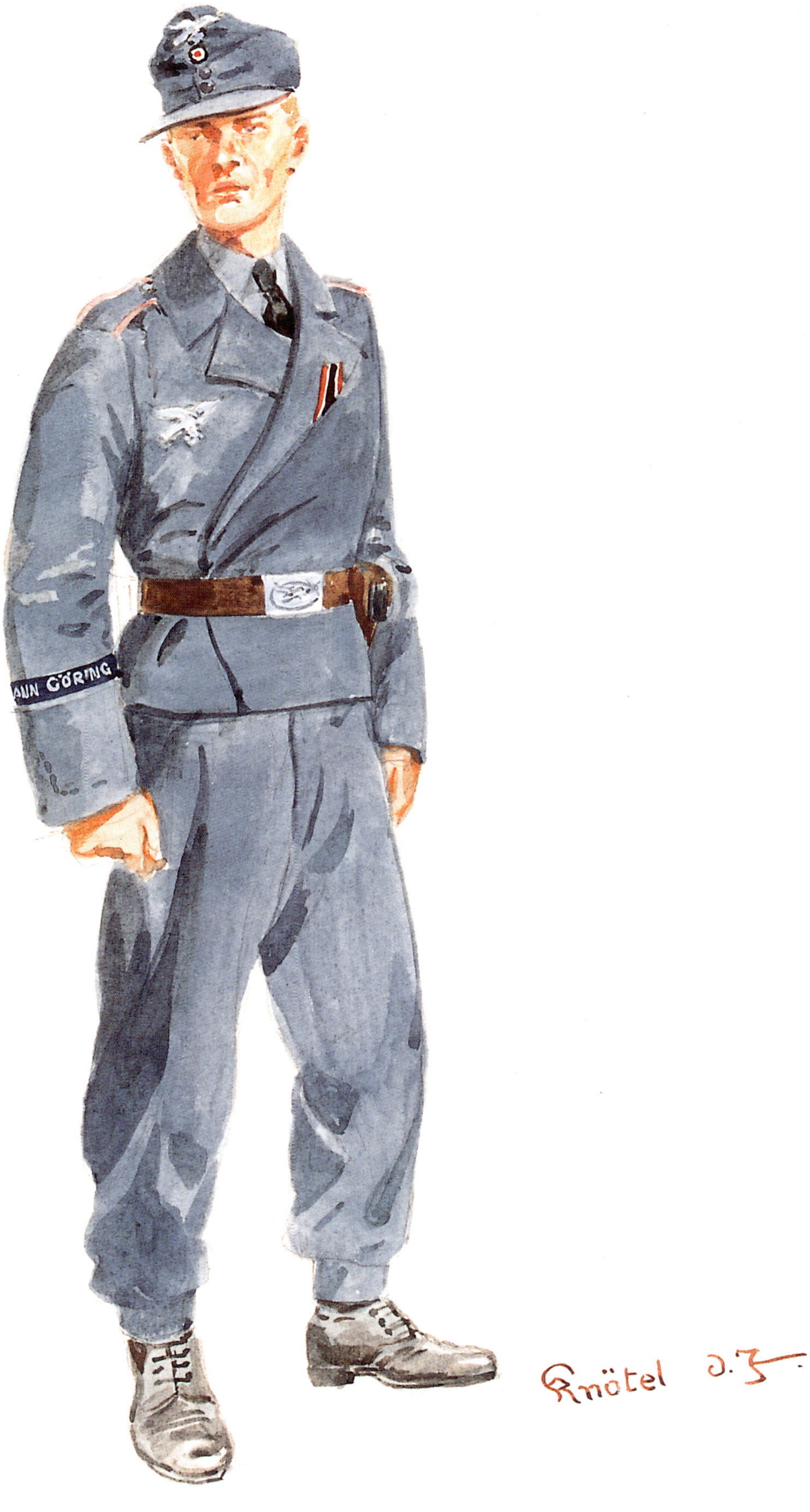

Tank gunner Hermann Göring Division, World War II.

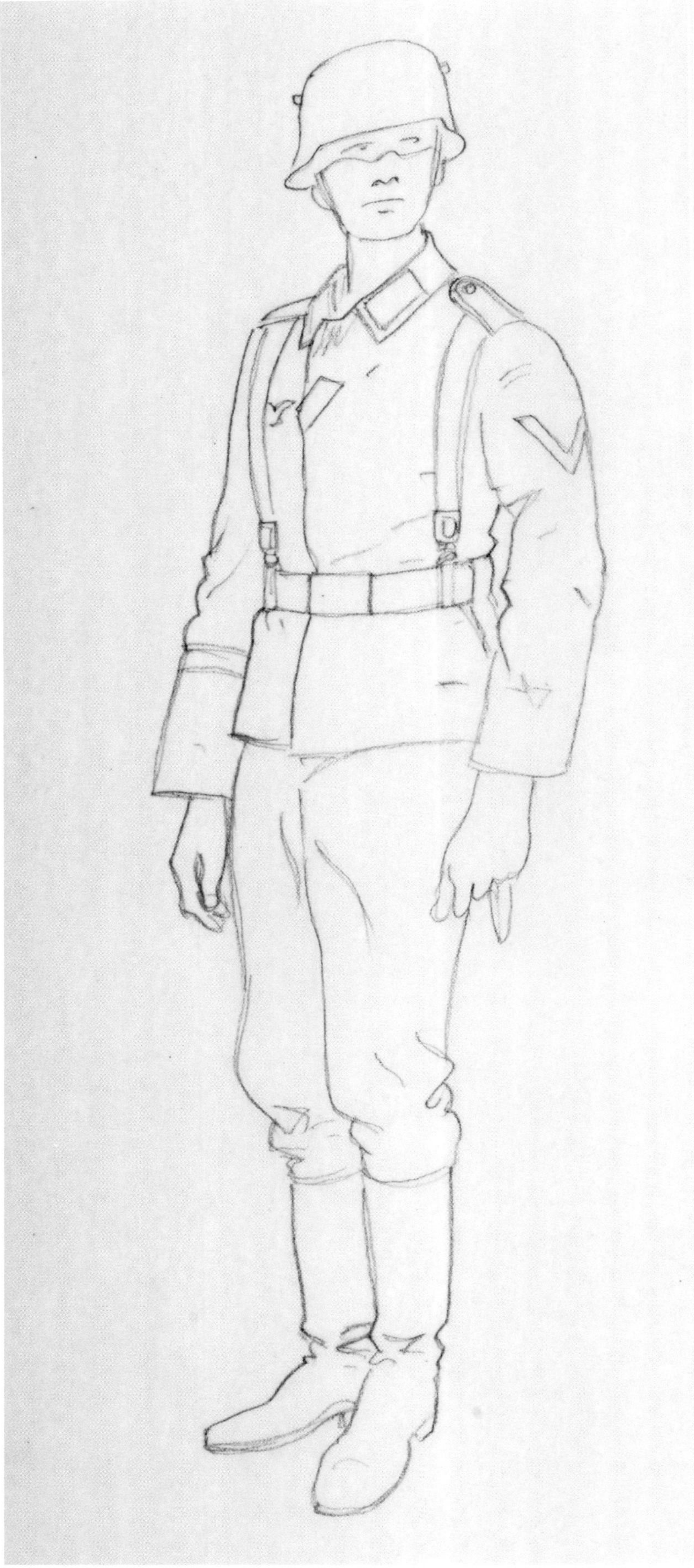

Artillery Bombardier sketch, Hermann Göring Division, World War II.

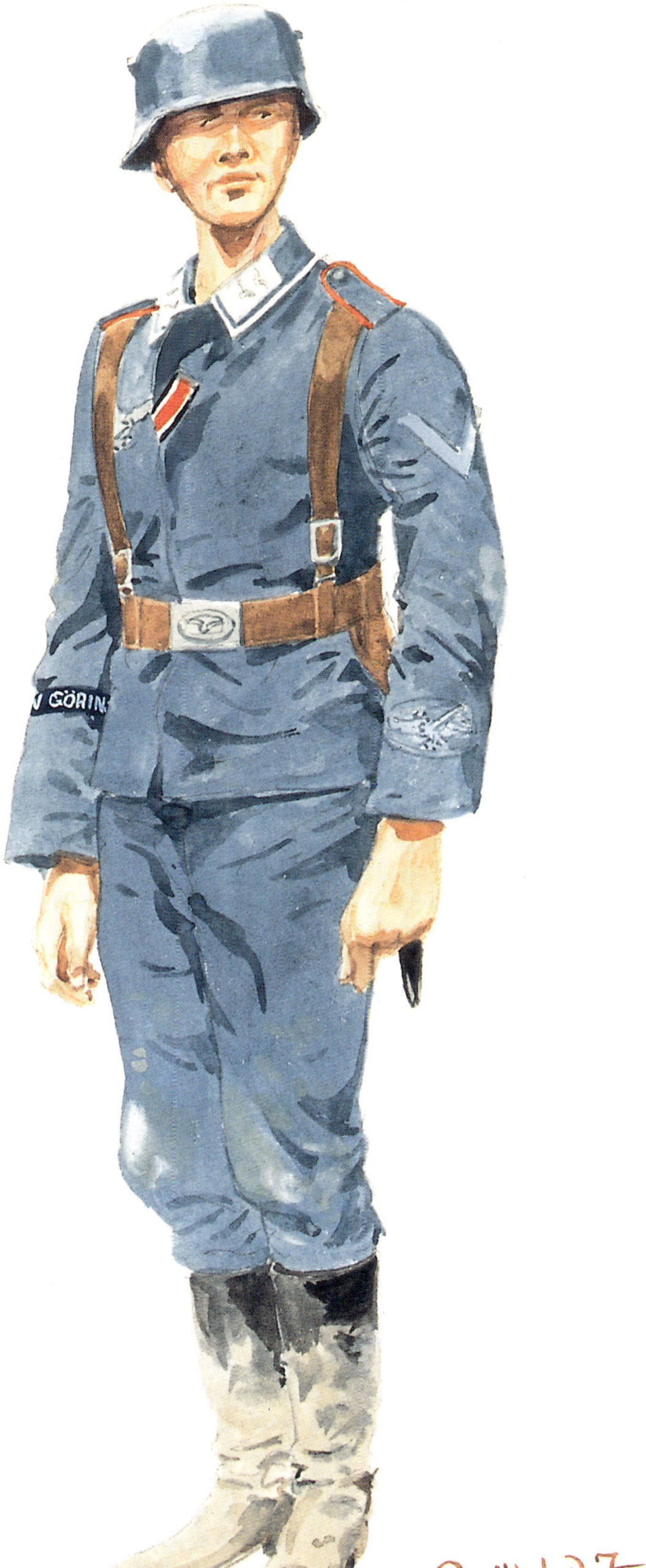

Artillery Bombardier, Hermann Göring Division, World War II.

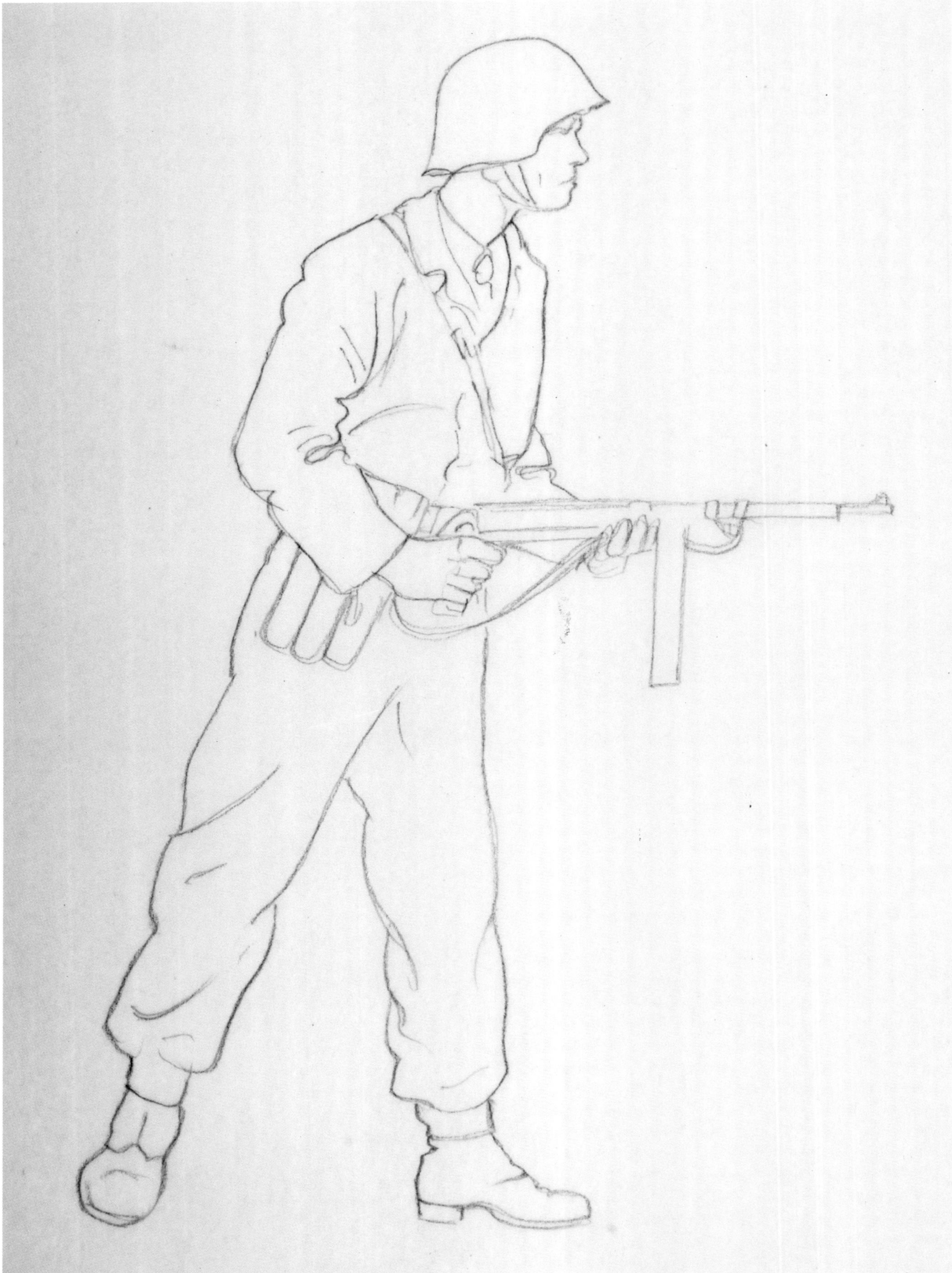

Noncommissioned officer in camouflage sketch, German, World War II.

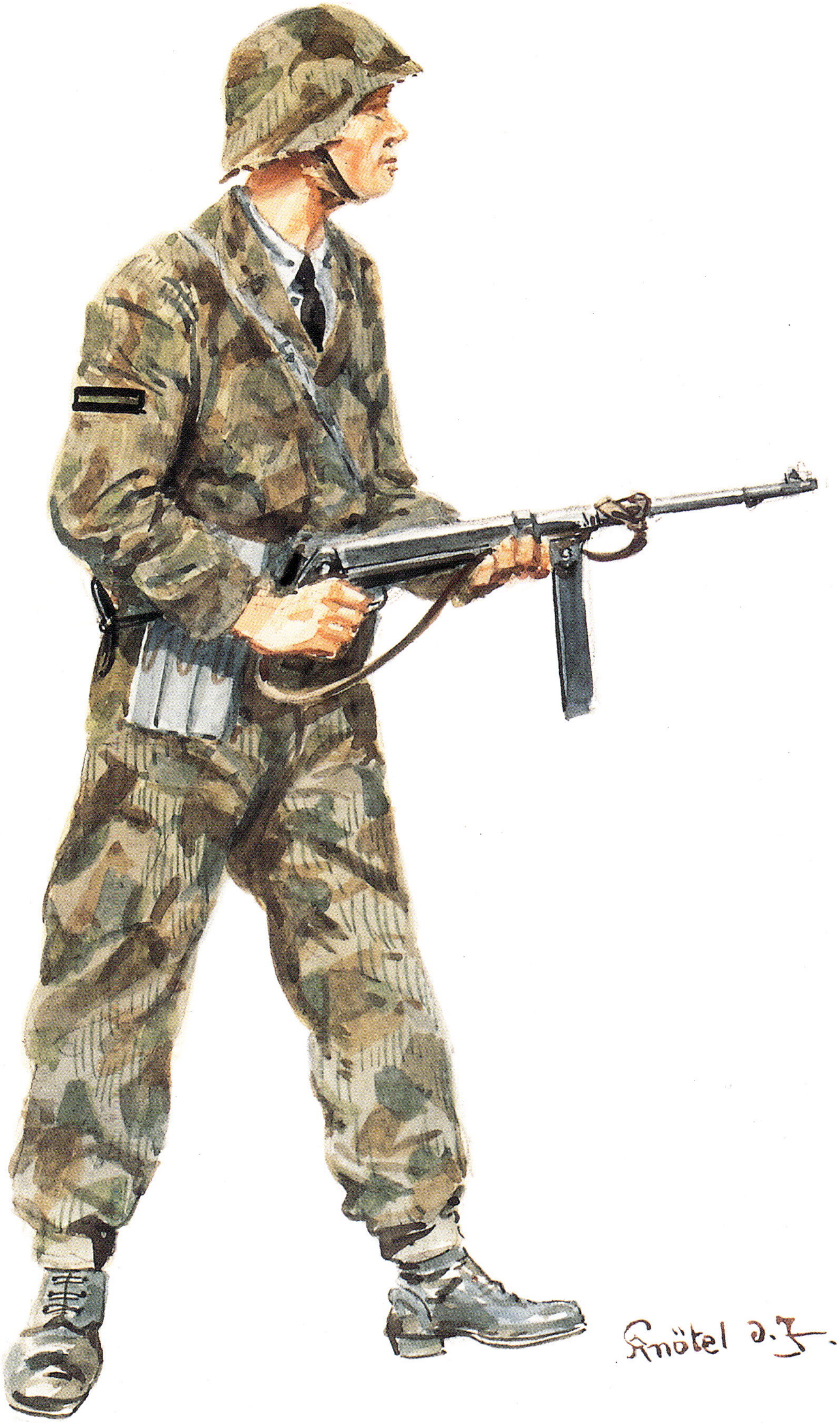

Noncommissioned officer in camouflage, German, World War II.

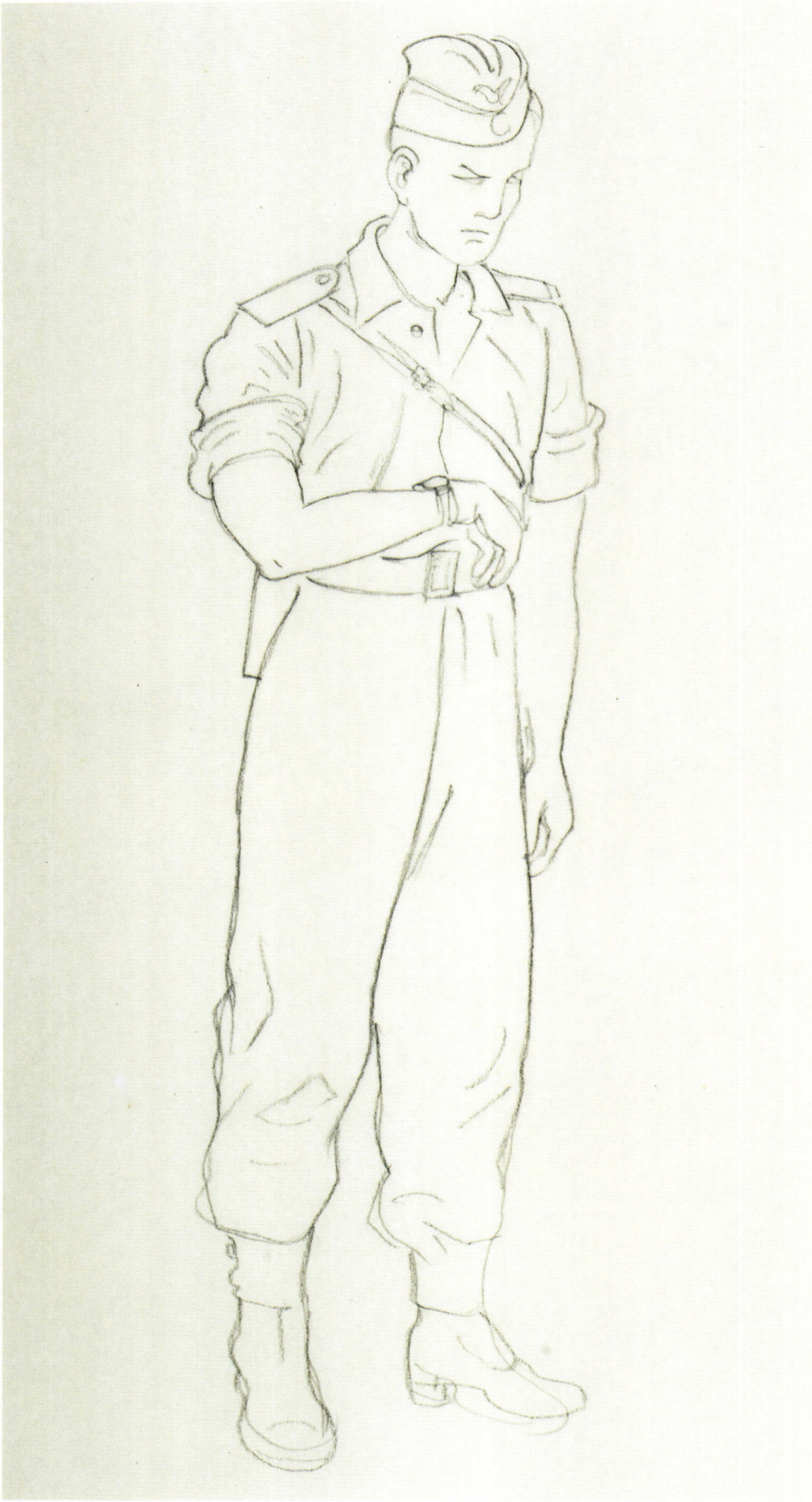

Lieutenant checking the time sketch, German, World War II.

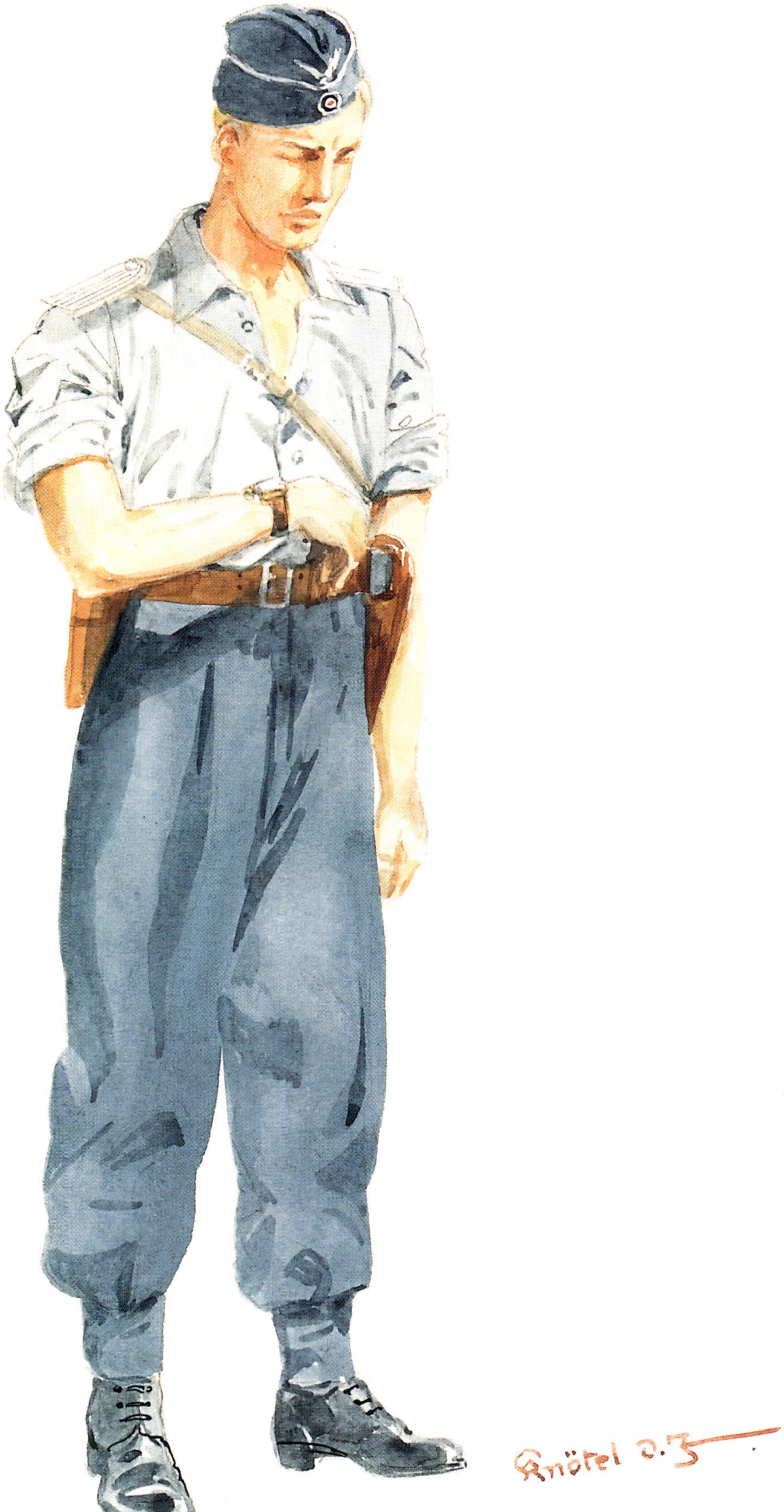

Lieutenant checking the time, German World War II.

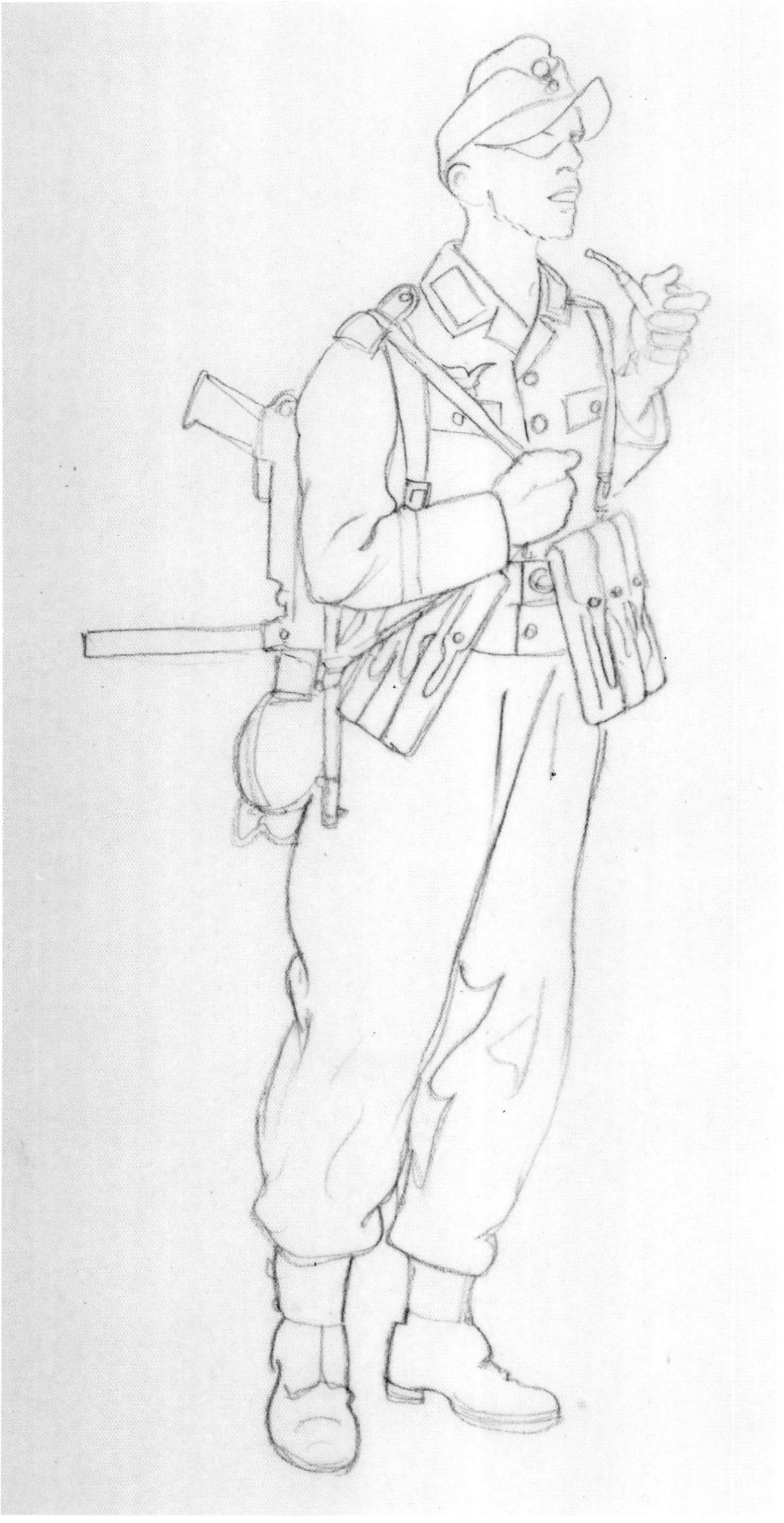

Grenadier smoking pipe in standard uniform sketch, German, World War II.

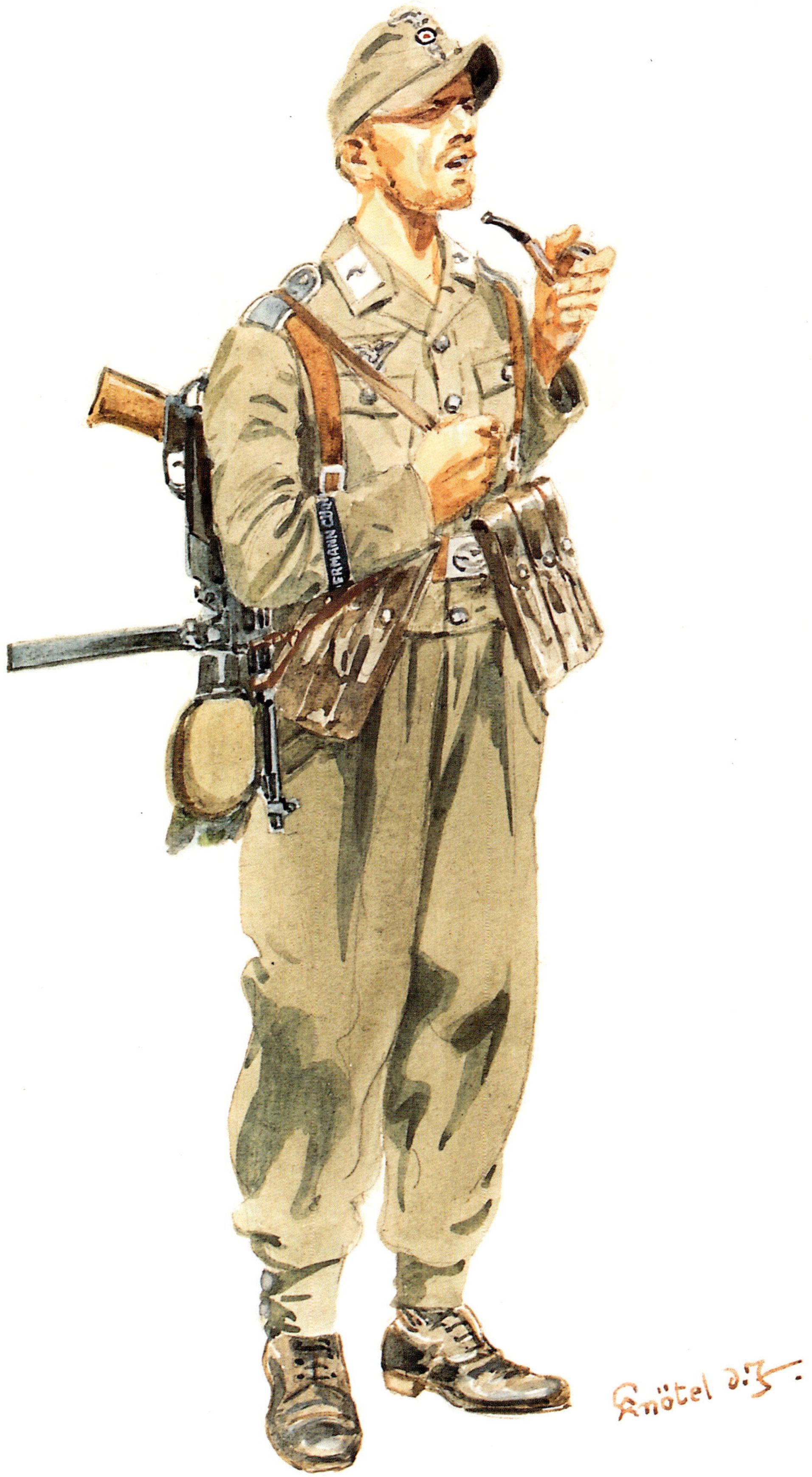

Grenadier smoking pipe in standard uniform, German, World War II.

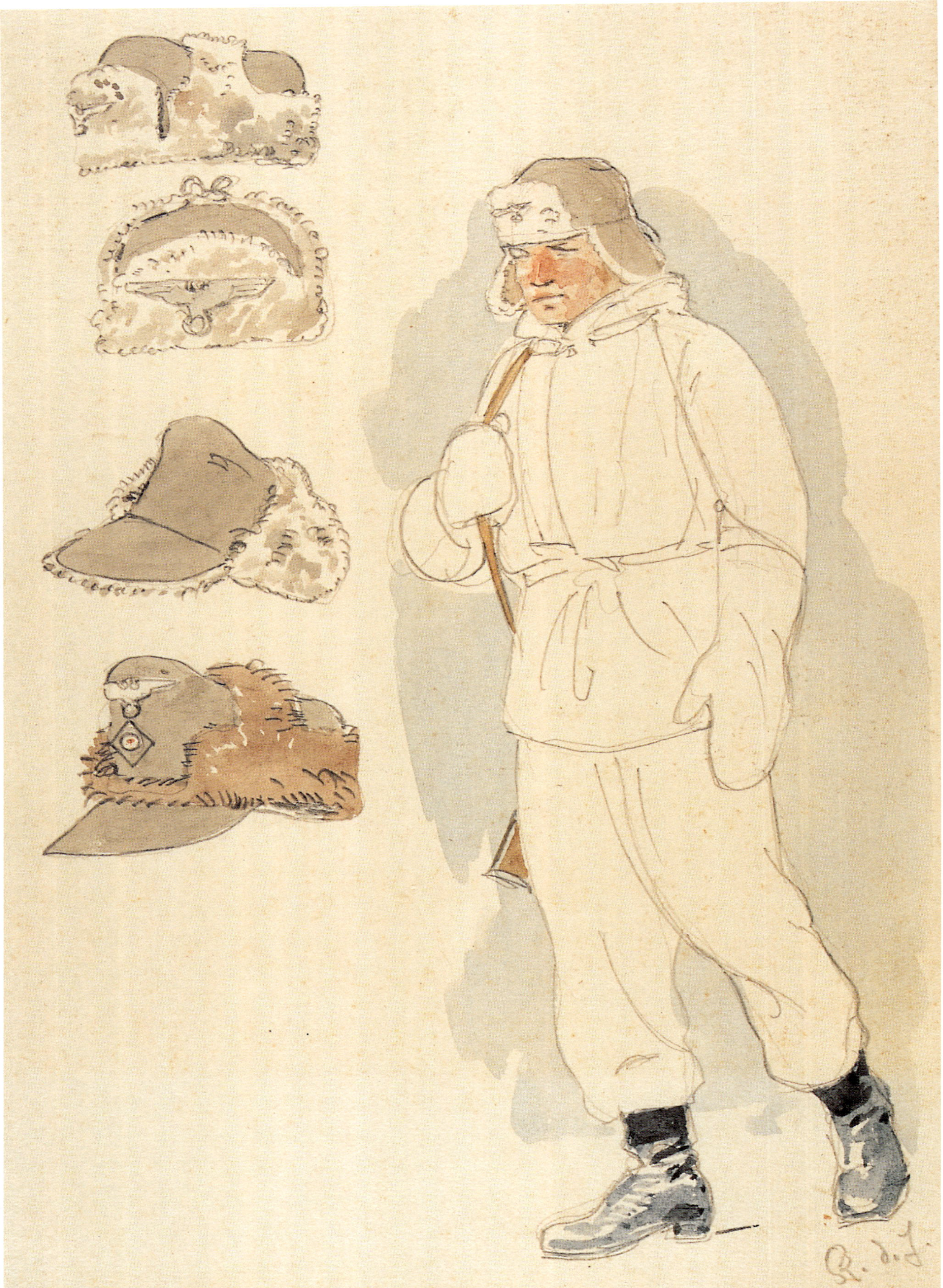

Trooper in winter whites, German, World War II.

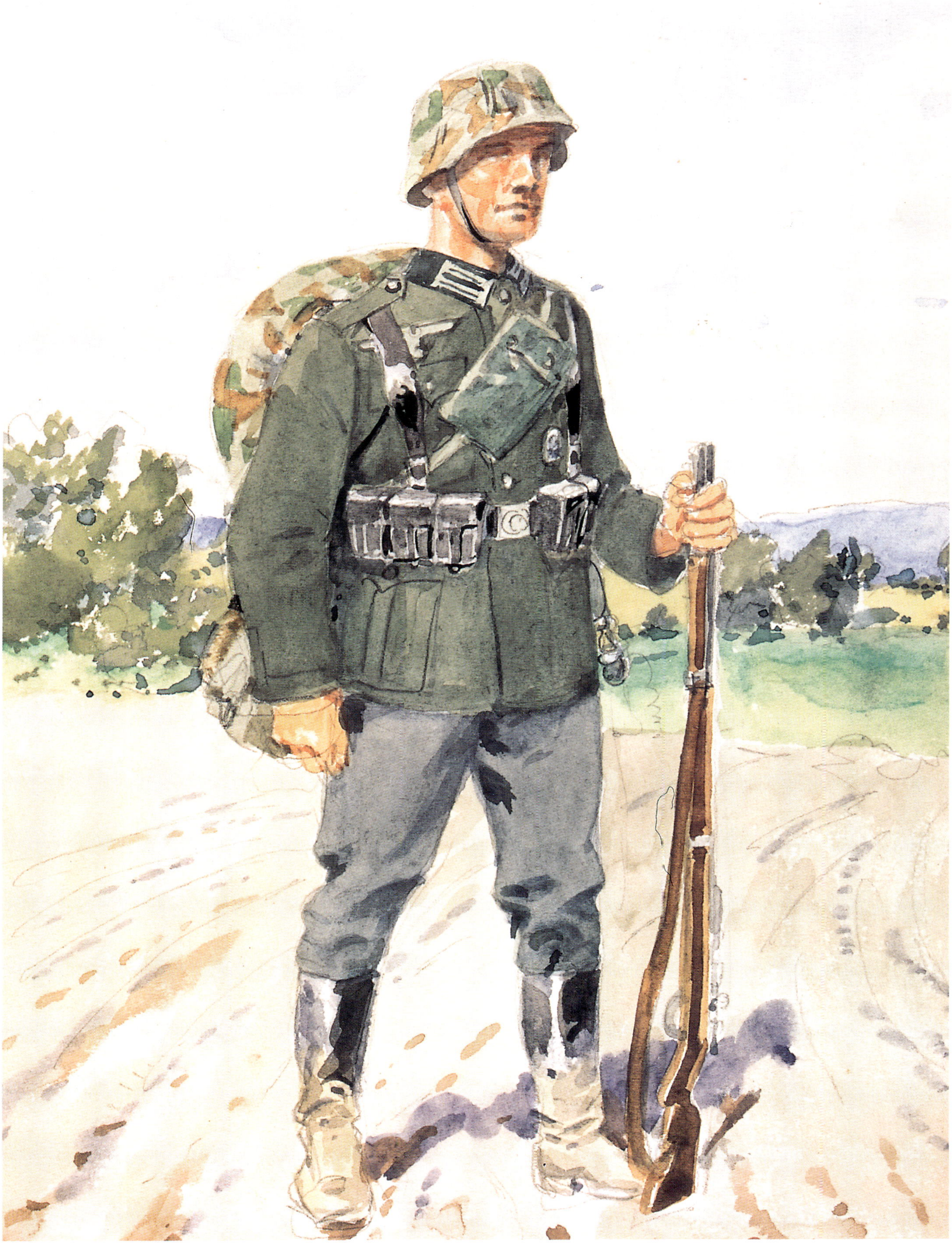

German soldier 1940

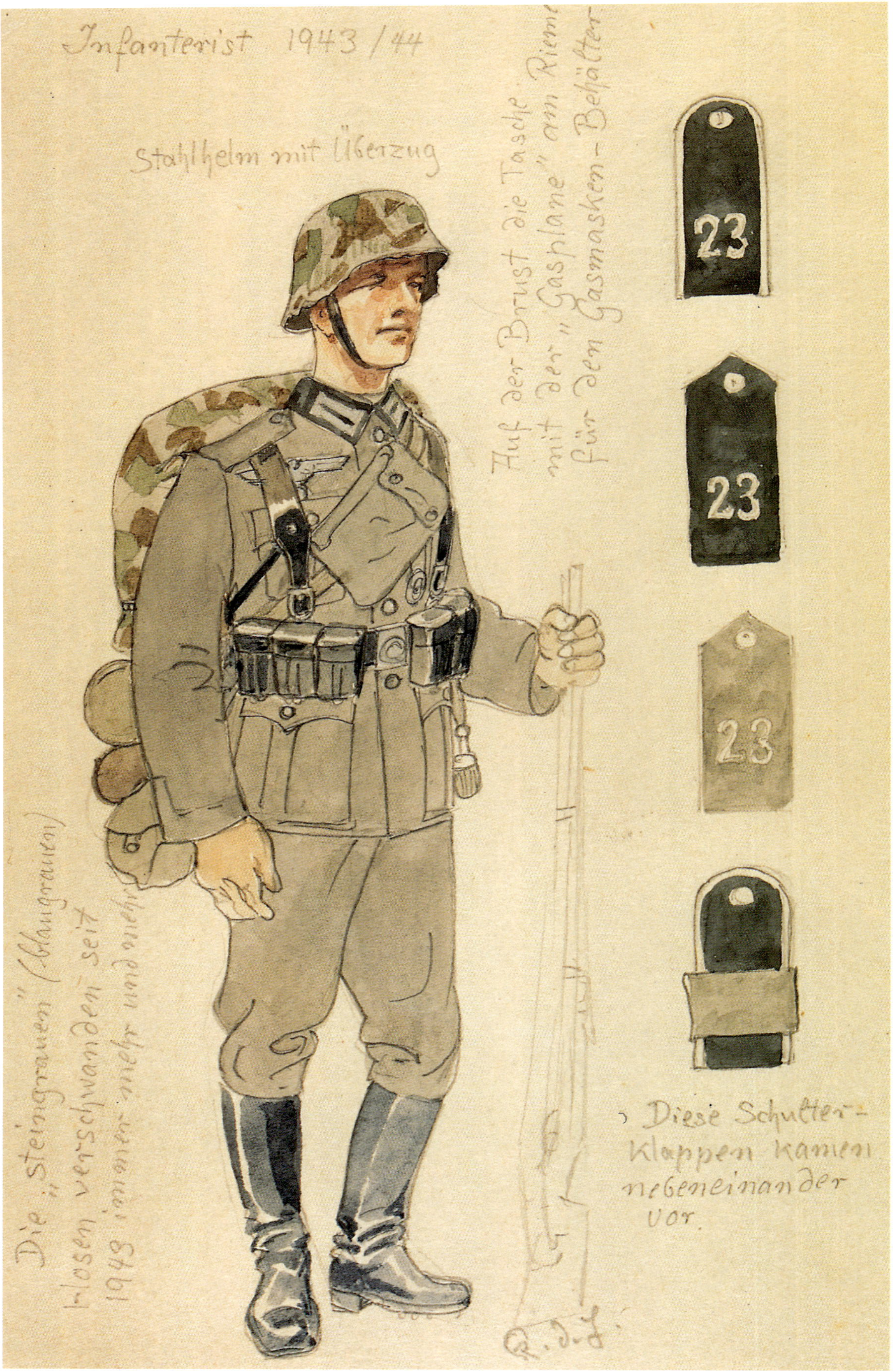

German Infantryman 1943-1944. The stone gray pants increasingly went out of use starting in 1943. The shoulder epaulets come one after another. His steel helmet is covered for camouflage. The device on the right front strap is a Gaspiane, used with a gas mask.

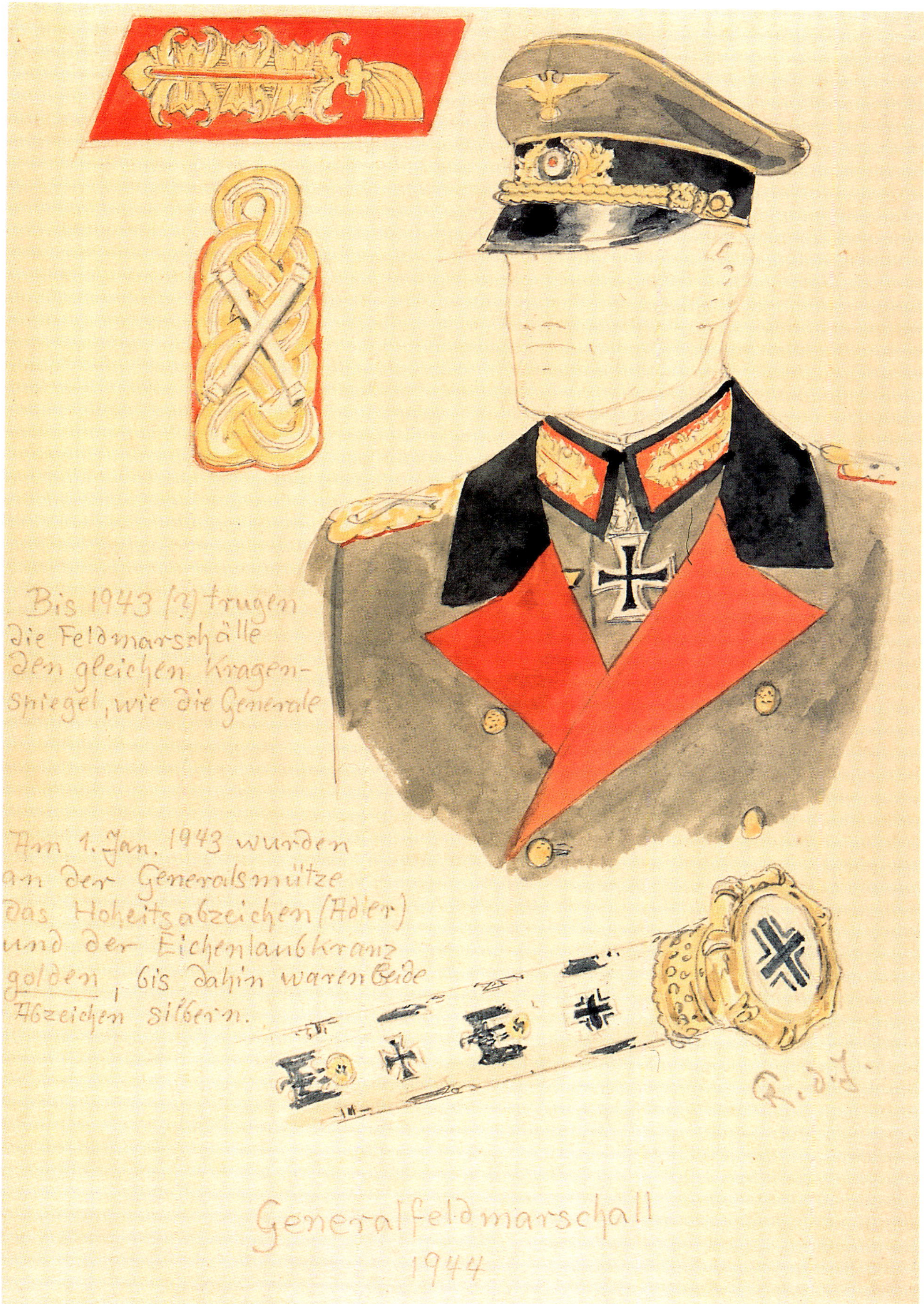

German General Field Marshall 1944. Until 1943 Field Marshals wore the same collar insignia as generals. On January 1, 1943, the national markings (eagle) and the oak leaf garlands on the general's cap were in gold. Until then both had been in silver.

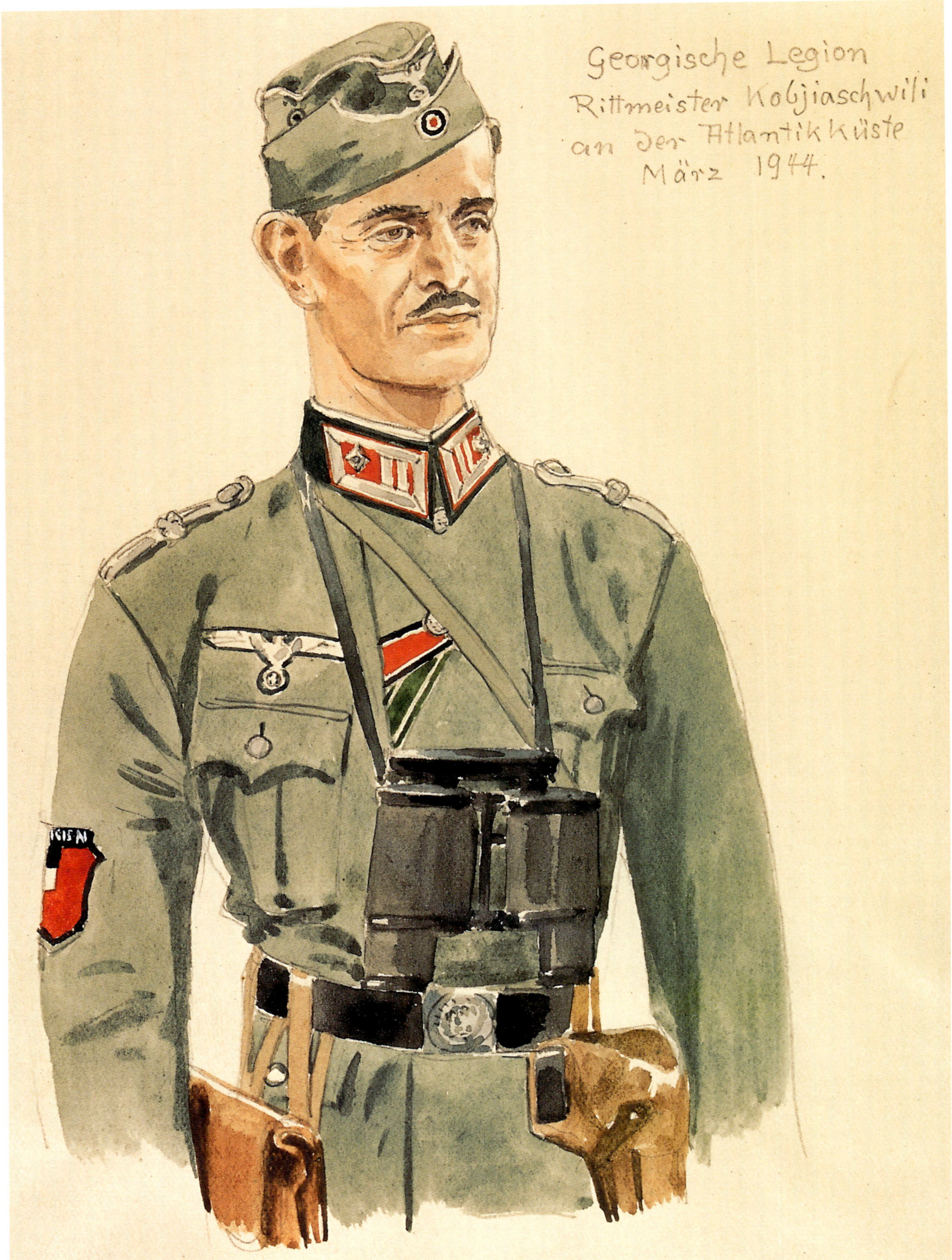

Georgian Legion, Atlantic coast March 1944.

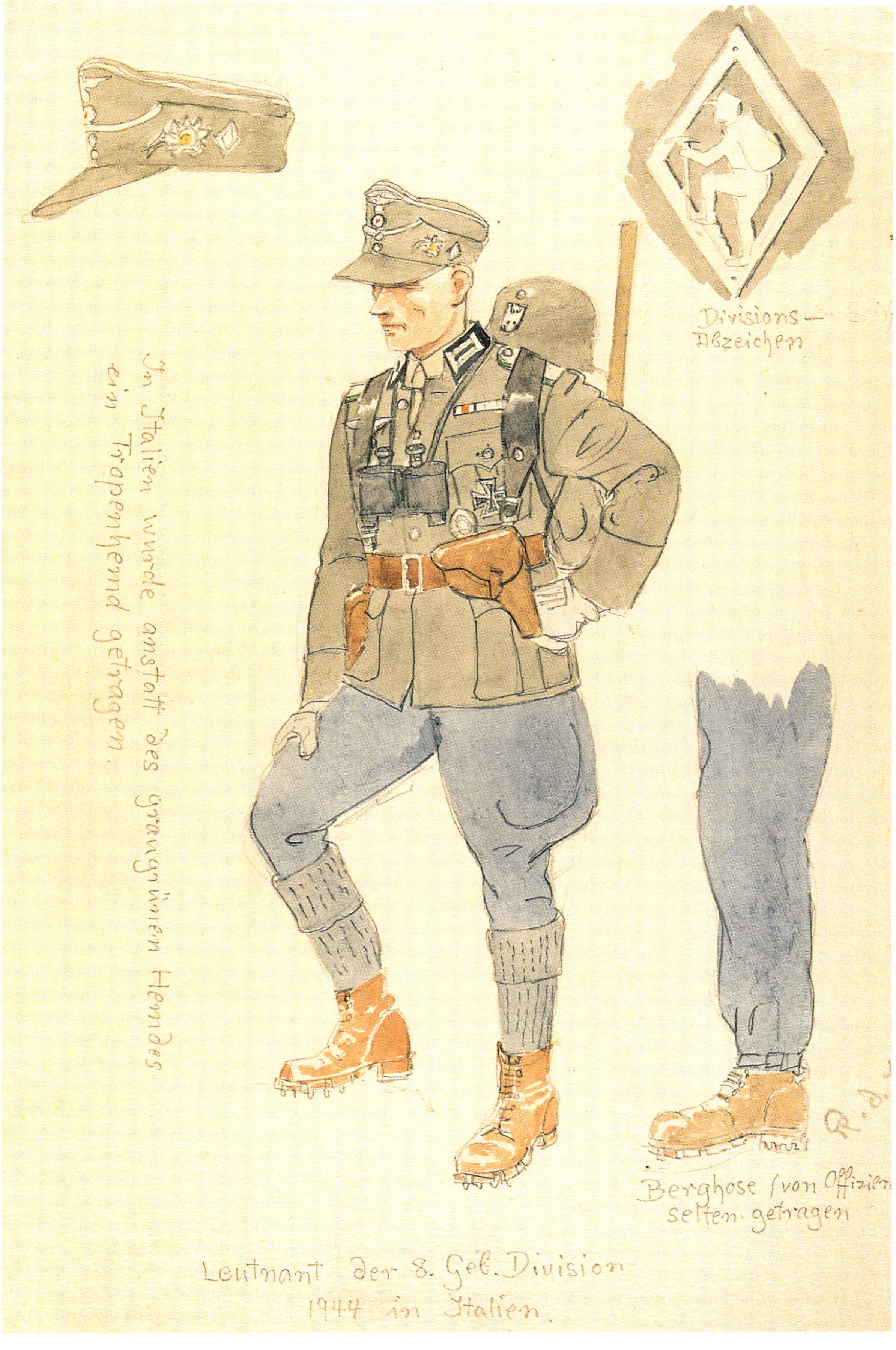

German Lieutenant of 8th Mountain Division, Italy 1944. In Italy, the tropical shirt was worn instead of the gray-green shirt. Mountain pants were rarely worn by officers. The patch with the soldier climbing is the divisional marking.

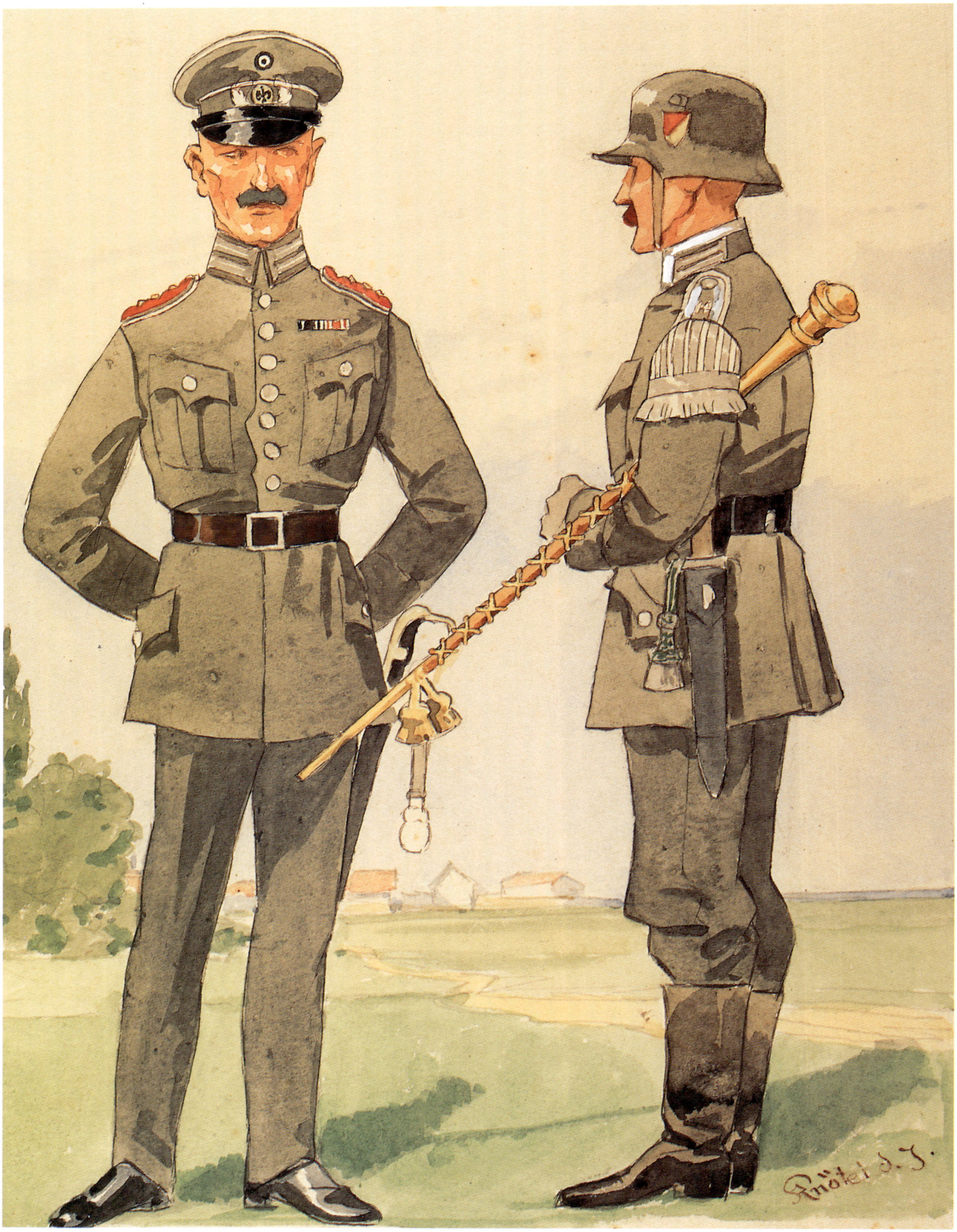

Officer and Drum Major, German, World War II.

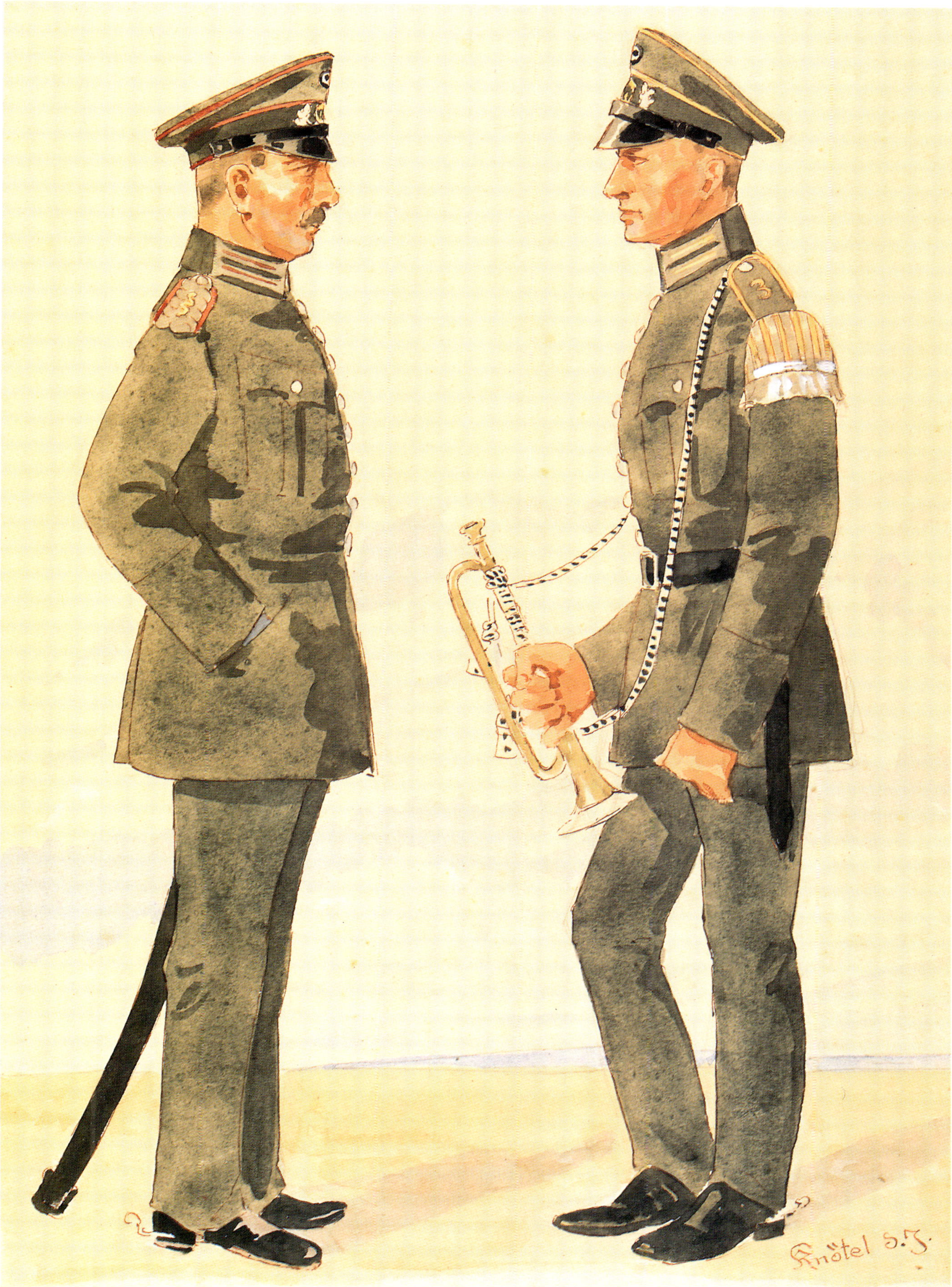

Officer and Trumpeter, German, World War II.

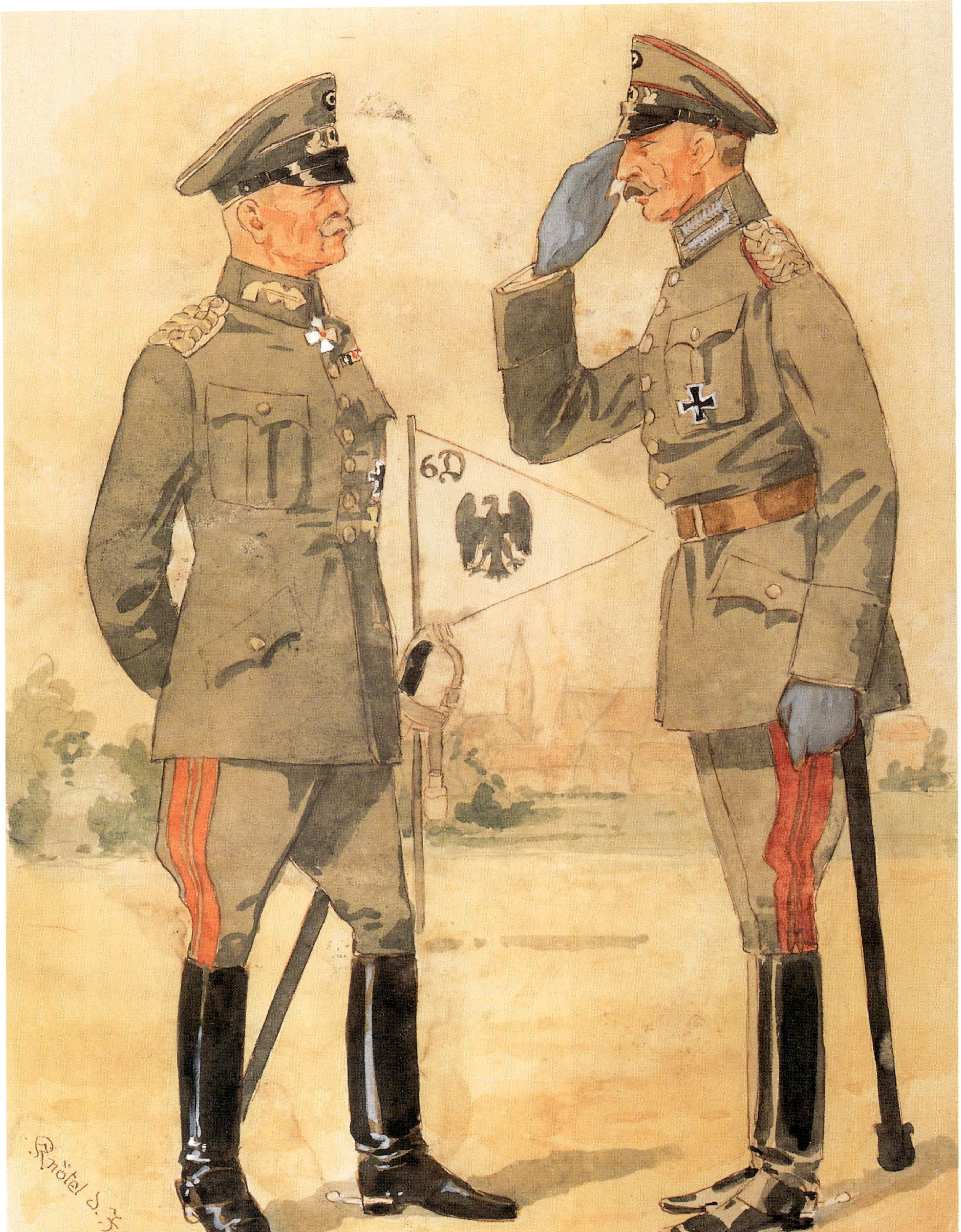

Staff Officers, German, World War II.